# External Perceptions of the European
# Union as a Global Actor

This book provides the first detailed analysis of perceptions of the European Union throughout the world.

Through a wide range of policies, from international trade to global environmental agreements, the EU has not only carved an important space for its international outreach, but it has also presented itself as a 'distinctive' global power, whose actions are based more on shared values and principles rather than national interests. This book attempts to test this 'distinctiveness' theory by unveiling what the rest of the world thinks of the EU.

Carrying out the first global analysis of perceptions of the EU, the book considers:

- political and economic elites, public opinion, civil society organizations and the media in other global powers (US, Russia and China), emerging markets (Brazil, India, Mexico, South Africa), the Middle East (Iran, Israel, Lebanon and Palestine), and the developing world (the ACP countries and the African Union),
- international agencies (UN and World Bank), non-Western media (Al Jazeera) and diplomatic circles.

Providing insights about attitudes of the European Union, which may run counter to the assumptions of EU policy makers, this book will be of major interest to students and scholars of European Studies, Politics and Area Studies.

**Sonia Lucarelli** is Lecturer of International Relations at the University of Bologna, Italy. **Lorenzo Fioramonti** is Research Fellow at the University of Bologna, Italy and at the Department of Political Sciences at the University of Pretoria, South Africa.

## Routledge/GARNET series: Europe in the world

Edited by David Armstrong
*University of Exeter, UK*

Karoline Postel-Vinay
*Centre for International Studies and Research (CERI), France.*

The Routledge GARNET series, *Europe in the World*, provides a forum for innovative research and current debates emanating from the research community within the GARNET Network of Excellence. GARNET is a Europe-wide network of 43 research institutions and scholars working collectively on questions around the theme of 'Global Governance, Regionalisation and Regulation: The Role of the EU', and funded by the European Commission under the sixth Framework Programme for Research.

# External Perceptions of the European Union as a Global Actor

Edited by Sonia Lucarelli and
Lorenzo Fioramonti

LONDON AND NEW YORK

First issued in paperback 2011
First published 2010
by Routledge
2 Park Square, Milton Park, Abingdon, Oxon OX14 4RN

Simultaneously published in the USA and Canada
by Routledge
270 Madison Ave, New York, NY 10016

*Routledge is an imprint of the Taylor & Francis Group, an informa business*

Typeset in Times by Wearset Ltd, Boldon, Tyne and Wear

*British Library Cataloguing in Publication Data*
A catalogue record for this book is available from the British Library

*Library of Congress Cataloging in Publication Data*
A catalog record for this book has been requested

ISBN10: 0-415-48100-7 (hbk)
ISBN10: 0-415-61961-0 (pbk)
ISBN10: 0-203-86691-6 (ebk)

ISBN13: 978-0-415-48100-7 (hbk)
ISBN13: 978-0-415-61961-5 (pbk)
ISBN13: 978-0-203-86691-7 (ebk)

# Contents

# Figures

# Tables

# Contributors

**Eugenia Baroncelli** is assistant professor of Political Science at the University of Bologna (Italy) and has been professorial lecturer in Introduction to Development at SAIS, Johns Hopkins University. Between 2001 and 2006 she worked at the World Bank in the DECRG Trade Group (Washington, DC) as a trade consultant and served as a trade specialist for MENA, SASIA and Africa regions. She holds a PhD in Political Science and has published widely on international political economy and development.

**Franziska Brantner** is a PhD candidate at the University of Cologne (Germany) with a thesis on the role of the European Union in the United Nations reform process. She is a graduate of the School of International and Public Affairs at Columbia University and the Institut d'Etudes Politiques at Sciences Po-Pari (France), and a research associate at the European Studies Centre of Oxford University (UK).

**Caterina Carta** holds a PhD in Comparative and European Politics and is currently post-doctoral fellow in European Foreign and Security Studies with a grant of the Compagnia di San Paolo, Riksbankens Jubileumsfond and Volkswagen Stiftung. She collaborates with the University of Siena (Italy) and the London School of Economics (UK) in the framework of the RECON project. Her research interests cover European foreign policy and diplomacy and the EU's external relations.

**Alejandro Chanona** holds a PhD in political science and government and a master in Western European politics from the University of Essex (UK). He is a full-time research professor of the School of Political and Social Sciences of the National Autonomous University of Mexico, where he also founded the Centre of European Studies. His research fields include regional integration, compared regionalisms and international security. Chanona is also a member of the Honorary Council of the Mexican International Studies Association and an associate member of the Mexican Council on Foreign Relations.

**Donatella Della Ratta** is a specialist of Arab media. She is the author of a number of essays and books concerning Arab newspapers and TV networks. In 2005, Della Ratta was invited to the international art exhibition 'Occidente desde

Oriente' (The West Viewed by East) organized by Centro de Cultura Contemporanea de Barcelona (Spain). In early 2008, she organized the two-day festival 'The West Viewed by the Arab Media' in Rome (Italy), featuring the most important Arab TV programmes dealing with 'the clash of civilizations', terrorism and broad cultural and social relations between Arab and Western cultures.

**Ole Elgström**, PhD, is Professor of Political Science at Lund University (Sweden). He has published on internal and international negotiations involving the EU in a number of journals such as the *Journal of Common Market Studies, Journal of European Public Policy* and *European Foreign Affairs Review*. He is the co-editor (with Christer Jönsson) of European Union Negotiations (Routledge 2005) and (with Michael Smith) of *The European Union's Roles in International Politics* (Routledge 2006).

**Lorenzo Fioramonti** holds a PhD in Comparative and European Politics. He is the author of a number of academic publications on EU external relations and EU–Africa policies, including the book *EU Democracy Aid: Strengthening Civil Society in Post Apartheid South Africa* (Routledge forthcoming). In the past six years he has been research fellow at the Department of Political Sciences of the University of Pretoria (South Africa) and, since 2007, he is also a fellow at the University of Bologna (Italy).

**Sonia Lucarelli** is senior researcher and lecturer of International Relations at the University of Bologna (Italy). She has published on international relations theory, EU foreign policy and the external image of the EU. Her most recent co-edited publications include *The Search for a European Identity. Values, Policies and Legitimacy of the European Union* (Routledge 2008) and *Values and Principles in EU Foreign Policy* (Routledge 2006). She was the guest editor of *Beyond Self Perception: The Others' View of the European Union*, special issue of the *European Foreign Affairs Review*, March 2007.

**Raffaele Mauriello** is an expert in contemporary Shia history and a translator from Arabic and Persian. He holds an MA degree in translation and interpreting from the Escuela de traductores de Toledo. He is a doctoral candidate in Islamic Civilization and his publications focus on identity in contemporary Shia communities, particularly in Iran and Iraq. He lives and works in Tehran (Iran).

**Mara Morini** works at the University of Parma (Italy). She holds a PhD in Political Science and Comparative Analysis of Democracies and is involved in a number of research projects concerning democratization in post-communist regimes and the relationship between Russia and the EU. Her research interests include party politics and political institutions in Russia, the consolidation of democracy in post-communist countries and Russia's foreign policy. In December 2003, Morini was appointed electoral observer by the Organization for Security and Cooperation in Europe with the task of monitoring the elections of the Russian Duma. She is also project manager of several Tempus Tacis Programmes with Eastern Europe.

**Rami Nasrallah** is the Head of the Board of Directors of the International Peace and Cooperation Center in East Jerusalem. He studied Middle East Studies and Political Science at the Hebrew University of Jerusalem, where he also received his MA degree in International Relations. He is currently a PhD candidate in Urban Planning at the TU Delft in the Netherlands and a Research Associate in the Architecture Faculty of Cambridge University (UK). From 1996 to 1998, Mr Nasrallah was the director of the Orient House Special Projects Unit. He is co-author of a number of publications on urban studies, divided cities and political and social transformation of the Palestinian society.

**Gerrit Olivier** is the director of the Centre for European Studies at the University of Johannesburg (South Africa) and president of the European Community Studies Association of Southern Africa. He has published numerous articles and monographic volumes on the EU and its relations with Africa and his op-eds are regularly featured in prominent South African newspapers. Olivier was the first South African ambassador to the Russian Federation.

**Sharon Pardo** holds a PhD from the University of Ghent (Belgium). He is Jean Monnet lecturer at the Department of Politics and Government, Ben-Gurion University of the Negev (Israel) and Director of the university's Centre for the Study of European Politics and Government (CSEPS). He is a Senior Fellow at the International and European Research Unit of the University of Ghent (Belgium) and a member of the National Executive of the Israeli Association for the Study of European Integration. He is one of the founders of the Israeli Ministry of Regional Cooperation and served as the director of the Ministry's Projects Division as well as a Senior Assistant to the Ministry's Director General. He is currently completing a book on Euro-Israeli relations (Rowman & Littlefield forthcoming).

**Roberto Peruzzi** is an historian specialized in international history, Chinese foreign policy and South East Asia, and Euro-Asian relations. He studied Chinese language in Kunming University (China) and received his PhD in International History at the University of Florence (2008). Currently, Peruzzi teaches History of International Relations at the universities of Bologna and Venice (Italy) and History of Contemporary China at the University of Florence (Italy).

**Arlo Poletti** is PhD candidate in Political Science (specialization in International Relations) at the University of Bologna (Italy). He has published on EU external relations in international journals such as *European Foreign Affairs Review* and *Third World Quarterly*.

**Ruth Hanau Santini** is a political scientist specializing in European foreign policy. She received her MA degree at the School of Oriental and African Studies in London (UK) and her PhD at the University Federico II, Naples (Italy). She is currently Compagnia di San Paolo Fellow at Johns Hopkins University, SAIS, Bologna Center (Italy).

**Simona Santoro** is Adviser on Freedom on Religion or Belief in the Tolerance and Non-Discrimination Department of the Office for Democratic Institutions and Human Rights of the Organization for Security and Cooperation in Europe (OSCE). From 2004 to 2007, she served in the OSCE Mission to Serbia as Senior Adviser on Minority Issues. In 2003, she worked on Common Foreign and Security Policy (CFSP) coordination on OSCE issues in the Department of Multilateral Affairs of the Italian Ministry of Foreign Affairs. She holds a PhD in Social and Political Sciences from the European University Institute. Her dissertation focused on Israeli-Palestinian joint committees as mechanisms of cooperation in the Oslo process.

**Daniela Sicurelli** is lecturer in Political Science at the Department of Sociology and Social Research of the University of Trento (Italy). She has been EAP Fellow of the University of California (Berkeley) and Marie Curie Fellow at the University of Birmingham (UK). She holds a PhD in Comparative and European Politics and has published a number articles on EU Union politics and external relations. In 2007, she published the volume *Divisi dall'ambiente. Gli USA e l'Unione europea nelle politiche del clima e della biodiversità* (Vita e Pensiero).

**James C. Sperling** is professor of Political Science at the University of Akron (USA). He held previous teaching appointments at the James Madison College, Michigan State University and Davidson College. He has published widely on German foreign policy, transatlantic relations, and regional and global security governance. He is co-author of *EU Security Governance* (Manchester 2007) and co-editor of *Global Security Governance* (Routledge 2007). He has published articles in *Review of International Studies*, *Journal of European Public Policy*, *British Journal of Political Science*, *German Politics*, *European Foreign Affairs Review* and *Contemporary Security Policy*.

**Lorenzo Trombetta** holds a PhD in Contemporary History of the Levant from the Sorbonne University (France). He is based in Beirut (Lebanon) and collaborates with a number of international newspapers and press agencies.

# Acknowledgements

This book is the result of a two-phase survey on *The External Image of the European Union* developed in the framework of the Network of Excellence *Global Governance, Regionalisation and Regulation: the Role of the EU* – GARNET (EU sixth Framework Programme 2005–2010; call identifier: FP6–2002-Citizens-3). All the chapters in the book (with the only exception of Chapter 9) draw on the research conducted for the survey.

This project has involved a number of researchers across the globe and benefited immensely from the support of several people in academia as well as from public institutions. We are particularly grateful to Furio Cerutti, Andrew Gamble and Mario Telò for having believed in the importance of this research by including it within their GARNET jointly executed research project. Also, a special recognition is due to Richard Higgott, Eleni Tsingou and Angela Liberatore for having supported the project since its inception. We also thank Martin Holland and Natalia Chaban from the National Centre for Research on Europe (University of Canterbury, New Zealand).

The research work was enhanced by the comments and suggestions of a number of colleagues, amongst whom: Ali Ansari, Shaun Breslin, David Camroux, Kenneth Chan, Mahrukh Doctor, Hanaa Ebeid, Maria Grazia Enardu, Laura Guazzone, Rajendra K. Jain, Knud Erik Jørgensen, Emil Kirchner, Angela Liberatore, Zhu Liqun, Arturo Marzano, Arrigo Pallotti, Daniela Pioppi, Walter Posch, Gareth Price, David Ringrose, Maria Stella Rognoni, Angela Romano, Federico Romero, Karen Smith, David Shambaugh, Xinning Song, Antonio Tanca, Nicola Todaro Marescotti, Alberto Tonini, Roberto Toscano, Zhang Yun and Loris Zanatta. We are grateful to Sirkku Salovaara and Giuseppe Sorgente of the Forum on the Problems of Peace and War (Florence, Italy) for their logistical support as well as to Lisa Tormena for her precious research assistance.

This research could have not been carried out without the financial assistance of GARNET and the Italian Ministry of Foreign Affairs.

Bologna
Sonia Lucarelli
Lorenzo Fioramonti

# Abbreviations

| | |
|---|---|
| ACP | African, Caribbean and Pacific countries |
| APEC | Asia-Pacific Economic Cooperation |
| ASEM | Asia Europe Meeting |
| AU | African Union |
| BRIC | Brazil, Russia, India and China |
| CFSP | Common Foreign and Security Policy |
| CIS | Commonwealth of Independent States |
| DG | Directorate-General |
| EBA | Everything But Arms scheme |
| EC | European Community |
| EDF | European Development Fund |
| EEC | European Economic Community |
| EMP | Euro-Mediterranean Partnership |
| ENP | European Neighbourhood Policy |
| EPA | Economic Partnership Agreements |
| ESDP | European Security and Defence Policy |
| EU BAM | European Union Border Assistance Mission for the Rafah Crossing Point |
| EULAC | European Union–Latin America and Caribbean |
| EUMFTA | EU–Mexico Free Trade Agreement |
| FTA | Free Trade Agreement |
| GATT | General Agreement on Tariffs and Trade |
| GSP | Generalized System of Preferences |
| IBSA | India, Brazil and South Africa |
| LAC | Latin America and Caribbean |
| LDC | Least Developed Countries |
| MDG | Millennium Development Goals |
| MENA | Middle East and Northern Africa |
| NAFTA | North American Free Trade Agreement |
| NATO | North Atlantic Treaty Organization |
| NGO | Non-governmental Organization |
| NPT | Non-Proliferation Treaty |
| NSS | National Security Strategies |

| | |
|---|---|
| OSCE | Organization for Security and Cooperation in Europe |
| PA | Palestinian Authority |
| PLO | Palestine Liberation Organization |
| SADC | Southern African Development Community |
| SIT | Social Identity Theory |
| UfM | Union for the Mediterranean |
| UK | United Kingdom |
| UN | United Nations |
| UNIFIL | United Nations Interim Force in Lebanon |
| UNSC | United Nations Security Council |
| USA | United States of America |
| USD | United States Dollar |
| VAT | Value Added Tax |
| WB | World Bank |
| WESP | World Economic Situation and Prospects |
| WESS | World Economic and Social Survey |
| WTO | World Trade Organization |

# 1   Introduction

## The EU in the eyes of the others – why bother?

*Sonia Lucarelli and Lorenzo Fioramonti*

> One Middle Eastern diplomat put the problem neatly: 'The US makes offers we cannot refuse; *the EU makes offers we do not understand!*' People may not like US policy, but at least its message is clear. The challenge facing the EU is different: people outside Europe are not certain what the Union stands for or whether it matters ... As the Union develops as a strategic player, ... [it] must speak to the world clearly, *and it must start listening to what the world thinks about it.*
>
> (Linch 2005: 11; emphasis added)

Considering the number of issues affecting the European Union (EU) internally, one might wonder why this book bothers to analyse its external image in the world. At a time of constitutional turmoil and growing Euro-scepticism, why should one pay attention to what non-Europeans think of the EU?

In fact, there are several reasons. The first reason is that the EU has become a rather consolidated player in the international arena. After more than a decade of fledgling movements in the global context, the EU is now legally represented in almost all countries and regularly interacts with governments, business, civil society, the media and other relevant groups. If the EU wants to have a chance to implement efficient policies, it cannot avoid taking into serious consideration expectations, images and perceptions in the rest of the world.

In second place, there is a gap in the literature that needs to be filled. The thesis of the EU's 'distinctiveness' (Lucarelli 2007), found widely in the literature dealing with the EU's specific role in world politics, needs to be further challenged. So far research has been undertaken on evaluating the EU's coherence and effectiveness, but very little has been done on how the other international players regard the EU. This area of enquiry, therefore, deserves further investigation.

In third place, looking at external images means looking at one of the variables that contributes to shaping a European political identity among the Europeans. As a matter of fact, self rhetorical representation, public debate and mirror images are fundamental components of a political identity in the making like the EU/ropean one. For this reason it is useful to understand what the external images are.

This introductory chapter deals first with each of these 'founding reasons' at a time. It then briefly evaluates what elements most shape external images; and finally it illustrates the structure of the book.

## The EU as a deaf global power?

In the past few years the global role of the EU has been widely recognized by a growing body of academic literature (Bretherton and Vogler 2006; McCormick 2008; Hill and Smith 2005). The international ambitions of the EU have been sealed by the establishment of the Common Foreign and Security Policy (CFSP) in 1992, the first out-of-area mission of the European Security and Defence Policy (ESDP) in 2003, and the significant growth of the various ramifications of the external policies carried out by the European Commission. The EU has furthermore asserted itself as the largest trade actor in the world, with significant leverage at various international forums such as the World Trade Organization. The EU's financial and economic policies reach governments, private corporations and non-governmental organizations across the globe. Finally, the EU is the largest donor of development aid, with offices and delegations in more than 120 countries.

At the educational level, the European Commission has been subsidizing research units on European Studies in various countries around the world. In the global arena the EU has also been leading a number of processes at the multilateral level, thereby increasing its power and influence. In short, what is decided at the EU does not only impact the European polity, but also has direct consequences on many countries around the world.

With increasing power comes increasing responsibility. In international diplomacy and foreign policy, mutual understanding is important if common objectives are to be achieved. For instance, the stalemate at the Doha Round has proven that a number of countries previously sidelined in international politics is increasingly demanding to be given a voice. The reform processes at the UN and at the international financial institutions such as the International Monetary Fund and the World Bank have also demonstrated that the traditional global governance set-up has been largely discredited. The growth of regional powers, such as China and India, as well as the creation of parallel institutions, such as the G20, are just a few examples of a growing trend.

Against this backdrop it becomes evident that the way in which the EU is perceived by other countries is likely to have a direct bearing on its success as a player in the international arena. What the world thinks of the EU is therefore an important factor in facilitating or opposing the achievements of EU-sponsored policies. Comprehending the perceptions of the EU can help gauge the extent to which the Union is seen as a credible and consistent actor in global politics. Furthermore, they can also help assess the extent to which the European 'soft power' is still a reality in the eyes of citizens around the world. Moreover, external images might tell us something of the degree of the EU's effective communication skills, which, according to the Middle Eastern diplomat mentioned in the incipit, is not high. In a way perceptions can be seen as 'early warning systems' for an actor such as the EU, which is still in the process of establishing itself as a credible international focal point.

## The images – self-images: gaps in the literature and the reality

A second reason for studying the external images of the EU is a gap in the literature. As early as the 1970s there was a tendency to describe the then European Community as a progressive international player that followed precise norms and values. Since then, particularly in the 1990s, the literature has rediscovered Duchêne's original concept of 'civilian power' Europe (1972, 1973). Terms such as *civilian power* (Telò 2006; Whitman 1998), *normative power* (Manners 2002), *structural foreign policy* (Keukeleire 2000, 2004), *normative area* (Therborn 2001), *gentle power* (Padoa-Schioppa 2001) and *norm-maker* (Björkdahl 2005; see also Checkel 1999) have been coined to capture the idea that the EU is a different (read 'better') international actor: a new form of global player, profoundly different from 'traditional powers'. Whether to enrich the concept (Telò 2004) or to revise it (Manners 2002), these authors share Duchêne's views that the EU is internationally different because its initial *telos* (peace through integration), its historical developments and its current institutional and normative framework make it better suited to spreading universal values. This scholarly image has been matched by a self-rhetorical representation in EU documents describing the EU as a global player with global responsibility, but also with the will 'to play a stabilizing role worldwide and to point the way ahead for many countries and peoples'; in other words, it is a player ready to 'shoulder its responsibilities in the governance of globalization' (European Council 2001).

For some years the combination of this self-representation and academic literature both supporting the idea of the EU as a 'distinctive' power created a highly self-referential attitude not only among EU scholars, but also in the limited-though-existent EU public debate. At this turn of the century there has been growing criticism towards the idea of the EU as a distinctive international actor and an increasing number of studies have started to criticize the very applicability of the concept to the EU (Diez 2005; Sjursen 2006) and to test empirically both the EU's coherence as a civilian power and its effectiveness (Panebianco 2006; Smith 2006; Scheipers and Sicurelli 2007; Elgström and Smith 2006; Balducci 2008). This literature has been extremely useful in pointing out the strengths and weaknesses of the EU's international conduct, its coherence and effectiveness. What this literature has not done so far is to investigate the impact and effectiveness of the EU's performance on the images that it projects of itself abroad: no systematic research has been conducted on 'external views' worldwide.[1] The failure to investigate external images not only results in a gap in the literature that deserves to be filled, but it might also have/have had important practical repercussions. This lack of information is rather worrisome for a new actor with global aspirations and high-flying rhetoric; moreover, it could even be dangerous as it might easily generate cognitive dissonances between what the EU 'says about itself' and what the rest of the world 'thinks', as we have seen above.

## Images and political identity

There is also another reason, which – we think – speaks directly to the hearts and minds of European citizens. Given the history of the European project and its cultural and social mix, a mass-based European political identity is still in the making.

Undoubtedly, various factors influence this process of identity-building. There is a debate in the literature regarding what affects identity-building the most. Authors tend to envisage a different approach to the relationship between political identity, on the one side, and factors such as culture, history and ethnicity, on the other.[2] We share the view that common identity for the Europeans can only be *political*, grounded in the set of social and political values and principles that Europeans are ready to recognize as theirs, that make them feel like a political group (Cerutti 2003: 27). According to this view, culture, history, policies and institutions are the frameworks in which the interpretation of political values takes place, thereby giving meaning to political identity (Cerutti and Lucarelli 2008; Lucarelli 2006). Next to these fundamental factors, however, there are other factors, frequently neglected in the literature, that play a relevant role. Probably the most important of these is the relationship with external Others.

The relevance of 'Others' (particularly of physical Others – other individuals, other states, etc.) is appreciated in both socio-psychological (Taylor 1994; Turner *et al.* 1987) and international relations literature (cf. Rumelili 2004; Neumann 1996b). On reviewing the available literature, 'Others' are seen to be treated as relevant to the self-identification process in four broad respects: *recognition*, *distinctiveness*, *labelling* and *bordering*.

Pizzorno reads recognition as 'the reciprocal attribution of identity, ... constitutive of any form of sociality ... that simply reflects the arrival on the scene of new actors' (2007: 190). Charles Taylor asserts that 'our identity is partly shaped by recognition ... often by the *mis*-recognition of others'. He also argues that 'a person or group of people can suffer real damage, real distortion, if the people or society around them mirror back to them a confining or demeaning or contemptible picture of themselves' (Taylor 1994: 25). Thus, we can maintain that the Others produce a second 'mirror' for 'us' as a group engaged in a self-identification process (the first 'mirror' being provided by the direct observation of our political action). Hence, images of the EU from the outside might contribute to consolidating a European political identity.

External views are also relevant as inactive objects of our comparisons. Self-categorization theory finds a key psychological motivation for an individual's endorsement of group affiliation in his/her need 'to differentiate [his/her] own groups positively from others to achieve a positive social identity' (Turner *et al.* 1987: 42). Such differentiation is not necessarily oppositional but entails assuming the positive distinctiveness of one's group with respect to comparable Others (see Neumann 1996a).

A further way in which external views are relevant to processes of identity formation is by contributing to 'labelling' the group and tracing its contours

(Huddy 2001). Others' labelling is an important element in that it creates cognitive boundaries between members of a group and outsiders. Boundaries are both created by the members of a group as a by-product of self-categorization processes, and imagined by outside Others. Moreover, they can be seen as identifying the contour of a group of people either sharing some similarities (for example, having a European passport) or having internalized the *meaning* of group membership (for example, the difference between having European citizenship and having a European identity). Boundaries as meanings are what count more in identity-formation processes.

Despite the relevance of external perceptions, traditional literature on European identity has not been interested in this topic. This literature fails to study *if* and *how* the EU's foreign policy and external images are relevant to the construction of a European political self-consciousness. Such a lack of interest is striking considering that, according to the Eurobarometer surveys, not only do Europeans have their own vision of the role of the EU in the world, but they tend to find the EU's international stance legitimate, positive and worth pursuing (Eurobarometer 2007; Transatlantic Trends 2006).

## What shapes images?

Before describing the way in which this book aims to study external images, a few words need to be spent on how these images are shaped – a fundamental question if the EU wants to have a chance to influence its future images.

In Social Identity Theory (SIT), social identity influences the group's perception of others, but at the same time is influenced by the cognitive relationship that the group establishes with others. One of the factors that influences external perceptions is the very identity of the group that perceives and its need to differentiate itself (Turner *et al.* 1987). However, this can be considered as one of the dimensions that shape external images. Drawing from both SIT and international relations, it is possible to identify a two-level model that pays attention to both long-term/framework variables and interactional/contingent factors. In line with SIT, we consider (i) political identity, (ii) historical memories and (iii) socially shaped conceptions of world order to be fundamental components of the prevalent cognitive maps within a society, the same maps that we assume influence the interviewees. Drawing from international relations and foreign policy analysis, we identify some more 'contingent' variables as relevant in the formation of a perception of an external 'other': (iv) positional variables (that is, those preferences, interests, perspectives, that the interviewee assumes as a player in a particular social role (that is, leader of a non-governmental organization or a political party)); (v) power-related variables that account for asymmetries with respect to the EU; (vi) interaction variables (e.g. the specific political interaction experience with the EU in an issue area within a bi/multilateral context).

Each chapter in the book will attempt to identify the variables that seem to have played a greater role in the specific case study.

## Structure of the book

The book is divided into two main parts. Part I is entitled 'Great powers, conflict areas and emerging markets' and includes a series of country case studies. These studies were conducted between 2006 and 2008 by local researchers and country experts. In some cases, chapters were co-authored by various specialists in order to combine a strong knowledge of local dynamics and culture with a deep understanding of EU policies.

The country studies identify images of the EU in the United States of America (USA), Russia and China, Iran and Lebanon, Israel and Palestine, Mexico and, finally, India, Brazil and South Africa. These countries were selected as they represent a diverse range of perspectives, which might allow for interesting generalizations while providing a good approximation of the whole range of global perspectives. While the USA provides the angle of the only 'superpower', the study of Russia and China includes the perspective of other 'great powers' with a strong voice in international affairs. Iran and Lebanon constitute two interesting examples of Muslim communities, though culturally and socially different from one another. Moreover, they are two important test beds for the external credibility of the EU due to direct post-conflict commitment in Lebanon and significant diplomatic efforts with the Iranian government. Israel and Palestine are crucial cases for assessing the perceived performance of the EU as a promoter of peace in the most well-known case of prolonged conflict in world politics. The chapter on Mexico aims to provide the perspective of a key regional player and important actor in Latin America, while the collective analysis of India, Brazil and South Africa surveys the critical stance of three emerging powers and leading nations of the so-called 'global south'.

Each chapter provides background on the political, social, economic and cultural relations between the EU and the relevant country/ies. The perception analysis is organized around four different groups: public opinion, political and business elites, civil society and the media. This methodological set-up proved quite useful in order to identify different images of the EU in the various groups, based on the conviction that different stakeholders within the same country might hold a diverse range of opinions about the EU.

Unlike Part I, which focused on specific countries, Part II deals with 'International organizations, regional institutions and the media'. The aim of this part of the book is to broaden the spectrum of analysis in order to include perspectives and perceptions from a wide range of intergovernmental and non-state actors. The first chapter analyses the perceptions of the EU as a commercial power through a survey of representatives of the African, Caribbean and Pacific (ACP) countries involved in negotiations for the Economic Partnership Agreements. The following chapter focuses more directly on the EU as a development actor by studying how the World Bank assesses the EU's contribution to the fight against poverty. This is followed by an analysis of perceptions within the UN General Assembly and the UN Secretariat. Another chapter looks at a regional institution like the African Union and provides a broad analysis of the appreciations as well as criticisms raised against recent EU policies in Africa. In a shift from institutions to international media, the case of the Arab TV network Al Jazeera is discussed as a key example of how the EU is perceived by news editors and then presented to the Arab audience. Moving closer to the EU, the final chapter of this part discusses how non-European delegates based in Brussels perceive the EU and its global roles. The book ends with a concluding chapter, which provides a detailed summary of the main findings and discusses some key recommendations for the EU.

## Notes

1 Indeed, there are very few systematic studies of the others' images of the topic of the EU. The two largest research initiatives on the EU's external image include the project that originated this book, coordinated by Sonia Lucarelli (and Lorenzo Fioramonti in Phase Two) in the framework of the Network of Excellence GARNET, and *The EU through the Eyes of Asia* coordinated by Martin Holland (www.europe.canterbury.ac. nz/appp/project_description/), which was recently published in Holland and Chaban 2008.
2 For a range of positions see: Huntington 1996; Jepperson *et al.* 1996 and Cerutti 2008.

## References

Balducci, G. (2008) *Inside Normative Power Europe: actors and processes in the European promotion of human rights in China*, EU Diplomacy Papers 8/2008, College d'Europe, Bruges. Online, available at: http://www.coleurope.eu/file/content/studypro-grammes/ird/research/pdf/EDP2008/EDP_8_2008.Balducci.pdf (accessed 31 January 2009).

Björkdahl, A. (2005) 'Norm-maker and Norm-taker: Exploring the normative influence of the EU in Macedonia', *European Foreign Affairs Review*, 10 (2): 257–78.

Bretherton, C. and Vogler, J. (2006) *The European Union as Global Actor*, 2nd edn, London: Routledge.

Cerutti, F. (2003) 'A Political Identity of the Europeans?' *Thesis Eleven*, 72 (1): 26–45.

—— (2008) 'Why Political Identity and Legitimacy Matter in the European Union' in F. Cerutti and S. Lucarelli (eds) *The Search for a European Identity: values, policies and legitimacy of the European Union*, London and New York, Routledge.

Cerutti, F. and Lucarelli, S. (eds) (2008) *The Search for a European Identity: values, policies and legitimacy of the European Union*, London and New York, Routledge.

Checkel, J.T. (1999) 'Norms, Institutions and National Identity in Contemporary Europe', *International Studies Quarterly*, 43 (1): 83–114.

Diez, T. (2005) 'Constructing the Self and Changing Others: reconsidering "Normative Power Europe"', *Millennium*, 33 (3): 613–36.

Duchêne, F. (1972) 'Europe's Role in World Peace', in R. Mayne (ed.) *Europe Tomorrow: sixteen Europeans look ahead*, London: Fontana.

—— (1973) 'The European Community and the Uncertainties of Interdependence', in M. Kohnstamm and W. Hager (eds) *A Nation Writ Large? Foreign policy problems before the European Community*, Basingstoke: Macmillan.

Elgström, O. and Smith, M. (2006) 'Introduction', in O. Elgström and M. Smith (eds) *The European Union's Roles in International Politics: concepts and analysis*, London: Routledge.

Eurobarometer (2007) *Public Opinion in the European Union. Standard Eurobarometer 67. First Results*, European Commission, public opinion analysis, Brussels. Online, available at: http://ec.europa.eu/public_opinion/archives/eb/eb67/eb_67_first_en.pdf (accessed 31 January 2009).

European Council (2001) *Laeken Declaration on the Future of Europe*, Attachment to the Presidency Conclusions, European Council Meeting in Laeken, 14–15 December 2001 (SN300/01 ADD1).

Holland, M. and Chaban, N. (eds) (2008) *The European Union and the Asia-Pacific: media, public and elite perceptions of the EU*, London: Routledge.

Hill, C. and Smith, M. (eds) (2005) *International Relations and the European Union*, Oxford: Oxford University Press.

Huddy, L. (2001) 'From Social to Political Identity: a critical examination of social identity theory', *Political Psychology*, 22 (1): 127–56.

Huntington, S. (1996) *The Clash of Civilizations and the Remaking of World Order*, New York: Simon & Schuster.

Jepperson, R., Wendt, A. and Katzenstein, P. (1996) 'Norms, Identity, and Culture in National Security', in P. Katzenstein (ed.) *The Culture of National Security*, New York: Columbia University Press.

Keukeleire, S. (2000) 'The European Union as a Diplomatic Actor', Discussion Paper no. 71, Centre for the Study of Diplomacy, University of Leicester, UK.

—— (2004) 'EU Structural Foreign Policy and Structural Conflict Prevention', in V. Kronenberger and J. Wouters (eds) *The European Union and Conflict Prevention: legal and policy aspects*, The Hague: Asser Press/Cambridge University Press.

Linch, D. (2005) *Communicating Europe to the World: what public diplomacy for the EU?* Working Paper no. 21, Brussels, European Policy Centre. Online, available at: www.epc.eu/TEWN/pdf/251965810_EPC%2021.pdf (accessed 31 January 2009).

Lucarelli, S. (2006) 'Values, Identity and Ideational Shocks in the Transatlantic Rift', *Journal of International Relations and Development*, 9 (3): 304–34.

—— (ed.) (2007) *Beyond Self Perception: the Others' view of the European Union*, Special issue of the *European Foreign Affairs Review*, 12 (3).

McCormick, J. (2008) *Understanding the European Union*, 4th edn, London: Palgrave/ Westview Press.

Manners, I. (2002) 'Normative Power Europe: a contradiction in terms?' *Journal of Common Market Studies*, 40 (2): 253–74.

Neumann, I.B. (1996a) *Russia and the Idea of Europe: a study in identity and international relations*, London: Routledge.

—— (1996b) 'Self and Other in International Relations', *European Journal of International Relations*, 2 (2): 139–74.

Padoa-Schioppa, T. (2001) *Europa, forza gentile*, Bologna: Il Mulino.

Panebianco, S. (2006) 'Promoting Human rights and Democracy in European Union Relations with Russia and China', in S. Lucarelli and I. Manners (eds), *Values and Principles in European Union Foreign Policy*, London: Routledge.

Pizzorno, A. (2007) *Il velo della diversità. Studi su razionalità e riconoscimento*, Milan: Feltrinelli.

Rumelili, B. (2004) 'Constructing Identity in Relating to Difference: understanding the EU's mode of differentiation', *Review of International Studies*, 30 (1): 27–47.

Scheipers, S. and Sicurelli, D. (2007) 'Normative Power Europe: a credible utopia?' *Journal of Common Market Studies*, 45 (2): 435–57.

Sjursen, S. (2006) 'What Kind of Power? European foreign policy in perspective', *Journal of European Public Policy*, 13 (2): 169–81.

Smith, K.E. (2006) 'The Limits of Proactive Cosmopolitanism: the EU and Burma, Cuba and Zimbabwe', in O. Elgström and M. Smith (eds) *The European Union's Roles in International Politics: concepts and analysis*, London: Routledge.

Taylor, C. (1994) 'The Politics of Recognition', in A. Gutmann (ed.) *Multiculturalism: examining the politics of recognition*, Princeton, NJ: Princeton University Press.

Telò, M. (2001) 'Reconsiderations: three scenarios', in M. Telò (ed.) *European Union and New Regionalism: regional actors and global governance*, London: Ashgate.

Therborn, G. (2001) 'Europe's Break with Itself. The European economy and the history, modernity and world future of Europe', in F. Cerutti and E. Rudolph, *A Soul for Europe: on the cultural and political identity of the Europeans*, Vol. II: *An Essay Collection*, Leuven: Peeters.

Transatlantic Trends (2006) *Key Findings 2006*. A project of the German Marshall Fund of the United States and the Compagnia di San Paolo, with additional support from the Fundação Luso-American, Fundación BBVA, and the Tipping Point Foundation. Online, available at: www.transatlantictrends.org/trends/doc/2006_TT_Key%20 Findings%20FINAL.pdf (accessed 31 January 2009).

Turner, J.C., Hogg, M.A., Oakes, P.J., Reicher, S.D. and Wetherell, M. (1987) *Rediscovering the Social Group: a self-categorization theory*, Oxford: Blackwell.

Whitman, R. (1998) *From Civilian Power to Superpower? The international identity of the European Union*, London: MacMillan.

**Part I**

# Great powers, conflict areas and emerging markets

# 2 American perceptions of the EU

## Through a glass, darkly or through the looking glass?

*James C. Sperling*

## Introduction

The founding and evolution of what has become the European Union (EU) constituted an important component of the postwar American strategy of containment. The EU remains an important component of the post-Cold War American foreign policy strategy, largely owing to Europe's continuing support of the American-designed international economic order and contribution to the tasks of global security governance. The EU's leading member states are unequivocally the most important military partners of the United States of America (USA): since 1990, they have made significant contributions to seven major military operations directly led by the USA or conducted within the North Atlantic Treaty Organization (NATO). The relative importance of the Atlantic economy has declined owing to the rise of China as a manufacturing and trading power that holds a significant amount of externally held US Treasury debt. Nonetheless, the EU remains as significant economic partner of the USA as before: it is the third largest trading partner after the North American Free Trade Agreement and the Asia-Pacific Economic Cooperation region; over 50 per cent of US direct foreign investment is in the EU and the EU accounts for over 60 per cent of foreign direct investment in the USA; and the EU states hold 35 per cent of externally held US Treasury debt (Sperling 2009).

The economic and financial importance of the EU to the USA is complemented by the military importance of the major EU states, particularly Britain, France, Germany and Italy, as American allies in governing global security. This complementarity is absent in the case of China. Many fear that Chinese economic capacity may be transformed into military power that would adversely affect American interests in the Asia-Pacific and endanger the security of its closest Pacific ally, Japan. The strategic alliance between the EU states and the USA, built up over historical time and reinforced by the shared ethnicities, religious traditions and foundational political philosophy, in conjunction with the emergence of the EU as a global actor, would suggest that the attention paid to the EU by American attentive foreign policy elites would be commensurate with that constellation of factors. Yet, it is not.

This chapter investigates the attitudes of four broad constituencies that shape, with differing degrees of influence and constancy of purpose, US policy towards the EU: the public, political and economic elites, organized civil society, and the media. The empirical findings are relied upon to answer three questions. What degree of 'actorness' do Americans ascribe to the EU? How important is the EU vis-à-vis the member states? How relevant is the EU to solving a wide variety of policy challenges facing the states of the transatlantic area?

## Public opinion

Public opinion belies a relatively low level of awareness of the EU as a discrete or important actor, a pattern parallel to (or caused by) the under-representation of the EU in the press (see below). Questions about the EU were absent from the major foreign policy public opinion surveys. Neither the public opinion surveys conducted by the Chicago Council on Foreign Relations nor the surveys conducted by the German Marshall Fund and Pew Global Attitudes Survey included questions about the EU until 2002. Both surveys demonstrate that the public perceives the EU as a positive force in global affairs, but its precise role is poorly defined. Respondents have consistently held that the EU should exert global leadership (ranging from 81 per cent in 2002 to 73 per cent in 2005) and that Europe and the USA should remain as close or even closer (77 per cent in 2004 and 63 per cent in 2006) (German Marshall Fund 2005, 2006).

There is also public support for the EU to emerge as a superpower, presumably on a par with the USA (rising from 33 per cent in 2002 to 47 per cent in 2005). For those believing that the USA should remain the only superpower, 45 per cent would allow that the EU become one if it shared the military burden of global governance, while 80 per cent of those who believe that the EU should emerge as a superpower did not change their mind with the prospect of an EU opposing US policies. The clear majority of the respondents, however, view the EU as an economic rather than military actor *and* they are not in favour of granting the EU a permanent seat on the United Nations (UN) Security Council. There is a great deal of ambivalence about the EU; even those who concede that the EU has attained global power status do not agree that the EU is the appropriate actor for assuming global security responsibilities. Perhaps more surprising is the view that the EU is not an economic power on the same level as the USA, China or Japan (Saad 2008). These public assessments of the EU as a foreign policy actor are consistent with the self-confessed lack of knowledge about the EU as revealed by a 2004 Gallup poll: only 22 per cent of respondents self-assessed themselves as having either a great deal (2 per cent) or fair amount (19 per cent) of knowledge about the EU, while 37 per cent claimed to have very little knowledge or none at all (40 per cent) (Gallup and Saad 2004).

## Political and economic elites

The divided nature of American government in combination with the diffused power and influence wielded by specific government bureaux and attentive foreign policy and economic elites, makes any generalization about the perception of the EU by American political and economic elites problematic. Elite attitudes towards the EU and the perceptions of it are divided into four general subcategories: the top executive branch (the Office of the President and the functional departments and agencies), the legislative branch (House of Representatives and Senate), the foreign policy community and peak economic interest groups.

### The US Congress

In Senate and House documents, hearings and prints between 1990 and 2007, China accounted for almost 39 per cent of document titles, followed by Europe (10 per cent), the Balkans and former Yugoslavia (11 per cent) and NATO (9 per cent). Japan, Russia and North Korea jointly accounted for 22 per cent of the titles and each individually exceeds the EU share of 4 per cent, which is equal to the share of the major EU member states. The EU was identified as the subject with an economic or security term in the 198 Congressional documents; where an economic or security term is the subject of the Congressional document, the EU is mentioned 22,289 times. Somewhat surprisingly, the Congress treats the EU as a security actor in 41 per cent and as an economic actor in 60 per cent of the time. Moreover, where the EU is mentioned in the text under a generic economic or security-related title, the rank order is reversed: security affairs account for 62 per cent and economic affairs 38 per cent of Congressional documents.

The American Congress endows the EU with a low level of actorness relative to the other major states in the international system. Actorness refers here to the extent to which the EU is considered a target of foreign policy or international economic policies or as capable of thwarting or furthering American domestic or international objectives. The EU remains subordinate to the geographic designation 'Europe', however. And the EU is only marginally more important than the major EU member states individually considered. As important, however, is the overwhelming attention paid to Asia (particularly China) and the Pacific orientation of the Congress despite the continuing material importance of Europe (and the EU) to the USA. What is remarkable, however, is the high profile accorded to the EU in the area of trade: over 70 per cent of the documents and hearings with the EU in the title referred to trade. Much of that attention is negative, however: it focuses almost exclusively on the trade distorting effects of the common agricultural policy or growing European energy dependence on Russia. And almost all of the attention paid to the EU as a security actor reveals the fear that Europe will seek greater autonomy from the USA or form a caucus within NATO.

### Executive branch: the Office of the President

In a title search of the public papers of the US presidents (with the exclusion of press releases) from 1990 to 2005, the EU emerges as a security rather than economic actor (63 per cent v. 37 per cent), but the EU is only relevant 7 per cent of the time in economic issues and 5 per cent of the time in security issues overall. Moreover, although Europe retains its place as the most important region of the world for the USA (54 per cent) as compared to the Asia-Pacific (20 per cent) and the Middle East (24 per cent), the EU as such is only mentioned 2 per cent of the time, far below the attention given to NATO (20 per cent), Russia (9 per cent) or any of the major European states, China, Iran, Iraq, Israel, Japan and North Korea.

A more focused statement of American foreign policy objectives may be found in the *National Security Strategies* (*NSS*) issued by the White House. Since 1990, there have been six *NSS*s issued by Presidents G.W.H. Bush (White House 1991), W.J. Clinton (White House 1996, 1997, 1999) and G.W. Bush (White House 2002, 2006). Two things emerge immediately: the relative importance of Europe in administration foreign policy calculations has steadily declined (from 66 per cent in 1991 to 18 per cent in 2006), while the preoccupation with Asia and the Middle East has correspondingly risen (from 20 per cent in 1991 to 36 per cent in 2006 and from 12 per cent in 1991 to 28 per cent in 2006, respectively). The EU only accounted for 2.5 per cent of the major foreign policy actors or regions identified and the EU escaped mention in the 2006 *NSS*. There has been a Pacific reorientation in the American foreign policy calculations independent of the War on Terrorism and the centrality of the Middle East to it. The post-Cold War *NSS*s do not recognize the EU as a major actor of consequence for US foreign policy. Not only has 'Europe' remained the policy reference point for the Office of the President, the importance of the EU (and Europe more generally) has progressively waned while that of the Asia-Pacific has waxed.

### Executive branch: departments and agencies

The departments and agencies of the Federal Government with a foreign policy mandate have differentiated perceptions of the EU, no doubt tracking the interests and preferences of their domestic constituencies. Table 2.1 provides the summary results of a content analysis of the documents and publications of those departments and agencies with a significant foreign policy mandate: the Departments of Agriculture, Commerce (International Trade Administration and Bureau of Industry and Security), Defense, State and Treasury, and the Centers for Disease Control, the Environmental Protection Agency and the Board of Governors of the Federal Reserve System. The departments most preoccupied with the EU are Agriculture, State and Treasury, while Commerce, Defense, the Centers for Disease Control, the Environmental Agency and Federal Reserve are either focused on the member states or on regions other than Europe. Only the Office of the Special Trade Representative privileges the EU over its member states. The Federal Reserve and Defense retain a largely state-centric orientation inside and outside Europe. The other major non-European states, particularly China, Japan and Mexico, have a higher degree of recognition than does the EU for most agencies and departments (see Table 2.1)

Table 2.1 Department and agency perceptions of the European Union as an actor, 1990–2007 (percentage share of total mentions for all categories)

| | Treasury (%) | State (%) | Special trade representative (%) | International trade administration* (%) | Bureau of industry and standards* (%) | Agriculture (%) | Defence** (%) | Centre for disease control (%) | Federal reserve (%) |
|---|---|---|---|---|---|---|---|---|---|
| EU | 8.49 | 7.52 | 12.40 | 3.79 | 4.83 | 8.90 | 2.20 | 2.88 | 0.45 |
| UK | 5.25 | 9.83 | 1.91 | 5.77 | 7.72 | 0.63 | 8.32 | 7.73 | 14.35 |
| France | 7.57 | 6.35 | 2.58 | 6.13 | 6.77 | 7.44 | 4.94 | 8.69 | 9.75 |
| Germany | 8.56 | 6.37 | 3.53 | 6.76 | 8.08 | 6.95 | 14.65 | 7.67 | 7.66 |
| Italy | 5.48 | 6.37 | 1.92 | 5.58 | 5.17 | 6.39 | 6.51 | 7.48 | 3.87 |
| China | 11.21 | 9.80 | 7.60 | 17.33 | 17.14 | 12.05 | 7.64 | 8.38 | 7.80 |
| Japan | 12.25 | 7.23 | 7.46 | 9.49 | 11.09 | 9.16 | 11.05 | 8.25 | 13.11 |
| South Korea | 1.59 | 4.82 | 0.97 | 2.21 | 0.29 | 5.21 | 4.03 | 1.75 | 4.51 |
| Russia | 8.24 | 7.44 | 2.86 | 5.25 | 8.50 | 6.58 | 8.08 | 4.66 | 0.86 |
| Mexico | 11.56 | 7.28 | 7.14 | 16.34 | 5.85 | 11.87 | 3.92 | 22.44 | 10.39 |
| Canada | 9.64 | 6.57 | 8.14 | 9.90 | 10.82 | 13.77 | 4.55 | 11.84 | 19.55 |
| India | 5.03 | 8.34 | 6.27 | 8.19 | 13.70 | 8.18 | 3.02 | 8.25 | 6.56 |
| NAFTA | 1.74 | 1.91 | 35.48 | 2.64 | 0.03 | 2.60 | | | 0.07 |
| ASEAN | 0.73 | 2.68 | 1.73 | 0.62 | 0.02 | 0.29 | | | 0.04 |
| NATO | | 7.11 | | | | | 20.85 | | |

Notes
*Department of Commerce.
**1994–2007.

What conclusions can we draw about the US government's perception of the EU as a foreign policy actor? The Senate and House endow the EU with a high level of 'actorness' vis-à-vis the member states; it is also treated as an important global actor. The House and Senate hearings portray the EU primarily as an economic actor (almost 60 per cent of the EU-titled hearings are on economic issues), although its profile as a security actor is not insignificant. The evidence drawn from the Office of the President underscores the continuing identification of Europe rather than the EU as an 'actor', particularly in comparison to NATO. Moreover, the EU is overshadowed by the states of the Asia-Pacific and North America in both the economic and security domains, despite the EU competencies for Europe's foreign economic policies. The departments and agencies with a foreign policy mandate focus on the EU only when the Union is the policy locus for decision making. Only the Defense Department, the Centers for Disease Control and the Federal Reserve privilege European states over the EU, a not too surprising result given the continuing locus of national responsibility for defence and epidemiological surveillance as well as the national responsibility for regulating national banking systems and capital markets.

### The attentive foreign policy elite

A 2007 elite survey, drawn from responses to an electronic questionnaire sent to members of the Foreign Policy Association and high-profile foreign policy experts in academia, concluded that there is not a uniform assessment of the EU as a relevant security actor or partner for the USA (Sperling and Tossutti 2007). The EU was considered as a relevant actor in two issue areas where the USA is perceived to be laggard rather than leader: macroeconomic stability and the mitigation of environmental threats. At the same time, it was seen as a relatively unimportant actor for addressing the threats posed by cyber-warfare or cyber-vandalism, conventional war or a nuclear (or radiological) attack. The EU is treated as a viable and important partner for the USA across a broad spectrum of other security threats, but it is not clear how that importance should be interpreted. A number of threats, particularly ethnic conflict and migratory pressures, would seem to be parallel rather than common threats insofar as ethnic conflict and migratory pressures are regionally localized, while the logic of transnational cooperation is manifest for mitigating the threats posed by biological and chemical attacks, narcotics trafficking and pandemics.

Questions addressing the impact of the European Security and Defence Policy (ESDP) on NATO and the US role in Europe also suggest the potential for the EU to emerge as a security actor of consequence. A near majority (46 per cent) believed that a more autonomous ESDP would weaken NATO some or very much, while only 26 per cent did not believe it would significantly affect NATO at all. The geopolitical consequences of a stronger ESDP on the American security commitment exhibited a greater degree of uncertainty: slightly over 40 per cent of the respondents believed that a stronger ESDP might weaken the US commitment, while only 23 per cent believed that it would lead to the retrenchment of the US effort. One difficulty in drawing any firm conclusion about the consequences of a stronger ESDP on the American commitment is the prior understanding of that commitment held by each respondent: if the American commitment is considered a function of the American national interest rather than a mixture of interest and community, then the ESDP is unlikely to have a marked impact on American intentions; if the respondent were an ideological Atlanticist, there would be a similar lack of concern. Either rationale could explain why 28 per cent of the respondents see no change in the intensity of the American commitment.

The perceived durability of the American commitment to Europe despite the evolution of the ESDP can also be explained by the importance ascribed to the American commitment to European security. A clear majority (85 per cent) hold that the American security commitment to Europe is important, and 55 per cent believe that that commitment is either essential or very important. Only 15 per cent believe that the American commitment is inessential or not very important. What is remarkable, however, is the implication of these results for the expected future relationship between the EU and the USA: the strong belief that the American commitment to Europe is essential is tied to the equally strong belief that a more autonomous ESDP will weaken NATO; and that weakening of NATO, in turn, will reduce the security of the transatlantic area. These findings provide some basis for drawing the following conclusion. This position on the complex relationship between the USA, NATO and Europe is similar to that found in the Congress and various American administrations: a stronger Europe is only in the American (and European) interest so long as Europe remains the political and diplomatic subordinate of the USA.

### Economic elites

Any generalization about the perceptions American capital holds of the EU is likely to be contestable and difficult to assess owing to divergent sectoral interests with American labour. Table 2.2 presents the relative presence of the EU in the policy studies, congressional testimony and press releases of American business and labour. Labour is represented by three labour unions, the real and financial sectors of the economy are represented by four agricultural interest groups, four industry peak organizations, three industry associations, four interest groups representing the services industry and three media groups.[1]

The private sector attributes a high degree of actorness to the EU. Yet, there are significant variations in the precise role ascribed to the EU across and within the six categories of interest groups. First, as compared to member states, the EU is the single most important actor for all of the industrial interest groups, two of the agricultural interest groups (NAEGA and IDFA), two services groups (SIA/ SIFMA and the American Bar Association) and one labour union (IAMAW). Second, the EU is eclipsed by the member states in the policy calculations of importance for two interest groups representing agriculture (NAEGA and NCC), services (AMA and AbA) and labour (UAW and IMU), and all three media

Table 2.2 Interest group perceptions of the European Union (percentage share of total mentions for each group across all categories)

| | EU | UK | France | FRG | Italy | European total | China | Japan | Russia | Mexico | Canada | India | NAFTA | ASEAN |
|---|---|---|---|---|---|---|---|---|---|---|---|---|---|---|
| *Agriculture:* | | | | | | | | | | | | | | |
| NAEGA | 11.41 | 1.63 | 1.09 | 1.63 | 1.63 | 17.39 | 16.85 | 20.11 | 0.54 | 20.65 | 16.85 | 4.89 | 2.17 | 0.54 |
| NCBA | 1.75 | 10.30 | 10.16 | 10.17 | 10.14 | 42.52 | 10.72 | 11.70 | 1.28 | 11.60 | 11.82 | 10.18 | 0.16 | 0.02 |
| IDFA | 23.68 | 6.23 | 5.48 | 4.04 | 4.86 | 44.29 | 6.57 | 5.89 | 2.67 | 15.47 | 18.07 | 2.94 | 4.11 | 0.00 |
| NCC | 6.27 | 4.32 | 1.72 | 7.81 | 3.08 | 23.20 | 17.75 | 12.66 | 2.01 | 17.75 | 5.38 | 17.04 | 3.85 | 0.36 |
| *Industry:* | | | | | | | | | | | | | | |
| AIA | 17.38 | 11.02 | 11.64 | 7.78 | 5.14 | 52.96 | 13.10 | 8.14 | 5.94 | 6.00 | 17.58 | 7.78 | 0.37 | 0.12 |
| Pharma | 7.21 | 5.41 | 4.50 | 4.50 | 2.70 | 24.32 | 13.51 | 12.61 | 5.41 | 5.41 | 17.12 | 18.92 | 0.90 | 1.80 |
| NAM | 16.96 | 7.78 | 7.23 | 7.04 | 3.80 | 42.81 | 15.01 | 7.41 | 3.15 | 8.80 | 7.60 | 7.78 | 6.02 | 1.39 |
| BR | 39.23 | 1.23 | 1.58 | 1.93 | 0.70 | 44.67 | 20.49 | 7.88 | 1.05 | 8.76 | 5.43 | 8.41 | 2.98 | 0.35 |
| ACC | 9.58 | 5.99 | 4.49 | 6.29 | 2.40 | 28.75 | 14.97 | 7.78 | 3.89 | 17.66 | 11.68 | 11.68 | 3.29 | 0.30 |
| USCC | 13.14 | 0.53 | 4.01 | 4.73 | 2.17 | 24.58 | 13.14 | 12.55 | 5.12 | 13.14 | 12.16 | 13.14 | 4.80 | 1.38 |
| USCIB | 29.37 | 2.33 | 7.36 | 5.10 | 3.94 | 48.10 | 16.98 | 13.78 | 6.63 | 7.51 | 9.99 | 8.75 | 4.30 | 0.44 |
| *Services:* | | | | | | | | | | | | | | |
| SIFMA | 43.30 | 7.45 | 6.19 | 4.70 | 4.70 | 66.34 | 8.71 | 6.76 | 1.49 | 3.78 | 8.71 | 3.89 | 0.23 | 0.11 |
| AMA | 5.15 | 18.88 | 7.85 | 8.45 | 3.23 | 43.56 | 15.97 | 8.12 | 2.38 | 8.32 | 13.07 | 7.85 | 0.59 | 0.13 |
| AbankA | 3.05 | 9.14 | 7.61 | 7.11 | 6.09 | 33.00 | 12.18 | 9.64 | 6.09 | 18.27 | 13.71 | 6.60 | 0.51 | 0.00 |
| ABA | 15.90 | 11.44 | 7.60 | 7.54 | 5.97 | 48.45 | 8.30 | 7.38 | 5.64 | 10.91 | 9.82 | 5.97 | 3.14 | 0.37 |
| *Labour:* | | | | | | | | | | | | | | |
| AFL-CIO | 1.16 | 2.01 | 1.35 | 1.03 | 0.57 | 6.12 | 13.84 | 2.45 | 0.65 | 57.75 | 6.68 | 3.62 | 6.93 | 0.01 |
| UAW | 1.93 | 1.64 | 2.21 | 4.49 | 0.71 | 10.98 | 20.33 | 7.13 | 0.36 | 20.61 | 22.33 | 2.43 | 15.83 | |
| IMU | 4.03 | 2.98 | 2.85 | 2.94 | 2.02 | 14.82 | 26.31 | 3.07 | 1.82 | 10.24 | 32.33 | 3.87 | 3.65 | 3.87 |
| *Media:* | | | | | | | | | | | | | | |
| MPA | 0.18 | 7.89 | 8.85 | 8.72 | 8.17 | 33.81 | 10.64 | 8.85 | 8.58 | 9.36 | 19.79 | 8.97 | | |
| MPAA | 1.13 | 3.76 | 2.26 | 4.14 | 1.88 | 13.17 | 14.85 | 5.26 | 4.70 | 11.28 | 46.99 | 3.76 | | |
| NAB | 3.20 | 15.60 | 5.20 | 4.40 | 10.00 | 38.40 | 6.80 | 16.00 | 3.60 | 12.80 | 20.80 | 1.60 | | |
| NAA | 4.35 | 36.65 | 8.70 | 14.91 | 3.73 | 68.34 | 18.01 | 13.66 | | | | | | |

groups. Third, Mexico and Canada are jointly the most important states for three groups representing agriculture (NCBA, IDFA, NCC), services (SIA/SIMFA, Aba, ABA), labour (AFL-CIO, UAW, IMU), media (MPA, MPAA, NAB), and two industry groups (AIA and ACC). Finally, China captures the primary attention of four interest groups (NAM, BR, USCIB and AMA) and Japan only one interest group (NAEGA), while India is the favourite of Pharma. Europe and North America, despite the popular, press and official preoccupations with China, remain the focus of American economic elites – a finding consistent with the markets for US goods and services.

The AIA and SIA/SIFMA represent two sectors of the American economy directly affected by the regulatory policies of the EU as well as competition in third markets. The preoccupation of the AIA vis-à-vis the EU consists of complaints about launch aid and export subsidies for Airbus commercial aircraft, non-competitive bidding practices that favour European aerospace manufacturers at the expense of American corporations, a restrictive regulatory environment and the extra-territorial application of EU law that has prevented the consolidation of the American aerospace industry (Commission 2002: 6–20). The AIA also points to the EU *Vision 2020* as a model of government–industry cooperation for the USA, particularly given the EU objective of pushing European aerospace manufacturing to the 'forefront of the global market' at the expense of American dominance (Douglas 2001, 2005). A final concern of the AIA reflects the likelihood that the world will adopt EU rather American manufacturing and safety standards, a development that will impose significant costs on American industry and lend an additional competitive advantage to European aerospace.

The SIA/SIFMA does not view the EU as imposing a regulatory burden on the financial services industry or providing European firms with protection from their American competitors. Instead, SIA/SIFMA has adopted the global perspective that the best outcome for Europe and the USA is an integrated transatlantic capital market that will benefit Europe and America equally; SIA/SIFMA is interested in assuring that common standards are adopted to facilitate trade in financial services (particularly accounting standards), that the extra-territorial application of law (e.g. Sarbanes-Oxley and Exon-Florio in the USA) does not constitute a barrier to capital market integration and that there is greater regulatory convergence between the USA and the EU. SIA/SIFMA also tracks specific EU directives that affect capital markets and market access; the commentaries are neither laudatory nor critical, but simply identify the changes in the law and the steps that firms must take to be in conformity with the new regulations (Security Industries Association 2002, 2003a, b; Lackritz 2006; Huet 2007). As is the case with AIA, the industry also looks to the EU as a model for US legislation, particularly the consistency of American law with the EU's Financial Action Services Programme (Litman 2003; USCC 2007; Thornburgh 2004; Lackritz 2005).

The four industry peak organizations (the BR, NAM, USCC and USCIB) recognize that the EU Commission regulates the European economy and that the EU is the most significant export market for US manufactures. They also share five categories of concern with respect to the EU. The first, and most important, is the divergent regulatory environment found in the EU and the USA, particularly the less 'business-friendly' regulatory environment in the EU, as a significant barrier to trade within the transatlantic area. EU directives and common policies have extra-territorial implications for American business and add to the cost of doing business in the European and American markets by creating divergent regulatory regimes in the two major markets for American goods and services (Vargo n.d.). A second set of concerns revolves around the value added tax (VAT). In addition to viewing the VAT as an export subsidy for EU manufacturers, the USCIB has criticized EU efforts to impose VAT on electronic trade at the origin of the sale, a decision that would leave American firms physically operating outside the EU subject to it (Nichols 2000). Third, these peak organizations also recognize the common ground that binds the EU and the USA together; namely, the need to enhance the competitiveness of European and American firms in third markets. Towards that end, the USCIB recommends, for example, creating a transatlantic legal framework affording greater protection to intellectual property rights and more effective policing of counterfeit goods in third markets, establishing a common or equivalent set of accounting standards and fostering greater regulatory cooperation to remove barriers to trade (USCIB 2004). Fourth, industry has expressed concerns about the trade-diverting consequences of third-party EU free trade agreements and bilateral investment treaties that disadvantage US firms (National Association of Manufacturers 2004, 2006; USCC 2004; Business Roundtable 2001). Finally, these peak organizations view the external projection of the EU regulatory regime to third markets as a threat to American competitiveness as well as a model for externalizing the American regulatory regime (Business Roundtable 2006).

American agriculture, preoccupied with the tariff and non-tariff barriers to transatlantic trade in agricultural products, takes the position that the EU Common Agricultural Policy not only prevents the deeper market penetration of more efficiently produced American agricultural goods in the European market, but also drives American producers out of third markets owing to EU export subsidies. American agriculture also focuses on the non-tariff barriers to trade posed by the EU regulatory environment, especially the reliance upon the precautionary principle in assessing the safety of genetically modified foodstuffs, food hygiene (particularly sanitary and phytosanitary measures), the banned importation of hormone treated beef, the possible introduction of geographic indications and product designation of origin for a broader range of agricultural products, particularly cheeses, which would leave American manufacturers bereft of categories now considered generic (e.g. asiago, parmesan, brie, etc.) (IDFA n.d.; Tipton 2005; NAEGA 2007; NCC 2001: 9; Powell 2004).

American labour views the EU as an ally in its quest to staunch the loss of American manufacturing jobs to lower cost producers, particularly in Asia. American labour looks to European labour as an ally in passing trade legislation that effectively provides non-tariff barrier protection to US and European manufacturing jobs; namely, mandating that firms operating outside Europe and the USA meet common safety, environmental and remuneration standards (European Trade Union Confederation and AFL-CIO 2007). The natural alliance between US and EU labour, however, is qualified: the IAMAW, for example, has expressed concern over EU subsidies to Airbus Industrie and EADS in the commercial and military sector as a direct threat to American jobs (IAMAW n.d.).

American manufacturing and services industries focus on the EU owing to the prominent regulatory role assumed by Brussels, the EU role in and responsibility for creating a European standard around which manufactures coalesce, and the EU's role in representing Europe in global and regional trading negotiations. The precise orientation of an industry towards the EU, however, is dependent upon the size of the European market for American goods and the nature and height of the barriers to market access. But where industry perceives a 'national' rather than an 'EU' market, as is the case in media and retail banking, the EU plays a significantly less important role in the industry calculations. Interest groups in the financial, agricultural and real sectors of the economy – with the exception of retail banking and beef – treat the EU as the regulatory address for meeting their concerns, but the EU plays a minimal role in the calculations of those interest groups representing media, labour and services (with the notable exception of SIFMA/SIA). The relative importance of the EU (and its member states) for the private sector as compared to the other major economic powers varies significantly: the EU and its member states, taken together, may be considered very important for three interest groups (higher than 50 per cent share), important for 12 interest groups (between 25 and 50 per cent) and of little importance for seven interest groups (less than 25 per cent).

## Civil society: an overview of advocacy networks

Environmental and consumer protection advocacy groups generally point to the EU as an exemplar for regulating industry and improving environmental conditions nationally and globally. Environmental groups are represented by the Environmental Defense Fund, while the consumer advocacy groups are represented by the US Public Interest Research Group.

Environmental advocacy groups view the regulatory role of the EU from the other side of the looking glass used by American manufacturers: EU regulatory policies are presented as the templates for US legislation; the EU is viewed as a mechanism for enforcing higher environmental standards in the US through the extra-territorial application of law made possible by the importance of the European market to US industry; and the EU holds lessons for the USA in tackling the critical environmental task of reducing $CO_2$ emissions. The Environmental Defense Fund has praised EU efforts to comply with their Kyoto Treaty commitments as well as the REACH proposal to ensure the safety and mitigate the environmental consequences of over 30,000 industrial chemicals (Environmental Defense Fund 2004).

The concerns of Public Interest Research Group, the major consumers' advocacy group in the USA, overlap significantly with those of environmental groups.[2] The Public Interest Research Group has commended the EU's REACH programme and criticized the Bush administration for its efforts to hinder its full implementation. Moreover, it advocates the EU 'precautionary principle' rather than the American principle of 'safe until proven otherwise', the preference for preventing harm rather than managing risk, forcing producers rather than Federal agencies to bear the cost of screening tests, and the preference for enforceable rules rather than voluntary compliance with them (US-PIRG 2004). These two advocacy groups, and other advocacy groups, view the EU as an important actor, and in most cases the EU is seen as a progressive institution protecting civil society from rapacious industrialists and financiers. The EU is relatively more important than its member states for the Public Interest Research Group. The more important result from this analysis, however, is that the EU and the individual member states are not the primary target of their concerns; almost all have a parochial agenda that yields an external agenda focusing primarily on Mexico and Canada. Nonetheless, the EU is taken seriously as an actor with global impact and importance.

## The press

The three American newspapers that demarcate the parameters of the public foreign policy debate are the *Wall Street Journal* (hereafter *Journal*), the *Washington Post* (hereafter *Post*) and the *New York Times* (hereafter *Times*). One or all of these papers is read on a daily basis by members of the foreign policy, political and economic elites. As a business, these papers supply information relevant to the preoccupations and needs of its reading public. In that sense, newspapers reflect events that are of importance to its readership; resources (foreign bureaux or the allotment of column space) are distributed over time to areas of importance as defined by the target audience. What do the headlines in these three papers since 1990 tell us about the American foreign policy elite's perception of the EU as an actor? First, it is clear that the EU does not hold much interest as a discrete actor for readers of the *Times* or *Post* (see Table 2.3) The EU appears in less than 2 per cent of titles in those papers, although it has a higher profile in the *Journal*, no doubt reflecting the readership's interest in the consequences of the EU's regulatory role for American capital – an inference supported by the relatively low number of headlines devoted to Iraq as compared to the *Times* and *Post*. As important, the major member states appear more frequently in *Times* headlines than the EU by a wide margin, although the discrepancy is less pronounced in the *Post*. In contrast, the EU captures more headlines than the member states in the *Journal*. China and Japan, however, individually and jointly, capture an arguably disproportionately large share of the headlines: 49 per cent in the *Journal*, 29 per cent in the *Times* and 21 per cent in the *Post*.

A second line of enquiry questions how the EU is viewed as an actor. In Table 2.3, the EU is also categorized as an economic or security actor.

Table 2.3 Press perceptions of the European Union as an actor: *New York Times*, *Wall Street Journal* and *Washington Post* (percentage share of total mentions for each paper across all categories)

| Appearance in headlines | Wall Street Journal (1996–2007) | | New York Times (1990–2007) | | Washington Post (1990–2007) | |
|---|---|---|---|---|---|---|
| EU | 3,333 | 9.85 | 314 | 0.62 | 363 | 1.98 |
| NATO | 440 | 1.30 | 1,430 | 2.83 | 1047 | 5.71 |
| Germany | 1,895 | 5.60 | 2,901 | 5.73 | 645 | 3.52 |
| France | 2,193 | 6.48 | 3,392 | 6.70 | 588 | 3.21 |
| Italy | 1,120 | 3.31 | 2,107 | 4.16 | 278 | 1.52 |
| UK | 740 | 2.19 | 3,823 | 7.55 | 603 | 3.29 |
| Russia | 2,278 | 6.73 | 4,648 | 9.18 | 1714 | 9.35 |
| China | 9,460 | 27.95 | 7,398 | 14.62 | 2654 | 14.49 |
| Japan | 7,217 | 21.32 | 7,370 | 14.56 | 1154 | 6.30 |
| North Korea | 634 | 1.87 | 1,441 | 2.85 | 383 | 2.09 |
| Iran | 773 | 2.28 | 2,724 | 5.38 | 1431 | 7.81 |
| Iraq | 2,929 | 8.65 | 10,000 | 19.76 | 5580 | 30.46 |
| Israel | 588 | 1.74 | 3,055 | 6.04 | 1881 | 10.27 |
| ASEAN | 137 | 0.40 | 3 | 0.01 | 11 | 0.06 |
| APEC | 109 | 0.32 | 1 | 0.00 | 11 | 0.06 |
| Total | 33,846 | | 50,607 | | 18,343 | |

| Appearance in text | New York Times (1990–2007) | | Wall Street Journal (1996–2007) | | Washington Post (1990–2007) | |
|---|---|---|---|---|---|---|
| *Economic:* | | | | | | |
| Trade | 106 | 38.55 | 45 | 4.80 | 22 | 36.67 |
| Agriculture | 18 | 6.55 | 6 | 0.64 | 2 | 3.33 |
| Finance | 32 | 11.64 | 45 | 4.80 | 7 | 11.67 |
| Euro/EMU | 49 | 17.82 | 93 | 9.92 | 7 | 11.67 |
| Energy | 15 | 5.45 | 50 | 5.34 | 6 | 10.00 |
| Oil/natural gas | 28 | 10.18 | 24 | 2.56 | 7 | 11.66 |
| Globalization | 9 | 3.27 | 2 | 0.21 | | |
| Deregulation | 5 | 1.82 | 12 | 1.28 | | |
| Airbus | | | 660 | 70.44 | 4 | 6.67 |
| Dollar | 13 | 4.73 | | | 5 | 8.33 |
| subtotal | 275 | 45.75 | 937 | 87.33 | 60 | 42.55 |
| *Security:* | | | | | | |
| Security | 61 | 18.71 | 15 | 11.03 | 17 | 20.99 |
| NATO | 35 | 10.74 | 18 | 13.24 | 9 | 11.11 |
| Terrorism | 31 | 9.51 | 8 | 5.88 | 1 | 1.23 |
| War | 58 | 17.79 | 30 | 22.06 | 14 | 17.28 |
| Nuclear | 12 | 3.68 | 13 | 9.56 | 1 | 1.23 |
| Foreign policy | 34 | 10.43 | 8 | 5.88 | 15 | 18.52 |
| Immigration | 16 | 4.91 | | | 3 | 3.70 |
| Human rights | 37 | 11.35 | | | 11 | 13.58 |
| Iran | | | 23 | 16.91 | 3 | 3.70 |
| subtotal | 326 | 54.25 | 136 | 12.67 | 81 | 57.44 |
| Total | 601 | | 1073 | | 141 | |

Somewhat surprisingly (and consistent with government perceptions), the EU is viewed as a security actor in 54 per cent and 57 per cent of the articles published in the *Times* and *Post*, respectively. Consistent with the *Journal*'s readership, the EU is treated as an economic actor in 87 per cent of the published articles. Trade and the euro are the most important economic subcategories for the *Times* and *Post*, while Airbus and the euro are most prevalent in the *Journal*. The distribution of articles by subcategory in the area of security is not particularly insightful, although security, defence and war combined account for 49 per cent of the articles in the *Times*, 49 per cent of the articles in the *Journal* and 47 per cent of the articles in the *Post*. Terrorism, the policy area where the EU has played an active internal role, does not figure prominently in either the *Journal* or *Post*, reflecting perhaps the assumption that terrorism is a problem addressed unilaterally or bilaterally.

The *Times* and the *Post* endow the EU with a relatively low level of actorness as compared to the European member states and other major states of the international system, while the *Journal* treats the EU as the third most important actor in the international system, an importance no doubt derived from the readership's sensitivity to the impact of the EU on their quarterly profit and loss statements or stock portfolios. Similar to the political elites they serve, the *Times* and *Post* seem more preoccupied with the EU's role as a security actor, while the *Journal* treats the EU primarily as an economic actor, a treatment consistent with its prerogatives under the Maastricht, Amsterdam and Nice Treaties. Most striking, perhaps, is the low level of significance ascribed to the EU compared to China and Japan, and to states of the Middle East, particularly Israel and Iraq.

## Understanding the American image of the EU

Do Americans view the EU through a glass, darkly or from the other side of the looking glass? There is no answer to this question that holds across (or even within) the four foreign policy constituencies considered. The political and economic integration of Europe constituted an important instrumental goal of American foreign policy over the course of the postwar period. The asymmetry of information about the EU, the interpretation of that information even when shared and the perception of the EU's relevance to the interests of the different constituencies influencing American foreign policy, should not come as a surprise. The American relationship with Europe and individual European countries is complicated and has always been so.

For Americans of European extraction, Europe exerts a wistful pull on those who have retained a strong ethnic identity or believe that it holds the key to discovering a grander familial past. Many instinctively accept that the American history before America is that of Europe; that American culture is a derivative of or at least deeply indebted to European culture, but possibly superior to it. Americans frame Europe's relationship with the USA in terms of the successive waves of immigration over the course of the nineteenth and early twentieth centuries, the American entanglement in European affairs that spawned two world wars and left Europeans and Europe as supplicants and dependent upon the USA for its postwar economic recovery and military security. These historical, linguistic and ethnic commonalities nevertheless stand in opposition to the American sense of exceptionalism and moral rectitude contrasted to European world-weariness and amorality; it is accompanied by a scarcely repressed fear that European culture is superior to that found in America, and it sometimes finds expression in a profound disappointment that Europeans are not as grateful as they should be for American protection and munificence since the middle of the twentieth century.

These psychological and cultural entanglements, and the contradictory impulses it has engendered, have become exacerbated by contrary American and European conceptions of world order and their respective roles in it. The American liberal internationalism of the Cold War period was arguably embedded in the DNA of the US foreign policy establishment, the legitimacy of which remained robust until the end of the twentieth century. Within this context and the Soviet–American competition to achieve European hegemony, the American preference to rely upon multilateral institutions and an unwillingness to flaunt international law was consistent with European sensibilities, although differences certainly existed at the margins of transatlantic diplomacy, particularly outside Europe.

With the end of the Cold War, however, different conceptions of international order produced transatlantic schisms that reflected changes in the American foreign policy elite, the nature and origins of the threats facing Europeans and Americans, and varying degrees of discomfort with the emergence of the USA as a *hyperpuissance*, the American triumphalism that it engendered and a new-found willingness to act alone.

The EU has played a central role in consolidating and sustaining Europe's relevance in the international system, despite the continuing dominance of national governments in the execution of Europe's foreign policies. The USA has historically championed, at least rhetorically, the goal of European integration. Yet the prospect of a Europe politically, diplomatically and militarily unified under the aegis of the EU promises a multipolar world that could negate rather than reinforce American prerogatives. The broadening and deepening of the EU set in motion with the Maastricht Treaty in 1992 have continued to produce the paradoxes of resentment that have vexed European–American relations since the French Revolution. Thus, American support for European integration has been always tempered by a corresponding suspicion that a more politically and economically unified Europe, particularly a French-inspired and autonomous Europe, would complicate American strategy vis-à-vis the Soviet Union and now Russia; that it could pose a serious challenge to American leadership within the transatlantic alliance or hinder the realization of American foreign policy objectives.

Just as Europeans rarely deviated from an 'Atlanticist' catechism, American rhetoric rarely questioned openly the benefits of European integration for the American global strategy of containment. While the material and strategic importance of the EU to the USA should be beyond question, the perception of the EU by America's political and economic elites appears problematic and puzzling. The political classes, while willing to acknowledge the EU as an actor, remain preoccupied with the nation state and wedded to a traditional understanding of security, while the economic elite views the EU as a regulatory behemoth hell-bent on destroying the American market economy. Similarly, the print media is likewise infatuated with the national policies of European states, even where the EU is the dominant institutional player, and tend to invert the real prerogatives the member states have endowed the EU; namely, they treat the EU as having a security function that is more important than its economic one. Arguably, three of the four foreign policy constituencies view the EU through a glass, darkly: the foreign policy and security roles of the EU are overestimated at the expense of the important economic role that the EU does play. Advocacy groups, which represent a fourth constituency, would appear trapped on the other side of the looking glass by comparison: they see the EU as a global regulatory and environmental actor capable of shaping global norms and American legislation for the better. The EU remains an ill-defined actor in American foreign policy discourse, although economic interest and advocacy groups are best attuned to the continuing importance of Europe to the USA and the global reach of the EU.

## Conclusion

The three questions raised in the introduction produce something of a paradox: the aggregate economic and financial capabilities of the EU are not dissimilar in magnitude to those possessed by the USA *and* the interaction level – economically, diplomatically and strategically – is inconsistent with the systematic discounting of the EU by important constituencies of the American foreign policy establishment. The EU is not generally endowed with a high degree of 'actorness' as either a facilitator or barrier to US foreign policy objectives. Why?

The least complex explanation for this paradox is the continuing pull of the Westphalian state on the imagination of the American foreign policy elite. Many discount the importance of the EU as an autonomous actor, preferring to see it as a cipher for the national interests of the individual member states or as an impenetrable bureaucratic maze. Moreover, it could as well reflect a deeply engrained American nationalism that is simply projected externally, despite the continuing expectation that the states of Europe abnegate their own national interests in deference to American ones. While the empirical evidence suggests that many constituencies accept that the EU is an economic actor with major responsibilities and prerogatives independent of member state governments, the consideration of the EU as a security actor is seen as an over-the-horizon eventuality that could diminish American prerogatives, not only in Europe but anywhere Europe has a vital interest. Consistent with American pragmatism and the irrepressible habit of mind to 'follow the money', the empirical evidence supports the proposition that where the EU *is* in fact the actor governing a specific policy domain, the constituent members of the American foreign policy establishment directly affected will beat a direct path to the Commission's door. American business – industry, agriculture, finance and services – and advocacy groups have recognized the significant and sometimes autonomous prerogatives that the EU possesses and have decamped to Brussels. Despite the best efforts to consolidate the Common Foreign and Security Policy and the ESDP, the member states have retained a virtual monopoly in the critical domains of foreign and defence policy. So long as that national monopoly persists, the member states rather than the EU will remain the only address for military-strategic or diplomatic correspondence from Washington.

## Notes

1 The labour organizations (and their acronyms) are AFL-CIO, the United Auto Workers (UAW) and the International Association of Machinists and Aerospace Workers (IAMAW); the four agricultural interest groups are International Dairy Farmers Association (IDFA), North American Export Grain Association (NAEGA), National Cattlemen and Beef Association (NCBA) and the National Cotton Council (NCC); the four industry peak organizations are the Business Roundtable (BR), the National Association of Manufacturers (NAM), the United States Chamber of Commerce (USCC) and the United States Chamber of International Business (USCIB); the three industry associations are Aerospace Industry Association (AIA), American Chemicals Council (ACA) and Pharma; the four services industry groups are Securities Industry Association/Securities Industry and Financial Management Association (SIA/SIFMA), the American Marketing Association (AMA), the American Banking Association (AbA) and the American Bar Association (ABA); and the three representative media groups are the Magazine Publishers of America (MPA), Motion Pictures Association of America (MPAA) and the National Association of Broadcasters (NAB).

2 Of the consumer advocacy groups, only the National Taxpayers Union reads from the same script as the manufacturing industry. A full accounting of the assessments of the EU as a global actor from the perspective of civil liberties, environmental and consumer advocacy groups can be found in Sperling (2009).

## References

Business Roundtable (2001) *Information Privacy: the current legal regime*, Washington, DC: Business Roundtable.

Business Roundtable (2006) *Expanding Economic Growth Through Trade and Investment: a blueprint for US leadership in the 21st century*, Washington, DC: Business Roundtable.

Commission on the Future of the United States Aerospace Industry (2002) *Final Report*, Washington, DC.

Douglas, J.W. (2001) 'Statement by John W. Douglas, President and Chief Executive Officer, AIA' before the House Science Subcommittee on Space and Aeronautics, hearings on *On the Aerospace Industrial Base*, 15 May

Douglas, J.W. (2005) 'Statement by John W. Douglas, President and Chief Executive Officer, AIA' before the House Committee on Transportation and Infrastructure, Subcommittee on Aviation, hearings on *The US Jet Transport Industry: global market factors affecting US producers*, 25 May.

Environmental Defense Fund (2004) *The Heat is On: a white paper on climate action*, New York.

European Trade Union Confederation and AFL-CIO (2007) *Transatlantic Cooperation for a Just and Sustainable Global Economy*, 30 April.

Gallup, A. and Saad, L. (2004) 'Americans know little about European Union'. Online, available at: www.gallup.com/poll/12043/Americans-Know-Little-About-European-Union.aspx (accessed 31 January 2009).

German Marshall Fund (2005) *Transatlantic Trends: topline data 2005*. Online, available at: www.gmfus.org (accessed 31 January 2009).

German Marshall Fund (2006) *Transatlantic Trends: topline report 2006*. Online, available at: www.gmfus.org (accessed 31 January 2009).

Huet, B. (2007) *Transatlantic Regulatory Convergence*, London, 18 September.

IAMAW (n.d.) 'Aerospace Jobs Issues'. Online, available at: www.goiam.org/copntent.cfm?cID=11873 (accessed 31 January 2009).

IDFA (n.d.) 'The World Trade Organization Built-In Agenda: US diary industry negotiating priorities'. Online, available at: www.idfa.org/intl/letters/051200b.cfm (accessed 31 January 2009)

Lackritz, M. (2005) 'The US–EU Relationship: what comes next?' testimony before the House Financial Services Committee, Subcommittee on Domestic and International Monetary Policy, Trade and Technology, 16 June.

Lackritz, M. (2006) 'Testimony' before Committee on Financial Services, Subcommittee on Capital Markets, US House of Representatives, 29 March.

Litman, G. (2003) 'Statement before the Subcommittee on European Affairs of the Senate Foreign Relations Committee', 16 October. Online, available at: www.uscc.com/issues/testimony/2003/03101litman.htm (accessed 31 January 2009).

NAEGA (2007) 'Letter to Marcia Holden (National Institute of Standards and Technology)', 19 October.

National Association of Manufacturers (2004) 'NAM Submission on Enhancing the Transatlantic Economic Relationship: federal register request for comments.... improving regulatory cooperation to create a seamless economic partnership', 22 December.

National Association of Manufacturers (2006) 'Letter to President George Bush, President Wolfgang Schüssel, and President Jose Manuel Barroso', 16 June.

NCC (2001) *National Council Report to Members 2000*. Online, available at: www.cotton.org/about/report/loader.cfm?csModule=security/getfile&pageid=19420 (accessed 6 September 2008).

Nichols, D.I. (2000) 'USCIB Letter to European Commission on Proposed Directive Regarding VAT Applicable to Electronically Delivered Services', 14 July. Online, available at: www.ucsib.org/index/asp?document=ID1425 (accessed 31 January 2009).

Powell, K.T. (2004) *Voters in Seven California Counties Consider Banning Genetically Engineered Agriculture: a white paper*, US PIRG Education Fund, July.

Saad, L. (2008) 'Americans See China Crowding Out U.S. as Economic Leader'. Online, available at: www.gallup.com/poll/104479/Americans-See-China-Crowding-Out US-Economic-Leader.aspx (accessed 31 January 2009).

Security Industries Association (2002) 'RE: EU financial conglomerates directive', 14 January.

Security Industries Association (2003a) 'RE: EU transparency obligations directive', 1 October.

Security Industries Association (2003b) 'RE: proposed reciprocity provisions to EU takeover directive', 7 May.

Sperling, J. (2009) 'Report on American Perceptions of the EU', in S. Lucarelli and L. Fioramonti (eds) *The External Image of the European Union (Phase Two)*. Online, available at: www.garnet.eu.org/fileadmin/documents/working_papers/6209.pdf (accessed 1 February 2009).

Sperling, J. and Tossutti, L. (2007) 'National Threat Perception: survey results from the United States', in E.J. Kirchner and J. Sperling (eds) *Global Threat Perceptions: elite views and national security culture, GARNET Working Papers No. 18.11/07*. Online, available at: www.garnet-eu.org/fileadmin/documents/working_papers/1807/5.3.2%20 contents.pdf (accessed 25 November 2008).

Thornburgh, R.E. (2004) 'The US–EU Financial Markets Dialogue: transatlantic good news', testimony before House Services Committee, Subcommittee on Domestic and International Monetary Policy, 17 June.

Tipton, C.E. (2005) 'Testimony', Senate Agriculture, Nutrition, and Forestry Committee, *Hearing on the Status of the World Trade Organization Negotiations on Agriculture*, 21 September.

US-PIRG (2004) *Trouble in Toyland: the 20th annual survey of toy safety*, US PIRG Education Fund, November.

US-PIRG (2005) *Duty to Disclose: the failure of food companies to disclose risks of genetically engineered crops to shareholders*, US PIRG Education Fund, August.

USCC (2004) *International Institutions Impacting Industrial Relations: how international employment policy is made and why you should care*, Washington, DC: USCC, 1 December.

USCC (2007) *Optimizing the Transatlantic Market*, Washington, DC: USCC.

USCIB (2004) 'USCIB Submission to USTR on Enhancing the Transatlantic Economic Partnership', 15 December.

Vargo, F. (n.d.) 'Manufacturing Trade Agenda: leveling the international playing field', *Solutions: a white paper series*, Washington, DC: National Association of Manufacturers.

White House (1991) *National Security Strategy of the United States of America*, Washington, DC: White House, August.

White House (1996) *National Security Strategy of Enlargement and Engagement*, Washington, DC: White House, February.

White House (1997) *National Security Strategy for a New Century*, Washington, DC: White House, May.

White House (1999) *National Security Strategy for a New Century*, Washington, DC: White House, December.

White House (2002) *National Security Strategy of the United States of America*, Washington, DC: White House, September.

White House (2006) *National Security Strategy of the United States of America*, Washington, DC: White House, March.

# 3 Eastern giants

## The EU in the eyes of Russia and China

*Mara Morini, Roberto Peruzzi and Arlo Poletti*

## Introduction

This chapter is dedicated to the analysis of China's and Russia's perceptions of the European Union (EU) with a view to assessing the extent to which some key self-representations of the EU are mirrored in the image it casts in two of the most important nations on the international stage.[1]

China and Russia share important similarities as far as their respective relationships with the EU are concerned. For instance, the EU is the main trading partner and an important source of foreign direct investments for both countries. At the same time, both countries pose great challenges to European economic growth and stability. Indeed the EU is heavily dependent on Russia's policies concerning energy supplies and vulnerable with respect to China's export-led economic growth. Against this background, since the mid 1990s both countries have experienced growing institutionalization in their economic and political cooperation with the EU. Finally, China and Russia have established themselves (or 're-established' in the case of Russia) as key players in world affairs and have become a crucial test bed for the EU's ambitions as a global actor. In addition, these countries share a long-term tradition of realist-based foreign policy culture and, more generally, a deeply rooted tendency to perceive other international actors according to specific beliefs and preferences in their foreign policy (Shambaugh 2008; Morini 2008).

Despite these similarities, the comparison between the two countries also reveals different perceptions of the EU, whose analysis will help us evaluate the relative weight of different factors in shaping these external images. Indeed by assessing the relative importance of factors such as geographical proximity/distance or cultural affinity/diversity in shaping images of the EU in these countries, this comparative exercise allows us to investigate what variables – long-term/structural or rather short-term/contingent – are relatively more important in accounting for different perceptive patterns.

## Images of the EU

The images analysis is structured around three different groups of stakeholders: public opinion, political elites and the media. Unlike the other studies presented in the book, no data concerning organized civil society are available. As far as China is concerned, the very nature of its political system does not allow for a meaningful investigation of how the EU is perceived by civil society organizations. The few interesting existing insights available have been drawn from research conducted on the Chinese community of 'European watchers'[2] and are included in the 'political elites' part of the chapter (Jing 2006; Zhu 2008). Similarly, in the case of Russia, legal and political constraints make it rather difficult to gather relevant and objective information on what the main Russian NGOs, associations and movements think of the EU.

## Public opinion[3]

Although specific information concerning the level of knowledge of the EU in these countries is not available, existing public opinion polls seem to suggest that the EU is not a well-known entity among the populations of these two countries. In 2001, more than three-quarters of the Chinese had no knowledge of or opinion about the EU (World Values Survey 2001). In 2007 half of the respondents in an opinion poll in Russia were not aware that their country was not a member of the EU (Public Opinion Foundation 2007). Although by no means exhaustive, this generic data is in line with the findings of previous research conducted in other countries (see Holland and Chaban 2008; Lucarelli 2007), which has highlighted the scarce knowledge of the EU as an element of concern for its global ambitions.

With respect to comparative perceptions of the EU and other international actors/organizations, public opinion polls reveal strikingly similar patterns in China and Russia. In both countries, most respondents express a positive view of Europe's role in the world (see Table 3.1).

When public attitudes towards the EU and other international actors are compared, further similarities emerge. Overall, it seems that the Russians and Chinese are more favourably inclined towards the EU than the United States of America (USA) or a US-led organization such as the North Atlantic Treaty Organization (NATO). First of all, the USA receives a much lower approval rating as a world power than the EU/Europe (see Table 3.1). While 44 per cent of Russians believe Europe has a positive impact on world affairs, only 12 per

*Table 3.1* Chinese and Russian views of European and US influence in the world

|  | Europe has a mainly positive influence in the world | | The USA has a mainly positive influence in the world | |
| --- | --- | --- | --- | --- |
|  | *Russia (%)* | *China (%)* | *Russia (%)* | *China (%)* |
| Agree | 44 | 54 | 12 | 38 |
| Disagree | 35 | 27 | 72 | 48 |

Source: Globescan, 19 nation poll on global issues, 2004 (Online, available at: http://65.109.167.118/pipa/pdf/jun03/Globallss_Jun04_quaire.pdf (accessed 31 January 2009).

cent are of the same opinion in the case of the USA. Similarly, only 38 per cent of the Chinese believe the USA has a positive influence on the world as opposed to 54 per cent who approve of the EU's role. Public opinions in these two countries, therefore, seem to share the perception that indeed there is a qualitative difference between the EU and the USA. In the case of Russia, the analysis can go further by using a specific survey gauging Russian attitudes towards Western organizations in general (Table 3.2).

Most Russians show positive attitudes towards the idea of 'Europe'. This can also be explained by the fact that Russia itself is historically and geographically part of the European continent. The EU ranks in third place, right after the Commonwealth of Independent States (CIS), with 56 per cent of positive attitudes. The USA and NATO, on the contrary, rank at the bottom in the positive perception scale and at the top in terms of negative perceptions. A more recent opinion poll conducted in Russia confirms these trends: the EU is perceived quite positively by 42 per cent of Russians (only 15 per cent harbour negative feelings about the EU) whereas perceptions of NATO are overwhelmingly negative (only 12 per cent of the respondents see it positively).[4]

Chinese and Russian perceptions of the EU also follow similar trends when it comes to a more substantial evaluation of the EU's role in the international system. As opposed to data concerning generic impressions, neither the Chinese nor the Russians believe that the EU is a strong international actor. The results summarized in Table 3.3 indicate that most respondents do not believe the EU is a relevant global power in today's world. Even lower is the number of those who think the EU will become more relevant in the future. This is a particularly worrying finding for the EU's external credibility with potentially negative effects on its future projection as a global power.

In addition, only a small minority of respondents believe that the EU should become a stronger voice in the quest for peace and stability. This is particularly surprising given the EU's proclaimed emphasis on peace and stability as its founding values and cornerstones of its global actorness.

Again, further evidence drawn from recent opinion polls conducted in Russia

*Table 3.2* Russian attitudes towards Western countries and organizations

|  | *Positive feeling* | *Negative feeling* | *No reply* |
|---|---|---|---|
| Europe | 77 | 11 | 12 |
| Western countries | 52 | 31 | 17 |
| Asia | 56 | 24 | 21 |
| USA | 34 | 50 | 16 |
| CIS | 59 | 21 | 20 |
| EU | 56 | 18 | 26 |
| WTO | 49 | 19 | 32 |
| NATO | 19 | 57 | 24 |
| IMF | 42 | 21 | 37 |

Source: Russian Public Opinion Research Centre 2007 (Online, available at: www.wciom.ru – Russian version).

*Table 3.3* Evaluation of world powers

| How many of you agree that… | … the EU is a world power today | … the EU will be a world power in 2020 | …the EU should play a more important role in maintaining peace and stability in the world | …cooperation between your country and the EU should be strengthened |
|---|---|---|---|---|
| Russia | 25% | 17% | 20% | 96% |
| China | 17% | 14% | 22% | 89% |

Source: TNS Emnid, 'World Powers in the 21st century' survey, Berlin, June 2006.

*Table 3.4* Russians' opinions about which countries and organizations will play the most important world role in the next 10–15 years (%)

| | |
|---|---|
| EU | 32 |
| 'The G8' | 29 |
| NATO | 28 |
| Organization of Petroleum Exporting Countries | 17 |
| World Trade Organization | 14 |
| United Nations | 13 |
| Shanghai Cooperation Organization | 8 |
| Commonwealth of Independent States | 8 |

Source: Russian Public Opinion Research Centre (VCIOM), 30 August 2007.

confirms these trends. Indeed only a minority of respondents answered positively when asked whether they believed the European nations would become a single state (13 per cent). A more recent opinion poll conducted in Russia, however, comes to different conclusions, pointing to an existing perception that the EU is indeed going to become an important world player in the near future (Table 3.4).

Nevertheless a surprisingly majority of respondents (89 per cent in China and 96 per cent in Russia) believes that the relationship between their country and the EU should be strengthened (see Table 3.3 above). Thus, in spite of its limited effectiveness and relevance, there seems to be a widespread perception that relations with the EU are likely to produce beneficial results for Russia and China. Further evidence from Russia reveals that the largest share of respondents perceive cooperation with the EU as more successful than cooperation with the USA (Table 3.5). More recently, opinion polls have shown that a large majority of Russians are in favour of closer cooperation with the EU (36 per cent supporting Russia's accession to the EU and 33 per cent believing in a strengthened cooperation with EU member states) as a means to achieving beneficial results in technological, economical and security terms.[5] In general, it appears that public opinions in these countries have a generally positive perception of the economic advantages generated by the EU. Although there is little or no clear confidence in the EU's ability to take a role as a leading international actor, the EU is nevertheless viewed as a partner with which to develop beneficial relations. Thus,

*Table 3.5* Russia and Western cooperation (Russia is more successful in cooperation with…)

| EU | USA | EU and USA equally |
| --- | --- | --- |
| 45% | 11% | 44% |

Source: The Public Opinion Foundation 2003–2007 (Report 11 June 2003).

while in doubt about its effectiveness and power as a global player, most Chinese and Russians believe the EU is exerting a marginal though positive impact on world politics. Possibly, this final element might confirm the EU's self-representation as a *qualitatively* different actor in world affairs. Indeed, the EU is consistently perceived as a 'better' international actor with respect to the USA.

### Political elites[6]

As already mentioned, the foreign policies of China and Russia are rooted in a well-consolidated and long-standing consensus as to what principles and priorities should guide their international strategies. As has been acknowledged, the Chinese foreign policy outlook needs to be understood in the wider context of broader Chinese hopes for developing an international order based on non-hegemony, dispersion of power and regional multipolarity, political equanimity, cultural diversity and economic interdependence (Shambaugh 2008). Similarly, Russia's foreign policy discourse and practice is rooted in a broad public and political consensus according to which foreign policy is a tool to stimulate economic growth and provide the optimal conditions for Russian influence in the region (Morini 2008; Kaveshnikov 2007; Fisher 2007). Such a policy is clearly stressed in the major Russian foreign policy documents and presidential speeches, which underline the concept of sovereignty (against the threat of interference), centralization and territorial integrity (against the threat of autonomy and separatism) as a way of strengthening the 'Russian Statehood' in the name of 'national interests' (Kratochvi'l 2008). In such a perspective Russia should create partnerships and agreements in order to improve its international standing and, in the economic sphere, to guarantee the 'defence of national economic interests' (Putin 2004).

Against this background, it must be emphasized that the political elites' views of the EU present both similarities and important differences. At a very general level, political elites in both countries acknowledge the existence of shared values and converging preferences with respect to global governance issues. In China's case, this perception of a strong political convergence of views is consistent across time and reinforced by the fact that 'there is no fundamental conflict of interests between China and the EU and neither side poses a threat to the other' (Ministry of Foreign Affairs of China 2003: 2). As far as the political dimension of the EU's image is concerned, therefore, the latter is consistently praised by Chinese leaders for its contribution towards the multipolarization of the international order, its support for a more balanced and democratic system of global governance and its preference for multilateral approaches. On different occasions, for instance, Premier Wen Jiabao has expressed the view that both China and the EU represent important forces for world peace and stability committed to multilateralism, the promotion of democracy and the rule of law in international relations (Wen 2004).

Interestingly, current global concerns over the financial crisis have not changed this perception. At the seventh Asia Europe Meeting (ASEM) held in October 2008, for instance, it was stressed both that 'Europe shares many similar views with Asia in terms of climate change, multilateralism and reform on global economic order. Asia-Europe cooperation will be more helpful for both sides to pursue its own policies.'[7] It was also mentioned that strategic interests between the Asian and European partners have kept extending as it was confirmed by the 'opposition to the practice of unilateralism' and the common belief that 'their cooperation has exerted a growing impact on the global setup' (Pan Guang 2008). The EU is also perceived as a development-friendly actor. Official documents and the speeches of Chinese officials often refer to the EU as a power committed to promoting sustainable development through poverty elimination (Ministry of Foreign Affairs of China 2003) and as a force that contributes to the sound and balanced development of globalization and to the narrowing of the North–South gap (Xinhua 2008). Another important component of this largely positive image is represented by the appreciation of the European integration project for its implications in international affairs, for providing new opportunities to deepen EU–China relations (Ministry of Foreign Affairs of China 2004) and as model for integrative efforts in other areas of the world (Mei 2004; Song 2008). Broadly speaking, therefore, there is a widespread perception among Chinese political leaders that the EU's and China's views of the world fit comfortably with each other and that this convergence is reinforced by the absence of a serious prospect of security and geopolitical conflict (Peruzzi *et al.* 2007: 322). Interestingly, the perception of the EU among Chinese scholars and commentators specialized in EU-related issues largely mirrors that of the political elites insofar as it is acknowledged that the goals of China's modernization and of European integration are both consistent with the trend towards a multipolar international order and that existing historical and social differences can be overcome through peaceful confrontation (Peruzzi *et al.* 2007). Whether these statements reflect truly shared worldviews, however, is open to debate. It has been suggested, for instance, that the Chinese elites' views of the EU are characterized by a cognitively dissonant character, that is, they have a consolidated habit of reading the European position through the lenses of their own political preferences and expectations concerning the international system. Quite possibly, this attitude has been strengthened by the optimistic statements elaborated by the European Commission in its official documents on China (Algieri 2008; Shambaugh 2008).

With respect to the economic side of the external images, again the EU is mainly perceived as an opportunity for China to achieve its development goals.

The political elites perceive the Chinese and European economies as complementary. Foreign direct investments and technological cooperation are the fields in which the EU's contribution to China's economic development is given most praise. As a top-ranking Chinese official clearly put it: 'Thanks to their respective advantages, namely that the EU has advanced technologies and strong financial resources while China boasts a huge market, increasingly deepened cooperation has brought mutual benefits and win–win achievements' (Ministry of Foreign Affairs of China 2004). The current global financial crisis has reinforced the perception of the need to strengthen cooperation with the EU. At the seventh ASEM summit, for instance, it was stressed that 'it is increasingly more essential for China and the EU to work for mutually-beneficial and win–win cooperation, because they are currently in a critical juncture of history'.[8]

Similar arguments can be identified in Russia's political discourse. Former President Putin, for instance, on the occasion of the EU's fiftieth anniversary celebrations declared that:

> Russians share the values and principles of the vast majority of Europeans. Respect for international law, rejection of force to settle international problems and preference for strengthening common approaches in European and global politics are factors that unite us ... We always feel we share a common view of the world.[9]

On another occasion, he also stressed the importance of mutual trade relations for Russia's development goals (Putin 2006). More recently, President Medvedev stressed that Russia's successful development depended on transparent and equal international relations and subsequently declared he wanted to 'start discussing together the future of our common European continent', meaning by this 'the role of Europe in the global economy and the establishment of a just world order'.[10]

Important differences, however, seem to exist between Russia and China with respect to how these claims about a perceived convergence of interests with the EU relate to the negative side of the perceptual pattern. In China's case, positive perceptions of the EU concentrate on long-term/structural issues while negative ones concern mostly divergences and problems between the two sides. The EU's critical approach to human rights issues in China, for instance, has been considered a serious obstacle for the development of cooperation between the two sides (Ministry of Foreign Affairs of China 2000) as it touches upon a sensitive issue for Chinese political elites, which are traditionally concerned with national sovereignty and independence. As a result of the evolution towards a less confrontational stance by the EU in the last decade (Baker 2002), however, the tones of the declarations on the Chinese side have significantly improved. At the economic level, Chinese government officials and most Chinese scholars have, on many occasions, pointed to the EU's arms sales embargo against China[11] and the problem of the recognition of China's full market economy status as examples of the EU's unfair and discriminating attitude towards China (Ministry of Foreign

Affairs of China 2005; Ministry of Foreign Commerce of China 2005). Despite the existence of this contingent friction, which impacts negatively on how Chinese political elites perceive the EU, however, the overall impression is that it is very unlikely to create a major setback in mutual relations. The positive image of the EU among Chinese leaders rests on solid ground: the EU poses no threats to China, either politically or economically.

In Russia's case, on the contrary, these rhetorical declarations about a perceived commonality of interests and shared worldviews are coupled with a number of negative perceptions associated with structural features of the European integration process and the EU's international standing. The fifth EU enlargement process, for instance, has undoubtedly worsened EU–Russia relations and raised security concerns among Russian political leaders. Another important problem related to the EU enlargement process stems from the anti-Russian attitude of some new member states. According to Putin, this has contributed to raising fears about the possibility that 'some countries have transposed their bilateral problems with Russia on to the European level' and, therefore, that 'overt opponents of closer relations with Moscow ... have decisive influence on EU relations with Russia'.[12] As a result, it has been suggested that Russia should work more actively with those EU countries that are interested in cooperation with Russia and want to see Russia as their strategic partner, and proposed that interactions and bilateral programmes with those EU states 'that don't heed the voice of reason' should be limited or curtailed.[13] Thus, tensions following the last round of enlargement have had a negative impact on the perception of the EU as a unitary actor and have increased Russia's political incentives to take advantage of existing divisions among EU member states. Moreover, the analysis of the discourse of Russia's foreign policy elite[14] reveals that the concept of state centrism, Russia's great power status and the conviction that Russia has frequently been treated unfairly are the main principles underlying the predominantly negative attitude towards the EU foreign policy. In particular, the state-centric view of the world has paved the way to the preference for bilateral relations with individual member states in contrast to the unacceptable principle of harmonization with EU law or other actions that are perceived by Russia as similar to a teacher–apprentice relationship. This is strongly related to the feeling that Russia is treated unjustly by the outside world: for some, this proves that there are 'attempts to ignore the interests of the Russian Federation' and 'efforts ... to weaken Russia's position in political, economic, military, and other spheres' (Kontseptsiya natsionalnoi 2000).

Other important problematic issues concern EU–US military cooperation within NATO as well as NATO's enlargement towards Ukraine and Georgia and their implications for Russia's security. More specifically, US plans to deploy elements of its missile defence system in Eastern Europe have stirred up angry reactions from Russian political leaders. Sergei Lavrov, Russian's Foreign Affair Minister, for instance, described the US missile defence plan relaunched by the G.W. Bush administration as an attempt by Washington 'to use the continent as its own strategic territory' and 'an affront to Europeans, as it would devaluate the continent's pan-European and multinational organizations'.[15] Vladimir Putin added that the US plan would turn Europe into a powder keg and create 'new and unnecessary risks for the entire system of international relations'.[16] The importance of these issues in shaping perceptive patterns on the Russian side is well exemplified by a recent declaration by President Medvedev regarding the prospect of NATO membership for Ukraine and Georgia:

> Admitting these countries would be victory over Russia, while keeping them out would be tantamount to capitulation. But the real issue is that NATO is bringing its military infrastructure right up to our borders and is drawing new dividing lines in Europe, this time along our western and southern frontiers. No matter what we are told, it is only natural that we should see this as action directed against us.[17]

Unsurprisingly, tensions arising from the security sphere have generated mutual recriminations and suspicion in other areas too. In response to critical statements concerning the alleged Russian political use of the energy weapon against neighbouring countries, former President Putin stressed that 'the interests of Russia and the EU will not always coincide' and warned its European counterparts against attempts 'to superimpose Cold War ideological labels on legal and quite understandable actions aimed at protecting our national interests'.[18]

Moreover, Russian political leaders perceive any attempt by the EU to 'lecture' Russia on democracy as an illegitimate intrusion in Russia's internal affairs. In response to Western criticism of Russian human rights policies, for instance, Putin argued that given

> the death penalty ... secret prisons and torture in certain Western countries and problems with the mass media and immigration legislation in some European countries that does not correspond with the commonly accepted norms of international law ... it would be hypocritical to talk as if we are dealing on one side with clean and furry partners and, on the other side, with monsters who have just come out of the woods and have hooves instead of feet and horns.[19]

In other words, EU–Russia relations are characterized by a number of potentially troubling issues. Differently from EU–China relations, however, these are neither contingent nor short term. The problem of the definition of EU borders, the relationship between the EU and its Eastern neighbours and the implications of these developments on Russia's geostrategic outlook are likely to become a key issue for the future of mutual relations. Similarly, the integration within the EU of countries in which anti-Russian sentiments have strong historical and cultural roots is likely to continue exasperating tensions and to cause setbacks at different levels. Again, it is not clear what shape the relationship between the EU's common foreign and security policy and the NATO framework will take and, thus, it is not unlikely that frictions and tensions concerning future developments

*Table 3.6* Main issues associated with perception of the EU in the political elites' discourse

|  | China | Russia |
|---|---|---|
| Positive | Multipolarity of global arena<br>Democratization of global governance<br>Commitment to multilateralism<br>Promotion of development-friendly policies<br>Model of regional integration<br>Source of foreign direct investments and technological cooperation | Shared values<br>Preference for common approaches to international problems<br>Respect for international law<br>Economic cooperation<br>Model of regional integration |
| Negative | Critical approach to human rights issues as interference in internal political affairs<br>Arms embargo<br>Opposition to China's full market economy status in the WTO | Enlargement process<br>Bilateral problems with new EU member states<br>US missile defence plan<br>Critical approach regarding Russia's democratic standards and human rights issues |

within Europe's security system will remain high on Russia's foreign policy agenda. We do not argue that negative perceptions of the EU will necessarily overshadow positive ones. Our argument is that, differently from China, it is difficult to attempt a prediction of how Russian perceptions of the EU will evolve. In light of both the relative uncertainty concerning future developments in mutual relations on all relevant dimensions of cooperation – political and geostrategic above all – and the importance of structural conditions of EU–Russia relations in shaping these patterns, it is very difficult in this particular historical moment to put forward any tentative remark concerning future trends in perceptual patterns. In Table 3.6, we summarize the positive and negative images of the EU stemming from the analysis of Chinese and Russian political elites.

## *The media*[20]

The analysis of the media in China and Russia confirms that there are both similarities and substantial differences in how the EU's image is depicted in the two countries. A first element of comparison concerns the volume of coverage of the EU in daily newspapers (Tables 3.7 and 3.8).

Table 3.7 reports data for some major Chinese newspapers during four months in 2006, while Table 3.8 reports data on Russian newspapers throughout the whole of 2004. Proportionally speaking, the magnitude of coverage is relatively similar in the two countries. China's popular newspaper, *People's Daily*, runs an average of 61 news stories referencing the EU per month. Two other newspapers also present rather high volumes of EU coverage – 54 news stories

*Table 3.7* Number of EU news items in the Chinese press (January to June 2006)

| Media | January | February | March | April | May | June | Total |
|---|---|---|---|---|---|---|---|
| People's Daily | 77 | 68 | 48 | 47 | 67 | 59 | *366* |
| International Finance News | 50 | 51 | 81 | 44 | 36 | 24 | *286* |
| China Daily | 48 | 48 | 56 | 45 | 68 | 59 | *324* |
| CCTV-1 | 17 | 14 | 12 | 8 | 11 | 10 | *72* |

Source: Peruzzi *et al.* 2007.

*Table 3.8* Mentions of the EU in the Russian press in 2004 (number of articles for the whole year)

| Ios/countries | NG | Izvestiya | VN | Vedomosti | Kommersant |
|---|---|---|---|---|---|
| EU | 380 (84) | 306 (73) | 495 (117) | 422 (65) | 757 (113) |
| CIS | 127 | 327 | 633 | 541 | 684 |
| NATO | 122 | 232 | 347 | 90 | 433 |
| United Nations | 545 | 342 | 555 | 174 | 686 |
| OSCE | 167 | 99 | 176 | 53 | 149 |
| USA | 2,393 | 2,211 | n.a. | n.a. | n.a. |
| France | 788 | 881 | n.a. | n.a. | n.a. |
| Poland | 294 | 300 | n.a. | n.a. | n.a. |
| Ukraine | 903 | 745 | n.a. | n.a. | n.a. |
| Kazakhstan | 366 | 214 | n.a. | n.a. | n.a. |
| China | 852 | 503 | n.a. | n.a. | n.a. |

Source: Kaveshnikov 2007: 399.

Note
The number of articles included in which the EU is the key topic is given in brackets. The total number includes articles mentioning the EU in the text but not dealing with the EU as the main topic.

per month on average in the case of an English-language newspaper (*China Daily*) and 47 in a business newspaper (*International Finance News*). In Russia's case, the two main business newspapers – *Vedomosti* and *Kommersant* – lead the group of Russian newspapers in terms of EU coverage. Moreover, Table 3.8 shows that the EU is the international organization with the most significant volume of coverage in Russian newspapers. It slightly overtakes the United Nations and more than doubles the volume of coverage of NATO, the Organization for Security and Cooperation in Europe (OSCE) and also CIS.

Similarities can be also identified in the extent to which news concerning the EU is framed in the domestic discourse of the country under analysis. In fact, in both countries the EU is mainly localized in the domestic discourse. The Russian newspapers' articles concerning the EU are devoted in the majority of cases to commenting and analysing EU–Russian relations (59.5 per cent) (see also

Kaveshnikov 2007). Similarly, Chinese newspapers refer to the EU mainly through news focusing on Chinese domestic matters. However, the results are quite different with respect to the relative importance of news focusing solely on the EU. While in Russia's newspapers 35.3 per cent of EU news concentrates on EU domestic policy developments and only 5.2 per cent on EU relations with third countries, Chinese newspapers take a different perspective, devoting more attention to EU dealings with third countries (40 per cent) than to EU internal affairs (18 per cent). Despite these differences, however, the importance of the 'local' angle is a relevant factor for the present analysis. Arguably, this type of framing may indicate to the readership that the EU and its actions have immediate consequences on local developments, thus turning happenings in the EU into 'zones of relevancy' (Schulz 1964) in the readers' minds.

Data available on Chinese TV news coverage of the EU shows a partly different picture.[21] Quite expectedly, the EU is given less visibility in TV news than in the newspapers. Time restrictions and different news approaches (as opposed to the press) limit the TV coverage of the EU to about 12 news items per month. Arguably, such a limited exposure is not only due to the specific constraints of TV bulletins but also to the fact that the institutional and political complexities of the EU make it less appealing to TV audiences.

The available data allows us to make a qualitative assessment of the contents of EU representations in the media (press and TV) in the two countries. In general, the 'quality' media representations in the two countries, analysed in terms of both evaluations on the EU and contents of the news stories featuring the EU, seem to show that the EU is a much more directly relevant actor for Russia than it is for China.

Let us first consider China.[22] Research conducted in China, for instance, reveals that the media used predominantly 'neutral' evaluations of the EU (Peruzzi *et al.* 2007: 29). There were no negative assessments found in the EU news on the television. As far as the content of news is concerned, the press divided their equal attention between presenting the EU as an 'economic' and a 'political' power (41 per cent for each theme respectively). The TV represented the EU mainly as a 'political' actor (58 per cent of all news stories), while images of the EU as an 'economic' player were much less visible (21 per cent news). With regard to the political element, the media concentrated its attention on representing the EU as an audible voice in the international arena, rather than focusing its reporting on the EU's internal developments. In the first six months of 2006, 86 per cent of the newspaper stories reported on the EU's foreign policy. As regards the economic framework, the most visible images described the EU as a trade power (49 per cent of all newspaper news), followed by reports on the EU's actions in the field of industry and business and finance (21 per cent for each theme). These three themes were the most prominent on television too, although in this case trade/industry led with 40 per cent each, and business/finance topics occupied 20 per cent of news space. Within the economic coverage of the EU, the most frequently reported events were ones revolving around EU–China trading relations, as well as around the EU's actions in the field of

*Table 3.9* Contents of EU representations in Chinese media

| | The EU as a political power | The EU as an economic power | The EU in social affairs |
|---|---|---|---|
| Press | **41%** | **41%** | **18%** |
| | Main sub-representations: <br>• EU in world politics (diplomacy, foreign affairs, etc.) | Main sub-representations: <br>• EU as a trade power <br>• Industry <br>• Business and finance | Main sub-representations: <br>• Health care <br>• Education and research <br>• Social legislation |
| TV | **58%** | **21%** | **21%** |
| | Main sub-representations: <br>• EU in world politics (diplomacy, foreign affairs, etc.) | Main sub-representations: <br>• Trade <br>• Industry <br>• Business and finance | Main sub-representations: <br>• Health care <br>• Environmental issues <br>• Education and research |

Source: Peruzzi *et al.* 2007.

energy production. The priority given to trade is not a surprise as it is a fundamental part of the relationship between the two parties. Finally, the analysis also considered the news reporting on the EU in social affairs, a residual category describing cultural, social and human stories. In this regard, most news touched upon the EU's health care systems and health concerns (more specifically, the EU's reaction to the 2006 bird flu epidemic). These were followed by news on the EU's dealings with education and research enterprises, developments in EU social legislation and EU environmental policies.

Differently from China, representations of the EU in Russian newspapers seem to be characterized by a less neutral orientation and a certain degree of polarization. Indeed, some have argued that EU-related news in Russia is bipolar: those describing the EU in negative terms and those describing it positively balance each other out (Kaveshnikov 2007). Newspapers' positive characterizations of the EU tend to concentrate on the value-based nature of the EU. References to the EU's democratic principles, rule of law, respect of human rights (as opposed to Russia's standards) and promotion of peace and prosperity are all described as distinguishing features of the EU as a political system. At the same time, these representations are coupled with negative characterizations with respect to the perceived existence of a democratic deficit, disparities in the economic development of the various member states, high levels of bureaucratization, inefficiencies in the decision-making process and interferences in the member states' domestic political affairs. This polarization of views on the EU is epitomized by existing perceptions of the EU's enlargement process. Indeed, while in some cases the enlargement is described as a significant breakthrough towards unity, in other instances it is considered as an obstacle to deeper integration, as a potential cause for political and economic tensions and as a modern type of colonization.

Representations of the EU as an economic actor are mainly positive. The EU is seen as stimulating competitiveness among member states, as a promoter of consumers' rights and environmentally friendly policies as well as social programmes. Only a few articles criticize the EU, pointing to different aspects related to the EU's low rates of economic growth. Finally, there seems to be consensus on the idea that the EU is an influential power in world affairs, despite a cleavage in the Russian media concerning the overall evaluation of the EU foreign policy goals and their implications for Russia. Positive views of the EU's influence, for instance, are compensated by interpretations of its actions in the post-Soviet space in terms of competition or struggle between spheres of influence. Similarly, praise for the EU's efforts to promote human rights, to provide assistance to developing countries and to liberalize world trade are coupled with negative perceptions concerning the EU's interest-based foreign policy behaviour, double standards and protectionist trade policies.

The EU image spread throughout the Russian public opinion by the most important TV channels is related to the Kremlin's foreign policy and influenced by some specific political events within the framework of EU–Russian cooperation. All nationwide TV channels usually make a clear distinction between the European countries' attitudes towards Russia. More specifically, a distinction is made between friendly and unfriendly ones: the Baltic states and Poland are described as 'unfriendly' while those countries having a long-standing tradition of economic and cultural relationships with Russia, such as Germany, Italy and France, are described as 'friendly'. In 2008, the Caucasus crisis paved the way to a disagreement between Russia and the EU, which may still become an insurmountable obstacle to the rapprochement. Russian television has recently depicted the EU's role as potentially constructive even though it is unlikely to accept Russia's recognition of Abkhazia and South Ossetia. Interestingly, it appears that the USA and Europe are largely described as actors with increasingly divergent interests.

To sum up, while media representations of the EU tend to be shaped through the lenses of domestic priorities in both countries, there are important differences regarding the 'quality' of these representations. The fact that the news reporting the EU is overwhelmingly neutral in China and very polarized in Russia suggests that there is a difference in the degree to which EU political, economic and social developments are perceived as directly relevant for media audiences in the two countries.

## Understanding Russian and Chinese perceptions of the EU

Rhetorical declarations about a perceived commonality of interests and values with the EU are common in the speeches of both the Russian and Chinese leaders. Public opinions in these countries share the perception that, although not crucial, the EU's influence on the international scene is nevertheless positive and that strengthening cooperation with it would bring beneficial results. Once political rhetoric is taken out of the equation, one notices substantial differences in the way in which China and Russia's perceptions of the EU are framed. From China's perspective, frictions and tensions with the EU represent only minor setbacks in a context where neither security nor economic concerns are high on the agenda. To put it bluntly, the EU is a long way away and does not threaten China's fundamental security and economic interests. These permissive conditions allow for allegedly similar conceptions of world order to play a significant role in shaping patterns of perceptions. Alleged common preferences for a multipolar international order, for a multilateral management of international interactions and for the development of more balanced and democratic global governance structures are key elements in understanding the context within which Chinese perceptions of the EU develop. Interestingly, these represent fundamental and long-lasting components of the cognitive structures within which the Chinese elites frame their foreign policy objectives. Hence, Chinese perceptive patterns of the EU are highly likely to remain stable over time. Of course, contingent variables do hold some relevance. Interaction variables have played an important role in accounting for variations in public opinion perceptions and diplomatic frictions in a variety of areas. For instance, it is possible that the EU public opinion's negative attitudes towards China and Chinese citizens might have a detrimental feedback effect on Chinese views of the EU. Since 2006 there has been growing concern among Chinese 'Europe watchers' about growing anti-Chinese feeling among Western public opinions.[23] However, on the basis of the evidence available, it seems fair to argue that contingent variations in perceptive patterns are likely to remain within the boundaries of a context characterized by a structural convergence of interests. Beijing's main foreign policy priority is to address the existing contradiction between the general set-up of the international system and the Chinese aim to build an international multipolar order. From this point of view, the strengthening of a 'strategic partnership' with the EU is likely to remain one of the key priorities of Chinese diplomacy, irrespective of contextual dynamics.

On the contrary, the structural framework within which EU–Russian relations take place is more problematic. Russia is not only geographically closer to the EU but it also aspires to reassert its status of a great global power. The EU's internal developments and security arrangements as well as its difficult but increasingly assertive standing in international affairs have direct implications for Russia's security and development goals. The EU represents a crucial parameter for Russia's capacity to achieve its fundamental security and economic interests. Unsurprisingly, Russia's perceptions of the EU are much more polarized than their Chinese equivalents due to frictions and tensions that cannot be disentangled from the structural problems characterizing EU–Russian relations. Short-term tensions concerning US plans to deploy missile defence systems in Eastern Europe are necessarily entrenched with broader Russian concerns regarding future developments in the Atlantic security architecture in the European continent. Similarly, minor diplomatic reactions to anti-Russian demonstrations in some of the newly accessed member states are part of wider preoccupations as to the enlargement's security implications for Russia. In other words, Russia's perceptions of the EU depend on contingent issues that reflect the ongoing difficult process of redefining mutual relations following the Russian transition after the end of the Cold War confrontation. In contrast to China, therefore, it is very difficult to come up with even tentative conclusions as to what factors will prevail in shaping perceptions of the EU. Depending on broader future developments in EU–Russian relations, these power-related sources of negative perceptions might consolidate and become an integral component of the cognitive maps through which Russian elites and public opinion come to look at the EU or, rather, evaporate and are relegated to marginal problems in the context of a structural convergence of views and interests.

## Conclusions and recommendations

The evidence provided in this chapter signals that EU self-representations are only partially mirrored in the perceptions of Russia and China. While the EU may be viewed as a more collaborative and cooperative partner than the USA, it is equally perceived as a rather weak one except for its economic might. At the same time, differences in the strategic, security and political contexts in which relations between the EU and the two countries take place have important implications. While Chinese perceptions take shape in a context where 'hard' security and economic conflicts with the EU are not likely to be on the agenda, Russian views evolve within a much more dynamic, complex and potentially problematic framework of mutual relations. These crucial differences should be taken into account by EU policy makers.

As far as China is concerned, there is a strong need to strengthen existing initiatives aimed at deepening the Chinese understanding of real European political interactions, both at the EU level and for each of its members. Since an important concern for the Chinese is that the Europeans are trying to impose Western values, it is important that mutual interactions regarding human rights, democratic rule and other sensitive issues are addressed more pragmatically by avoiding projecting the all-too-frequent image of cultural superiority. At the same time, the EU needs to deepen its understanding of Chinese political, cultural and social dynamics in order to interpret interactions with its counterparts in the context of the wider cognitive framework within which this growing power's foreign policy takes place. It is also important to devise the appropriate communication strategies to avoid the spread of unmotivated anti-Chinese feeling within European society.

Needless to say, it is much more difficult to put forward recommendations for addressing Russia's perceptions of the EU since perceptive patterns are largely dependent on a web of factors, ranging from short-term competitive ambitions to cultural hostilities with a number of new member states. Having said this, it needs to be stressed that anti-Russian attitudes in some of the newly accessed member states play a substantial role in creating friction between the two parties. Any initiative, either cultural or political, aimed at tackling this problem cannot but represent a positive step forward in building mutual confidence. EU policy makers, in addition, should make use of all cooperative frameworks available to dispel potential Russian misunderstandings with regard to motivations and objectives behind EU internal security and political developments. Whenever such developments may raise concerns among the Russian counterparts, EU leaders should take these seriously into consideration and share as much information as possible. At a broader level, consistent engagement and a cooperative attitude from Russia within the EU and Atlantic security cooperation frameworks is in the interest of Europeans and might prove an essential component of a strategy aimed at strengthening and deepening mutual understanding.

## Notes

1  The chapter builds on research undertaken by the authors of this piece (see also Peruzzi *et al.* 2007; Morini 2008) as well as the very limited existing literature on the topic (cf. Holland and Chaban 2005; Kaveshnikov 2007; Kratochvi'l 2008; Rose and Munro 2008; Shambaugh *et al.* 2008; Jing 2006; Holland and Chaban 2008). Our surveys of the external image of the EU, like the others in the research project, drew on existent sources as well as on original interviews and press analysis. This means that the data available in the case of China and Russia, particularly as far as opinion polls are concerned, come from different sources and have been therefore collected in a different way. This represents a methodological limit to a perfect comparison, but we still deem a comparison possible and that the advantages of making an attempt are greater than its limits. We would like to thank Vladimir Gel'man, Natalya Yargomskaya, Elena Belokurova and Maria Nozhenko at the European University in Saint Petersburg.

2  The Chinese community involved in research institutes, university and, more broadly, academic circles that analyse and study European integration, EU policies and EU–China relations.

3  Data concerning both Russian and Chinese public opinions have been drawn from a variety of different sources. In China's case, these are the World Values Survey and a report based on a nine-country survey entitled 'World Powers in the 21st Century: Europe's Global Responsibility' commissioned by the Bertelsmann Stiftung and conducted by TNS-Enmid in January 2006 and a survey involving 23 nations coordinated by Globescan and the Program on International Policy Attitudes (completed during December 2004). In the case of Russia, the main sources were the surveys of the Russian Public Opinion Research Centre and the Public Opinion Foundation.

4  See online, available at: http://wciom.com/archives/thematic-archive/foreign-policy-general/europe-and-eu.html (accessed 31 January 2009).

5  See online, available at: http://wciom.com/archives/thematic-archive/foreign-policy-general/europe-and-eu.html (accessed 31 January 2009).

6  The research on the political elites' perception of the EU was based on a careful analysis of speeches, official documents and policy papers from government representatives and agencies as well as press releases from news agencies.

7  'A new chapter in Asia-Europe cooperation', *People's Daily Online*, 29 October 2008. Online, available at: http://english.peopledaily.com.cn/ (accessed 31 January 2009).

8  'Voices of Asia, Europe draw global attention', *People's Daily Online*, 27 October 2008. Online, available at: http://english.peopledaily.com.cn/ (accessed 31 January 2009).

9  See online, available at: www.hri.org/news/balkans/rferl/ (accessed 31 January 2009).

10  See online, available at: www.kremlin.ru/eng/speeches/2008/10/08/2159_type-82912type82914_207457.shtml (accessed 31 January 2009).

11  Undoubtedly, the European leaders' inconsistent positions on the issue have fuelled suspicion on the Chinese side.

12  See online, available at: www.hri.org/news/balkans/rferl/2007/07–05-index.rferl.html (accessed 31 January 2009).

13  See online, available at: www.hri.org/news/balkans/rferl/2007/07–05-index.rferl.html (accessed 31 January 2009).

14  The research, led by Petr Kratochvi'l, is based on a contents analysis of major Russian foreign policy documents (Kontseptsiya vneshnei 2000; Kontseptsiya natsionalnoi 2000, Part III; Voennaya doktrina 2000), presidential speeches (2002, 2004, 2006) and, in particular, a set of interviews with Russian foreign policy makers and academics most frequently in touch with the European Union. See Kratochvi'l 2008.

15  See online, available at: www.hri.org/news/balkans/rferl/2007/07–05-index.rferl.html (accessed 31January 2009).

16  See online, available at: www.hri.org/news/balkans/rferl/2007/07–05-index.rferl.html (accessed 31 January 2009).

17  See online, available at: www.kremlin.ru/eng/speeches/2008/10/08/2159_type-82912type82914_207457.shtml (accessed 31 January 2009).

18  See online, available at: www.hri.org/news/balkans/rferl/2007/07–05-index.rferl.html (accessed 31 January 2009).

19  See online, available at: www.hri.org/news/balkans/rferl/2007/07–05-index.rferl.html (accessed 31 January 2009).

20  As far as China is concerned, the analysis of both the press and TV draws mainly on research conducted by Shuangquan Zhang and presented in our survey on Chinese perceptions of the EU (see Peruzzi *et al.* 2007). Shuangquan Zhang is also a member of the research team for the project 'The EU through the Eyes of Asia', coordinated by Martin Holland at the University of Canterbury (New Zealand). We are grateful to the coordinator and to Natalia Chaban for their cooperation. In the case of Russia, we relied on two different sources. The analysis of the press is based on evidence provided in Kaveshnikov (2007). This research analyses 528 articles published in 2004 in seven Russian newspapers: *Vedomosti*, *Vremya Novostei* (*VN*), *Gazeta Izvestiya*, *Kommersant*, *Nezavisimaya Gazeta* (*NG*) and *Rossiisskaya Gazeta* (*RG*), equivalent to 26,178 centimetres of column space. The TV media analysis elaborates on existing reports by Elena Prokhorova – analyst and regular contributor to bbcrussian.com – published on the following website: www.eu-russiacentre.org/our-publications/tv-review. We also monitored the following TV channels in June and October 2008: Channel One, Channel 3, TV Tsentr, RTR, TV Centre and NTV.

21  This analysis refers to one television news broadcaster: China Central Television (CCTV-1) and specifically its prime time news bulletin. CCTV-1 was chosen due to the fact that this channel has the largest outreach in the country, with an audience of 1.18 billion people.

22  Our analysis of Chinese media heavily relies on the methodological framework and findings of Chaban *et al.* 2007.

23  See for instance, the 2007 survey *Rising Environmental Concern in 47-Nation Survey. Global Unease with Major World Powers* by Pew Global Attitudes, also online, available at: www.pewglobal.org (accessed 31 January 2009). The perception of China as an economic threat seems to have been the main factor in influencing this negative trend. Until spring 2008, human rights issues had only a limited impact on this trend, but they became central for the media and Western public opinion after the Tibetan riots in March and in the run-up to the Olympic Games.

# References

Algieri, F. (2008) 'It's the System that Matters: institutionalization and making of EU policy toward China', in D. Shambaugh, E. Sandschneider and H. Zhou (eds) *China-Europe Relations: perceptions, policies and prospects*, London: Routledge.

Baker, P. (2002) 'Human Rights, Europe and the People's Republic of China', *China Quarterly*, 169: 46–63.

Chaban, N., Holland, M., Ryan, P. and Nowak, A. (eds) (2007) *The EU through the Eyes of Asia: media, public and elite perceptions in China, Japan, Korea, Singapore and Thailand*, Singapore-Warsaw: University of Warsaw.

Fisher, S. (2007) *Russia: a difficult partner for the EU*, Paris: EU Institute for Security Studies.

Holland, M. and Chaban, N. (2005) *The EU Through the Eyes of the Asia-Pacific: public perceptions and media representations*, NCRE Research Series no. 4, National Centre for Research on Europe, University of Canterbury.

Holland, M. and Chaban, N. (eds) (2008) *The European Union and the Asia–Pacific: media, public and elite perceptions of the EU*, London: Routledge.

Jing, M. (2006) 'Chinese Perceptions of the European Union: a review of leading Chinese journals', *European Law Journal*, 12 (6): 788–806.

Kaveshnikov, N. (2007) 'The European Union in the Russian Press', *Journal of Communist Studies and Transition Politics*, 23 (3): 396–424.

Kontseptsiya natsionalnoi (2000) *Kontseptsiya natsionalnoi bezopasnosti Rossiiskoi Federatsii*, Moscow: Ministry of Foreign Affairs of the Russian Federation. Online, available at: www.mid.ru/nsosndoc.nsf/0e9272befa34209743256c630042d1aa/a54f9caa5e6 8075e432569fb004872a6?OpenDocument (accessed 31 January 2009).

Kontseptsiya vneshnei (2000) *Kontseptsiya vneshnei politiki Rossiiskoi Federatsii*, Moscow, Ministry of Foreign Affairs of the Russian Federation. Online, available at: www.mid.ru/ns-osndoc.nsf/0e9272befa34209743256c630042d1aa/fd86620b371b0cf7 432569fb004872a7?OpenDocument (accessed 31 January 2009).

Kratochvi'l, P. (2008) 'The Discursive Resistance to EU-Enticement: the Russian elite and (the lack of) Europeanisation', *Europe-Asia Studies*, 60 (3): 397–422.

Lucarelli, S. (2007) 'The European Union in the Eyes of Others: towards filling a gap in the literature', *European Foreign Affairs Review*, 12 (3): 249–70.

Mei, Z. (2004) 'Significance of EU Eastward Expansion and its Impact on International Situation and Sino-European Relations', *Foreign Affairs Journal*, 73: 1–7.

Ministry of Foreign Affairs of China (2000) 'Spokesperson on the adopted resolution on China's human rights situation by EP', 15 November. Online, available at: www. fmprc.gov.cn/eng/default.htm (accessed 31 January 2009).

Ministry of Foreign Affairs of China (2003) *China's EU Policy Paper*, October.

Ministry of Foreign Affairs of China (2004) Speech of Mr Zhang Yesui, Vice Minister of the Ministry of Foreign Affairs at the opening ceremony of the Sino-EU Policy Paper seminar. Online, available at: www.fmprc.gov.cn/eng/default.htm (accessed 31 January 2009).

Ministry of Foreign Affairs of China (2005) President of the European Commission meets with Foreign Minister Li Zhaoxing, 18 March. Online, available at: www.fmprc.gov. cn/eng/default.htm (accessed 31 January 2009).

Ministry of Foreign Commerce of China (2005) Bo Xilai's meeting with EU Trade Commissioner Peter Mandelson who visited Dalian to participate in the WTO informal ministerial meeting, 15 July. Online, available at: http://english.mofcom.gov.cn/ (accessed 31 January 2009).

Morini, M. (2008) 'Report on Russia', *The External Image of the European Union*, jointly integrated research project 5.2.1. of the Network of Excellence *Global Governance, Regionalisation and Regulation: the Role of the EU* – GARNET (EU Sixth Framework Programme 2005–2010). Online, available at: www.garnet-eu.org/ (accessed 31 January 2009).

Pan Guang (2008) 'Enhance Silk Road Spirit for Win–Win Asia-Europe Cooperation', *People's Daily Online*, 24 October. Online, available at: http://english.peopledaily. com.cn/ (accessed 31 Janaury 2009).

Peruzzi, R., Poletti, A. and Zhang, S. (2007) 'China's Views of Europe: a maturing partnership', *European Foreign Affairs Review*, 12 (3): 311–30.

Putin, V.V. (2004) *Vystuplenie na plenarnom zasedanii soveshchaniya poslov i postoyannykh predstavitelei Rossii*, 12 July, Moscow, Ministry of Foreign Affairs. Online, available at: www.kremlin.ru (accessed 6 November 2007).

Putin, V.V. (2006) *Vystuplenie na soveshchanii s poslami i postoyannymi predstavitel'yami Rossiiskoi Federatsii*, 27 June, Moscow, Ministry of Foreign Affairs. Online, available at: www.kremlin.ru (accessed 31 January 2009).

Rose, R. and Munro, N. (2008) 'Do Russians See Their Future in Europe or the CIS?' *Europe-Asia Studies*, 60 (1): 49–66.

Schulz, A. (1964) *Collected Papers* (Vol. 12), The Hague: Martinus Nijhoff.

Shambaugh, D. (2008) 'China Eyes Europe's Role in the World: real convergence or cognitive dissonance?' in D. Shambaugh, E. Sandschneider and H. Zhou (eds) *China–Europe Relations: perceptions, policies and prospects*, London: Routledge.

Shambaugh, D., Sandschneider, E. and Zhou H. (eds) (2008) *China–Europe Relations: perceptions, policies and prospects*, London: Routledge.

Song, X. (2008) 'China's View of European Integration and Enlargement', in D. Shambaugh, E. Sandschneider and H. Zhou (eds) *China–Europe Relations: perceptions, policies and prospects*, London: Routledge.

Voennaja doktrina (2000) *Voennaja doktrina Rossiiskoi Federaatsii*, Moscow: Ministry of Foreign Affairs of the Russian Federation. Online, available at: www.mid.ru/nsosn-doc.nsf/0e9272befa34209743256c630042d1aa/a54f9caa5e68075e432569fb004872a8? OpenDocument (accessed 31 January 2009).

Wen, J. (2004) 'Deepening China–EU Relations and Strengthening All-round Cooperation', speech at the China–EU Business Summit, The Hague, 9 December.

Xinhua (2008) 'Chinese Foreign Minister says ASEM Summit was Productive', 26 October. Online, available at: www.xinhuanet.com/english/ or http://english.peopledaily.com.cn/ (accessed 31 January 2009).

Zhu, L. (2008) 'Chinese Perceptions of the EU and the China–Europe Relationship', in D. Shambaugh, E. Sandschneider and H. Zhou (eds) *China–Europe Relations: perceptions, policies and prospects*, London: Routledge.

# 4    Taking the lead

## EU mediation role assessed by Iran and Lebanon

*Ruth Hanau Santini, Raffaele Mauriello and Lorenzo Trombetta*

## Introduction

This chapter fills a gap in the literature of European foreign policy towards the Middle East.[1] It provides a snapshot of the opinions and perceptions held by Lebanese and Iranian elites, civil society organizations and the media on the European Union (EU) and its policies on the ground. The relevant literature on the area rarely analyses the regional actors' expectations, ideas and beliefs, and focuses more on historical accounts of regional developments, the analysis of systemic features and geopolitical challenges and changes. Our analysis concentrates on Iran and Lebanon in light of several considerations. First, these countries have been at the centre of EU diplomat activity outside its 'natural' borders. They both represent crucial gateways for the EU in terms of economic and trade penetration into the Middle East and even Asia (through Iran). In addition to the historical ties with some European member states, Iran and Lebanon are also crucial from a geostrategic point of view as they pose several challenges to the stability of the wider political region, a neighbouring geographic area for the EU.

The chapter is organized as follows. We first sketch some crucial elements of the historical relations between the two countries and Europe. We then analyse the findings on elites, civil society and the media as well as some of the key factors influencing Iranian and Lebanese perceptions of the EU. We end with some concluding remarks and provide specific recommendations for the EU.

## Iran, Lebanon and the EU in historical perspective

During the First and Second World Wars, Iran was involved against its own will in international power politics and its territory invaded by British and Russian forces competing for their influence in the Middle East (Mokhtari 2005). Iran's own political independence and integrity was even more dramatically undermined by the United Kingdom (UK) and the United States of America (USA) in the 1950s, when a coup masterminded by both countries overthrew the then Prime Minister Mohammad Mossadeq. This created a widely shared lack of trust in external actors across the social and political spectrum. However, during the

Pahlavi period (1925–1979), a relevant part of the regime's bureaucracy as well as prominent political personalities received a European education and tried to promote reformist and modernizing policies (Digard *et al.* 2007). They encountered some resistance under the reign of Reza Khan (1925–1941), clashing with his conservative tendency and his will to profit from the fight between Western and Russian influences. Under Mohammed Reza Shah (1941–1979), the attitude towards the West prevailed, favouring allegiances to the USA at the expense of Europe. Nevertheless, the political elites continued to acknowledge the added value brought by European technicians and state officials in areas ranging from institution building to the army, the educational system and state finances. This climate of collaboration, however, was suddenly revoked by Khomeini, shortly after the proclamation of the Islamic Republic of Iran, despite his having stayed in France during the last months of his long exile: the special relationship with France, which had sympathized with some of Khomeini's ideals and claims (Foucault 1994; Afray and Anderson 2005), deteriorated with the further curtailment of personal freedoms, public executions and the role of 'Islamic' tribunals in liquidating leftists and opponents of the regime (Djalili 2005). With the UK, relations have not been any smoother, particularly since Khomeini pronounced his *fatwa* against the Indian-born British writer Salman Rushdie in 1989.[2]

On top of previous and ongoing tensions, during the 1980–1988 Iraq–Iran war, the USA and European countries sided with the Iraqi Ba'thists, thereby deepening the mistrust among Iranians and compounding the accusations of double standards, since Iraq was a country ruled by a ruthless dictator guilty in particular of having used chemical weapons both against the Iranians and political opponents in his own country.

Since the 1990s, especially under the presidency of Khatami (1997–2005), the distance between Europe and Iran was reduced to the extent that in 1998 a 'comprehensive' dialogue substituted the previous 'critical' dialogue (in place since 1993) with the aim of normalizing diplomatic relations.[3] The new format was devised to cover a broad range of issues from human rights and the Middle East peace process to the fight against terrorism and non-proliferation (Van Engeland-Nourai 2005). Since 2001, the EU has officially been developing prospects for structured economic cooperation in the form of a Trade and Cooperation Agreement. However, negotiations over the agreement were suspended in light of Iran's supposed breach of the Non-Proliferation Treaty (NPT). From 2003 to this day, the EU has been heading the diplomatic effort to reach an agreement over Iran's nuclear programme, an effort rendered more complicated by the election of the current president, Mahmoud Ahmadinejad, in June 2005.

The historical relations of Lebanese social and political groups with European countries tell a different story, based on the creation of deep ties with single communities and the implications of these bonds: the French with the Christian Maronite community on Mount Lebanon and, to a lesser extent, the British with the Druzes. The friendship and protection of these communities were reciprocated by the possibility of culturally influencing the domestic social fabric and keeping a foothold in the country (Corm 2005). Colonial rivalry between the UK and France peaked in the Middle East, where the competition for regional hegemony translated into alliances with regional powers (Egypt with France, the Ottomans with the British) and the creation of two separate Druze and Maronite districts on Mount Lebanon (*Qa'im Maqam*). This short-lived experiment was characterized by violent clashes and massacres between the two groups in 1840 and in 1860 (which would be repeated in 1982 and 1984).

At the institutional level, Lebanon became a French protectorate from 1920 to 1942, when France took control of the Levantine provinces (*Bilad ash-Sham*) of the dismantled Ottoman Empire. With independence, acquired in 1943, the new Lebanese political leadership severely weakened cultural and political ties with France.[4] The colonial relationship had been problematic long before being institutionalized by the League of Nations' mandate. Since the first cultural and political ties had been forged with the Christian community, the Maronites' sense of relative strength vis-à-vis the other social groups had been artificially invigorated by French promises, thereby increasing the social and religious divide.

With independence, all confessions formally agreed to forgo any loyalty to or potential alliances with foreign powers (France in the case of the Maronites, Syria being the first reference point for Lebanese Sunni). Sectarian, social and political tensions were played out mainly by international (USA, Soviet Union and France) and regional actors (Egypt, Syria, Israel and Iraq), starting in the 1950s and more dramatically in the 1970s (with the addition of Iran). This interference led to a 15-year civil war that only ended in 1990. With the end of the Cold War, Beirut officially fell under the influence of Damascus. Consequently, relations with Paris were given a deadly blow: the only assets left to French policy makers dealing with Lebanon were diplomacy and personal political relations.

Currently, Iranian and Lebanese domestic and foreign policies have been under the European spotlight in two issue areas in particular: non-proliferation and political instability, with regional destabilization and state failure as foreseeable long-term effects.

In the case of Iran, in addition to some European states' strong historical and economic ties, the EU has been at the heart of the international community contact group (the E3+3 or the 5+1)[5] engaged in negotiations over Iran's presumed secret nuclear weapons programme.

In the case of Lebanon, on the other hand, the domestic situation has deteriorated significantly since the assassination of former Prime Minister Rafiq Hariri in 2005, which was further complicated by the war of summer 2006 between Israel and Hizbullah and the ensuing constitutional and political crisis. The decision by many European states to deploy several thousand troops under the aegis of the United Nations Interim Force in Lebanon (UNIFIL), already present in southern Lebanon and later renamed UNIFIL-II, proves the European commitment to try to act as a conflict-management actor in the region. The aim of this presence is to defend Lebanese territorial integrity, to bring about positive spillover effects – that is, to allow the Lebanese army to redeploy in southern Lebanon, between the Litani river and the line of the 2000 Israeli withdrawal

(Blue Line) – and, partially at least, to act as an external constraint to those factions interested in polarizing existing communitarian dynamics. However, this presence should not be considered as a real transformative tool in the hands of the international community, but rather as a way to crystallize existing tensions, thus creating a possible window of opportunity for serious dialogue and negotiations among the different Lebanese stakeholders.[6]

This short historical overview paves the way for a deeper analysis, structured around two analytical constituents of the societies, namely the elites, understood in a broad sense as they emerge from a set of in-depth interviews, and the opinions held by the population as revealed by more or less targeted opinion surveys. These findings are integrated by a more comprehensive content analysis carried out on two of the most significant newspapers in each country.

## Survey data[7]

### *Political elites*

In neither country can one talk of a single, monolithic elite, especially as far as the political arena is concerned. In Iran, traditional conservatives, liberal reformists and radical neo-conservatives share very little in terms of global orientations and world affairs (Halliday 2001). For instance, liberal reformists share a pro-globalization orientation, manifested in the support of economic and technical progress per se and as a result of increased political and cultural cooperation with Europe (Perthes 2006: 9). With regard to recent diplomatic events, they tend to express their disillusionment with the short-lived progress of the high-level diplomatic talks held in the 1990s. According to most pragmatic leaders, the EU is driven foremost by its economic agenda to the detriment of democracy promotion. And yet our interviews revealed the belief in the potentially influential and constructive role Europe could play by building confidence among political actors in the region. Overall, the EU fails to be recognized as an effective actor on the world stage both due to its lack of internal unity and its Eurocentric attitude. Iranian traditional conservatives espouse a *realpolitik* view, whereby foreign policy is driven exclusively by national interests, and their main representatives sit in the Supreme National Security Council. Thus, Iran has to defend itself from Western interference and its political goals should only be gauged against long-term benefits and costs (Perthes 2006). At the other end of the spectrum, Iranian neo-conservatives manifest scepticism over the relevance of the EU as a mediator vis-à-vis the USA. The adoption of sanctions is quoted as an example illustrating the limited autonomy in foreign policy choices and double standards (in terms of the EU only imposing sanctions on certain countries). This group considers the nuclear programme an existential right of the Iranian nation and stigmatizes the international community's efforts to slow down the country's overall progress towards international recognition as a regional power.

In Lebanon, political elites tend to share a more positive view of the EU, especially insofar as economic relations are concerned. In the words of the former Lebanese Minister for Economy and Trade, Sami Haddad, Lebanon entertains a 'privileged' relation with the EU, which is also mentioned as the first strategic partner of the 'cedar country'.[8] However, two broad sets of inconsistencies are mentioned as exemplifying the biased attitude of the EU towards the Levantine country at the policy level. At the cooperation level, it is pointed out that European member states carry out several projects in an uncoordinated manner, duplicating existing initiatives and thereby hampering efficacy. Compared to UN efforts in the technical cooperation dimension, they believe that European efforts fare much worse. In terms of democracy promotion, an alleged pivotal element of European foreign policy in the region, inconsistencies and double standards make overall appreciation of such efforts difficult to substantiate.[9] For instance, the EU has been financing Hizbullah-sponsored nongovernmental organizations (NGOs) in the southern part of the country while officially boycotting Hizbullah as a national political force. Or, as pointed out by former Lebanese President, Emile Lahoud, the EU is seen as oscillating, unable to react to the flagrant violations of international law and the destabilization of the region perpetuated by Israel, often thanks to the endorsement of its 'international ramifications'.[10]

As in the case of Iran, the EU tends to be gauged against other international players, and obtains a lower level of appreciation. In the words of an academic, 'compared to the USA, the EU seems more friendly. But this does not translate into being influential'.[11] In short, while Iranian elites view the EU as a potential counterbalance to the USA (considered as the main potentially aggressive competitor to Iranian ambitions), in the case of the Lebanese elites, the picture is more blurred as there are several regional powers (Iran, Syria and Israel) whose actions can heavily impact on the evolution of Lebanese politics as opposed to the background role of international actors.

In Table 4.1, we have tried graphically to sketch the prevailing views held by Iranian and Lebanese elites. This information was gathered through a series of in-depth interviews conducted in both countries between February and July 2008.

### *Public opinion*

To a large extent, Iranian elites and public opinion share the same perceptions on foreign policy actors. In February 2006, World Public Opinion, PIPA and Globescan conducted a poll for the BBC on global views of the main world powers,[12] from which some unexpected findings emerged. For once, the EU came out as being more appreciated than some of its constituent members such as France and the UK (see Table 4.2).

The results of a more in-depth opinion poll conducted in January 2007 with nationwide face-to-face interviews[13] stand as a confirmation of our analysis of the elites' attitudes: almost half of the respondents held a positive view of the EU, expressing their desire to see a stronger Europe (48 per cent) in the future to counter the weight of the USA.

*Table 4.1* Perceptions of the EU by political elites in Iran and Lebanon

|  | *Economic actor* | *Ideological actor* | *Unimportant and ineffective actor* |
|---|---|---|---|
| Iran | The EU behaves as an economic power bloc, potentially exerting a positive and constructive role; scepticism over diplomatic negotiations after the missed chance under President Khatami; (view held mainly by Liberal reformists). | The EU is biased and behaves according to double standards, no room for negotiation over the nuclear programme, an indisputable Iranian right (view held mainly by neo-conservatives). | The EU, like other Western powers, should not interfere and Iran should focus on long-term interests; however, the nuclear programme can be part of a trade-off over a comprehensive package deal (view held mainly by conservatives). |
| Lebanon | European countries acknowledged as historically having enjoyed important cultural and economic relations with Lebanon. | The EU is considered to behave as a good friend of Lebanon without however possessing enough political clout to exert a significant influence over either the USA or the UN. | The EU is deemed inconsistent at two levels: at a purely operational level regarding its management of cooperation and democracy promotion policies and at a more substantive level in terms of different foreign policies espoused by different EU member states. |

*Table 4.2* Iranian views of world powers

| *Iranian views of the following world powers* | *Positive views (%)* | *Negative views (%)* |
|---|---|---|
| India | 71 | 21 |
| China | 66 | 25 |
| Japan | 57 | 33 |
| Europe | 53 | 36 |
| Russia | 50 | 44 |
| France | 35 | 58 |
| United Kingdom | 29 | 66 |
| United Sates | 26 | 65 |

Source: World Public Opinion, PIPA and Globescan, 2006.

In the same survey, a significant question was posed with regard to the level of appreciation of regional players: a high ranking was given to Hizbullah (75 per cent) and the Palestinians (73 per cent), then Syria (61 per cent) and Hamas (56 per cent). Interestingly, half of the respondents seemed to consider China and its economic growth as a potential threat, while more than half of the interviewees deemed India is having a positive influence in global affairs (60 per cent, however, down from 71 per cent in the 2005 BBC poll) and only 44 per cent held the same opinion about Russia (down from 50 per cent in the 2005 BBC poll).

From the annual Arab public opinion survey[14] conducted in November 2006, with 600 respondents divided into four categories (Sunnis, Shias, Druzes and Christians), one can derive some interesting findings concerning Lebanese attitudes: Shias are those who most intensely dislike the USA (80 per cent hold a very unfavourable view), followed by half of the Sunni respondents. Conversely, very little trust is placed in US foreign policy in the region and all communities identify Israel as the biggest threat to their security. On exploring possible alternative world orders, still within a unipolar system, and having to choose between five alternatives, Christians, Sunnis and Druzes would rather have France as the sole superpower, while Shias would choose Russia.[15]

In the hitherto only opinion poll conducted on relations between Lebanon[16] and the EU, European institutions appeared to be reasonably well known by the public (the European Parliament by 38 per cent and the European Commission by 35 per cent). The percentage declaring that the EU was an essential political partner rose to a considerable 70 per cent, while the Gulf states ranked second (36 per cent) and the USA third (27 per cent). More than half of the respondents deemed Europe a positive force in light of its freedom and democracy (54 per cent) as well as its respect for human rights (53 per cent). Almost two-thirds reckoned that Europe should improve its peace promotion policies on the global scene. Almost one-third of respondents thought that Europe should get more involved in Lebanese economic reconstruction, but only 10 per cent of them expressed the wish to see Europe more actively engaged in peace and security promotion in Lebanon.

### Civil society

The understanding of civil society in Middle Eastern countries has to be declined according to the individual historical and domestic contexts of each country. In Lebanon, civil society (*al-mujtamaa al-madani*) historically preceded the formation of the state (Khalaf 2004; Dawahare 2000). With the establishment of formal state structures, however, civil society suffered from an increasingly rigid sectarian categorization of its constituent parts. In the post-civil war period, particularistic allegiances have competed against a developing sense of national identity among the population. This was also reflected in the existing structure of the Lebanese political system, which was highly politicized and represented several parallel religious, social and political identities. Today, in addition to the political elite and intellectuals, the main elements active in the public sphere are human rights activists and development NGOs (Härdig 2008: 3).[17] An interesting case in point is the NGOs' non-confessional umbrella organization *Khalass* (Stop). Created in January 2007, *Khalass* was meant to put pressure on political leaders to go back to the negotiating table, pave the way for the election of a new president and elaborate a comprehensive electoral law reform. The foremost aim was to exclude the use of any violence for political purposes. As regards its links with Europe, *Khalass* complained of a lack of official contacts with Brussels and subsequent lack of support for its peace-making, reconciliation and reformist activities.

In Iran, what is known as civil society (*jame'e-ye madani*) can be described as an arena outside the state, to which different partly public and private organizations belong.[18] Under Khatami (1997–2005), liberal reformists exploited the opportunity to fill this space by interpreting it as an arena where public demands mainly concerning political and economic liberalization could be legitimately formulated and voiced. The most clearly identifiable analytical element of civil society in Iran is NGOs, thus far largely ignored even by the literature. In the view of the NGOs surveyed for this research,[19] the EU can count on incredible economic power and know-how that can be translated into precious technical assistance to offer to third countries, including Iran. With the adoption of international sanctions and the suspension of most cooperation programmes, Iranian civil organizations have been struggling, as this transfer of knowledge can be hardly replaced by non-Western countries. The critiques of European foreign policy match those articulated by the Iranian political elites (lack of independence in foreign policy choices, a political body internally divided and externally incoherent in its promotion of democracy). The EU is seen as passively receiving and accepting negative biases on Iran from other foreign policy actors. More importantly, Brussels and the European capitals fail to recognize the important role Iran plays and wants to play in the Middle East and still tend to treat it from a position of asymmetrical power.[20]

### *The press*

In Iran, the press is the main tool for political participation and propaganda. Currently, the most eminent newspapers are *Keyhan*, the long-time leading conservative mouthpiece, edited by the feared and powerful Hossein Shari'atmadari, and *E'temad-e Melli* (National Confidence), the voice of the reformist movement, founded by Mehdi Karrobi (a long-standing member of parliament) in order to try to keep together the coalition that had led to the victory of Khatami. Articles were chosen within a two-year time frame: from 22 December 2005 to 22 December 2007. We searched those articles containing in the headline or body of the text explicit reference to Europe, the EU and its institutions.[21]

*E'temad-e Melli* and *Keyhan* depict the EU as a politically jelly-shaped economic power, sometimes applying double standards and showing inconsistencies in its dealings with Iran. Nonetheless, European countries appear to be fairer than the USA in terms of credibility in the international arena. However, the scant coordination in the member states' external action negatively influences the overall picture of the EU as described by the press. Politically, the big three (the UK, France and Germany) are singled out as being at the forefront of European integration. Because of its lack of internal unity, it is difficult to translate EU economic clout into effective political capital, which leaves the Union with only half a voice in international affairs, and even less in the Middle East.

Between 2005 and 2007, the nuclear programme was the main issue debated by the Iranian media, in conjunction with the internal economic situation and the clash between reformists and conservatives. News related to this issue was always placed on the front page and largely exposed and commented on in newspapers. Voicing the apparently unanimous stance of Iranian society at large, both *E'temad-e Melli* and *Keyhan* referred to nuclear energy as 'a right' of Iranian people. Many driving factors help explain this consideration of nuclear facilities as a natural right, such as the idea that it represents an improvement in engineering know-how, energetic independence, a bid for national security vis-à-vis imperialistic stances and the search for international recognition as a major regional actor.[22]

*Keyhan* and *E'temad-e Melli* depict the EU in generally positive terms; however, they underline different facets and nuances. The former has a practical approach,[23] considering the EU an important economic partner, a key mediator in the international arena and a fair balance-maker, at the same time 'victim' of US power but worthy of dialogue and not to be blamed for imperialism. The reformists, on their part, show a more ideological approach, looking at the EU as a model of integration, an example to follow in matters of human rights, and a laboratory of constitutional development. Therefore, the overall image of the EU in these newspapers appears to be largely positive although with nuanced positions.

With all of its historical difficulties, Lebanon has managed to produce a highly literate, educated and critical populace, thanks also to a relatively diverse and sophisticated press and media landscape. Emerging from the bloody chaos of the war in the 1990s, the Lebanese press includes 105 licensed political publications, including 53 dailies, 48 weeklies and four monthly magazines. Two dailies, *An-Nahar* and *As-Safir*, were chosen as representative examples of the Lebanese press in light of their widespread circulation[24] and their political orientation. The analysis of the press was conducted from 1 January 2005 to 31 December 2006, which was chosen as the time frame in light of the highly significant political events that occurred in those two years within the long political and institutional crisis that lasted from 2004 to 2008. The amount of news was selected according to the occurrence of the expressions such as European Union (*al-Ittihad al-Urubbi*) and Europe (*Urubba*) and then further narrowed down according to the real relevance of the topics. Eventually, 66 articles were selected for *As-Safir* and 59 for *An-Nahar*. In both cases the articles mainly dealt with: (1) EU political, economic or cultural initiatives in Lebanon, (2) EU–Lebanese institutional relations and (3) events somehow linked to the EU.

*An-Nahar* (The Day) was founded in 1933 by the Orthodox Christian Tueni family. It is characterized by a liberal orientation, which, without denying its roots and Arab affiliations, looks to Europe and the West in general as a political and cultural reference point. With the deterioration in the domestic institutional crisis, worsened by the regional opposition between a pro-US bloc and the Iranian–Syrian axis, *An-Nahar* has become the voice of the popular campaign against Syrian interference in Lebanon. The paper has hence started to express criticism towards Hizbullah and its main regional supporter, Iran.

*As-Safir* (The Messenger) was founded in 1974 and belongs to Sunni Muslim, Talal Salman. It is today the leading reference point for the opposition, standing for a Hizbullah-led 'Islamic resistance' and, more broadly, for 'resistance against Israel and the USA'. At least since 2005, *As-Safir*'s political orientation has partly shifted towards more radical stances. For decades, and at least until 1989, it represented the secular and left-wing Arab Lebanese intelligentsia, opposed to Washington policies and loyal to pan-Arab ideals.

Currently, *An-Nahar*'s readers can be identified with the anti-Syrian parliamentary majority, supported by the USA, the EU and the Arab Gulf states (*imprimis*, Saudi Arabia), while *As-Safir*'s readers are mainly to be found among the Lebanese opposition, headed by Hizbullah and the Christian Maronite party of Michel Aoun, de facto backed by Iran and Syria.

*An-Nahar* and *As-Safir* express different visions of the EU: for the latter, EU policy in the country is described with deep scepticism, while for *An-Nahar* the EU is an honest and loyal partner of an independent, free and sovereign Lebanon. Both dailies agree in their depiction of the EU as forcefully backing the first Siniora government (2005–2008). When the domestic political crisis worsened before and after the legislative elections in June 2005, *As-Safir* reinforced its criticisms against the EU, while *An-Nahar* continued to express appreciation of European efforts to facilitate the emergence of a democratic and independent Lebanon. During the Hizbullah–Israeli war, *As-Safir* and *An-Nahar* reserved a limited space to EU policies in Lebanon, focusing on the condemnation by Brussels of the 'disproportionate Israeli reaction', thereby hinting at the scarce efficacy of EU policy beyond declaratory rhetoric. Starting from different political and ideological points of view, both newspapers insisted on the lack of coordination among European countries and on the overall European weakness vis-à-vis Washington's regional policy. In their columns, the EU was asked either to show a more concrete support of Lebanese 'democratic seeds' (*An-Nahar*) or to balance 'US–Israeli expansionism' (*As-Safir*).

## Explaining images

In general, the main political actors' worldviews have as much to do with historical narratives and political self-perceptions as with current readings of international relations and the preference for a specific international system that would most benefit their country. In the case of Iran, three different but somehow overlapping historically grounded perceptions mingle into each other justifying clear-cut political preferences. The first self-perception refers to a sense of betrayal both from regional countries and external powers, which have histori-cally threatened the country's territorial and political integrity. The second has to do with what is perceived as a culturally unique mosaic linked to the country's ancient language and the elegant poetry that preserves it; Iranian religious herit-age and its fusion with Islam towards popular Shiism; the multifaceted ethnic composition of its population (Persians, Kurds, Balouchis, Lors, Gilaks, Maz-andaranis, Torkamans, Qashqais, Azaris and Arabs); and, last but not least, a prestigious and specifically Iranic cultural tradition. The third self-image is tied to the glorious historical past of Persia, its regional domination and its centuries-long empire. From these three different but complementary images stems the conviction that only a multipolar world could guarantee the country's security against external interferences, as well as leaving room for extending its influence and projecting its power in the region. Within this approach, ideology espouses pragmatism as the core of the issue is not so much about exporting the Islamic Revolution in the region, but being in the position to influence regional events autonomously from international interference.

Lebanon possesses a strikingly different historical legacy, characterized by a recent national foundation, continuing regional games over its control and con-stant instability nurtured by different sets of domestic and external state and non-state actors. Two main opposing views of the world emerge and develop from these perceptions. On the one hand, the preference is for a multilateral world (not to be confused with a multipolar world order implying several competing power centres with their various spheres of influence) whereby the distribution of power at the international level is based upon international institutions. In other words it is on the interplay between different international players that the resilience and survival of Lebanon depend. In this view, the EU cooperation and democracy promotion agenda is positively evaluated: the Union is assessed not only in terms of concrete economic measures but is seen as a political actor investing in the country's stability. This Lebanese view of multilateralism is motivated by the self-perception of the state's weakness and the need to act within an international framework charged in the last instance with guaranteeing the country's survival. In a more cynical, typically realist reading also endorsed by certain newspapers such as *As-Safir*, the world is seen as an anarchic stage where Lebanon should be left to Middle Eastern power politics, characterized by different sets of rules in terms of understandings of democracy, human rights and the rule of law. In this view, Lebanon would opt to explicitly jump on the bandwagon with a regional power protector that would guarantee its survival and territorial integrity.

At a more contingent level, relations with the EU and the perception of the Union's actions are also influenced by another set of factors, namely the actors' preferences, the perception of power asymmetries and the interplay between dif-ferent issue areas.

In this regard, Iranian elites and citizens show a strong interest in enhancing their interactions and exchanges with Europe. This interest is rooted in the long struggle Iranians have undertaken in their quest for modernity, both in terms of technological and economic progress, and advances in the constitutional and civil law apparatus, all elements somehow identified with the EU and, particularly, with its most prominent member states (the UK, France, Germany and Italy). These elements should, however, be viewed in the framework of the strongly regional and Asian cultural 'affiliation' of Iranian's identity.

For centuries, Europe has been the closest 'foreign' shore for the Levant. Until today, a constant stream of economic, political and cultural contacts has continued to flow between the two sides of the Mediterranean. In comparison with other countries of the eastern Mediterranean, Lebanon boasts the highest proportion of citizens spread all over Europe.[25] Some Lebanese, members of a cultural elite conscious of its historical Arab roots, are aware of the dangers posed by the US strategy and regard Europe as a vital economic and cultural pole.

In the Iranian case, the perception of power asymmetries with Europe is an oft-quoted comment among elites, complaining about Brussels' self-centred attitude and lack of acknowledgement of changes in the regional landscape in terms of political equilibria and subsequent power shifts. Especially since the overthrow of Saddam Hussein, the leadership in Iran now feels reassured and, regionally, substantially stronger. There are several elements that can account for this feeling of increased relative and absolute strength. Culturally, it must be underscored the enhancement of the Islamic Republic's soft power thanks to the diffusion of Farsi in many neighbouring countries as well as of Shiism (Nasr 2006; Fuller and Francke 1999; Mauriello 2006). Politically, the key element was the informal regional networks of elite family relations spanning from Lebanon through Syria and Iraq. Domestically, despite external pressures, the Islamic Republic stands out in the region as an example of resilience and stability. In terms of regional alliances, Iran's few but long-established partners, namely Syria (through its defence-oriented and partly ideologically diplomatic alliance), Lebanon (through the culturally and Islamic-driven new assertiveness of its southern population) and Turkey (through its economic exchanges, favoured by the Iranian Azeri citizens), create a sense that Iran has become a regional power to be reckoned with. According to some Iranian commentators, neglecting these facts and dealing with Iran as if it were nothing more than part of an 'Axis of Evil' is what made the EU lose significant legitimacy as an honest broker. Again, the nuclear dossier is a case in point. Iranians show a sort of regret for the EU decisions not to pursue an independent and self-oriented line towards their country, abandoning the Paris Agreements and following the American line, thereby sacrificing its economic and energetic interests.

In the case of Lebanon, the EU, despite its good intentions, is also seen as exercising a power asymmetry mainly in two issue areas. Politically, as a result of not engaging in diplomatic dialogue with all political forces, but choosing 'legitimate' representatives of political stances and interests, and refusing to engage in dialogue with all political parties, most notably with Hizbullah, thereby directly interfering with the final domestic configuration of forces. The second issue has to do with individual member states, which are accused of poorly coordinating their cooperation and democracy promotion policies. The support of 'foreign' NGOs by single European states, compared with the European Commission's short-term support of single projects by 'local' NGOs are seen as detrimental policies in terms of efficacy, duplication of activities and lack of real empowerment of local civil society.

Economically, the power asymmetry is more evident in indirect financial dynamics out of the direct control of the EU, namely the strengthening of the euro that makes imported goods particularly expensive. The EU is perceived as being much stronger economically than politically, both in terms of its weak diplomatic output and its internal inconsistencies (a clear example being the lack of a comprehensive EU approach towards Syria). At the political level, however, the EU is acknowledged as an autonomous player in Lebanon and not as an executor of the US agenda, as opposed to the UN.

With Iran, EU economic and cultural cooperation is virtually non-existent, while some cultural and cooperation initiatives continue to be carried out by single member states' diplomatic representations[26] and by national private actors within the boundaries set by the international sanctions. At the political level, relations are limited to nuclear talks and even the previous negotiations conducive to a Trade and Cooperation Agreement or the human rights dialogue have been suspended by one of the parties (the Commission in the former case, the Islamic Republic in the second).

With Beirut, cultural cooperation is notoriously scarce, while cooperation programmes suffer from the same contradictions encountered in the analysis of political relations. Among EU-sponsored NGOs, some Hizbullah-funded projects have now been temporarily suspended for potential involvement in arms trading.[27] At the economic level, after the 2006 Hizbullah–Israeli war, the economic domestic context has deteriorated to such an extent that recovering the previous trade exchanges will be quite arduous.

## Conclusions and policy recommendations

Europe is perceived as a multifaceted and sometimes underperforming global player, whose diplomatic role is, however, far from negligible in Tehran's brinkmanship calculations. When it comes to European foreign policy, opinions differ sensibly. Some view the EU as an economically driven bloc, an actor falling prey of ideological considerations and thereby losing real leverage or a player acting on behalf of good principles but incapable of resisting the US agenda. More specifically, political commentators believe the EU is being played out by the Iranian leadership in order to mitigate Washington's decisions and potential hostile acts against Tehran (Thränert 2004). As an active diplomatic player, on the other hand, the EU is blamed for having missed a unique chance to upgrade political relations with the Islamic Republic during the Khatami presidency. In this reading, the Union failed to set up a new agenda for the region that took into account a more determining role for Iran and thereby missed the only window of opportunity open to the West to redesign regional and international relations with, and not against, Tehran. These images can be partly explained by the Iranian elites' understanding of international relations, characterized by the strength of political will and focus on the priority of pursuing national interests. According to this interpretation, the EU neither acts forcefully following an internally elaborated agenda, nor transforms its economic leverage into political capital.

Broadly speaking, the depictions of Europe in Iran show several nuances and are articulated across overlapping dimensions. In particular some big European countries, among which Italy, Germany and France, are acknowledged as historically good political and economic partners. With European high-level political relations, first established with the 'critical dialogue', whereby human rights abuses were a central element of talks, low politics and economic relations have also become more politicized. This somehow partly distanced Iranians from the EU as the inseparability of human rights issues from other political dossiers slowed down the overall pace of the negotiation process.

Images of Europe in Lebanon benefit from a real EU presence on the ground, compared to their absence in the Iranian case, which ranges from economic cooperation (epitomized by the European Commission 2002 Association Agreement and the 2007 European Neighbourhood Action Plan) to military involvements represented by the strong European elements within UNIFIL II.

EU endeavours to promote stability and democratization in the region are acknowledged, but are inevitably assessed against concrete policies on the ground in Lebanon, where the first policy goal – stability – has trumped the latter. Criticisms abound concerning the EU's bias towards a fundamental player such as Hizbullah. This view is in accordance with the widely shared conviction that Hizbullah is a political force without which no lasting domestic power-sharing agreement among confessions and their political representations can be found. Criticizing the EU for its excess of public diplomacy and limited understanding of the political dynamics on the ground is meant to signal a discrepancy between words and deeds, between rhetoric and concrete efforts to help Lebanon stabilize.

Militarily, on the other hand, the voice of Europe is barely heard next to that of Washington, particularly at the UN headquarters where decisions on UNIFIL II are taken.[28]

Several factors can help explain the prevailing depictions of the EU found in Iran and Lebanon. Long-term variables can be summed up as follows: the political identity of different social groups, historical experiences with the European continent and, last, the predominant worldviews of political elites. While the first two variables are relevant in explaining the Lebanese images, the third is fundamental to understanding the Iranian elites' views.

Summing up, the EU is considered an important and much-needed player both in Iran and Lebanon. In Iran, the EU can count on a rather positive image, a view shared by the elites and civil actors as well, irrespective of their specific political affiliations or ideological orientations. However, this image is partly nuanced by the perceived inconsistencies and misguided policies the EU pursues towards Iran. The nuclear dossier is a fundamental and unavoidable test bed for Iranian–European diplomatic relations. The traditionally good economic, energetic and cultural exchanges between the EU and Iran have been largely harmed by the EU's adoption of sanctions against the Islamic Republic. The Iranian perception that the EU has not elaborated its own policy agenda on the nuclear dossier limits both the prestige and the credibility of the Union as an international actor. Had the EU formulated its non-proliferation and regional agenda more coherently, it would have received a different evaluation by Iranian intellectuals and policy actors. It could have done so, for example, by pursuing a stronger economic policy with Iran and by taking into account the specificities of the regional security system and the long-established peaceful policies adopted by Iran. The EU could also enhance civil society and cultural exchanges, through easier access to visas for Iranians, in particular for young students and artists, thereby proving its appreciation of Iran's cultural heritage. Finally, the EU could get involved in the local media landscape with a Farsi version of its programmes, a rather successful road as demonstrated both by the long-running experiences of the BBC Radio[29] and the Voice of America, or the recently launched MBC TV entertainment channel and the BBC World News Service (January 2009).

In Lebanon, the EU's endeavours to promote stability and democratization are vastly recognized as one of its main foreign policy drivers. In the Lebanese case, however, the EU has so far failed to create a win–win situation out of a classic trade-off between stabilization and democratization, paving the way for several criticisms. In its political and diplomatic behaviour, the EU is sometimes accused of being biased, for example for cherry-picking its political and diplomatic interlocutors, or for behaving in an uncoordinated manner, as exemplified by the different outlooks held by the European countries on Lebanese policies.

All parts generally acknowledge a quantitative and qualitative increase in the European presence in Lebanon since 2006. Many praise the output of the technical and economic cooperation with the EU and with European countries. However, they complain about expensive European imports and the ongoing EU trade tariff barriers hindering transparent trade exchanges. The military engagement of some member states in UNIFIL II, while mostly praised, is sometimes criticized for either following the US agenda in the region, or for exerting no decision making. The international organization is often seen as a political arena where the USA and Israel drive the course of action.

Despite acknowledging the difficulty of engaging with a confessional society and a failing state, the EU and European countries are deemed to invest little in increasing cultural ties with the cedar country. The approach adopted so far by the EU and European countries, based on a combination of strong economic incentives, political support to the existing government and beefing up international peacekeeping, bears a negligible impact on cultural ties. What this package of tools fails to offer is a new strategic vision that embeds Lebanon in the changing regional balance of power or even puts forward effective policy changes.

Refraining from direct intervention in Lebanese domestic affairs, together with pushing for political reforms – by acknowledging the existing distribution of forces and legitimizing the political branch of Islamist political forces – looks like the most promising approach to resolving the ongoing stalemate.

## Notes

1  The existing critical literature, in fact, generally covers the state of the art of political relations, their historical evolution and their difficulties and stalemates.
2  Online, available at: http://news.bbc.co.uk/2/hi/middle_east/4260599.stm (accessed 31 January 2009).
3  Among other things, the statement by Khatami that Iran would not take any steps to pursue the implications of the *fatwa* regarding Rushdie helped to re-establish political relations with the UK and European countries.
4  As also demonstrated by the fact that three out of the first six Presidents of the Republic were not Maronites (Corm 2005: 92).
5  In the aftermath of the disclosure that Iran had been breaching its NPT obligations for the previous 18 years, the UK, France and Germany, known as the E3, took collective action by engaging in a comprehensive nuclear dialogue with Tehran. In autumn 2004, they were joined by the EU High Representative Javier Solana to become the EU3. After Iran resumed its uranium enrichment programme in 2005, in January 2006 the EU3 enlarged the coalition, taking on board Russia, China and the USA (to become the EU3+3) with the objective of referring the matter to the UNSC and paving the way for sanctions.
6  Speech given by General Commander Graziano of UNIFIL II, Naqura, Lebanon, 28 November 2008.
7  The following data are taken from: in-depth interviews conducted in Iran and Lebanon between February and June 2008, an analysis of the existing surveys and polls as well as an elaboration from secondary sources in the literature. In Lebanon, we interviewed government officials, members of parliament, scholars and journalists, members of the so-called 'civil society' and of the political section of Hizbullah. In Iran we interviewed former politicians, journalists, members of civil society (NGO activists, academics, think tank experts). For a complete description of the data, please see the Iran and Lebanon reports online, available at: www.garnet-eu.org/fileadmin/documents/working_papers/6209.pdf (accessed 31 January 2009).
8  On the first remark, see the address by H.E. Minister Sami Haddad to the EU in Brussels. Online, available at: www.economy.gov.lb/NR/rdonlyres/6CD551CE-B496-45D2-BC13-6142FA41EA53/0/17EUinBrusselsen.pdf (accessed 31 January 2009). On the second consideration, see online, available at: www.economy.gov.lb/MOET/English/Panel/StrategicPartners/EU.htm (accessed 31 January 2009).
9  Face-to-face interview with a Hizbullah member of the Beirut-based Centre for Documentation.
10  Address by His Excellency President Lahoud at the Arab Summit in Algiers, 22 March 2005. Online, available at: www.presidency.gov.lb/president/president.htm (accessed 31 January 2009).
11  Face-to-face interview with a professor from the America University in Beirut
12  Online, available at: www.worldpublicopinion.org/pipa/articles/views_on_countries-regions_bt/168.php?lb=btvoc&pnt=168&nid=&id= (accessed 30 October 2008).
13  Online, available at: www.worldpublicopinion.org/pipa/pdf/jan07/Iran_Jan07_rpt.pdf (accessed 31 January 2009).
14  'Annual Arab Public Opinion Survey: the war in Lebanon', The Sadat Chair for Peace and Development, University of Maryland, Prof. S. Telhami principal investigator, 6–11 November 2006. Online, available at: www.brookings.edu/topics/~/media/Files/

events/2008/0414_middle_east/0414_middle_east_telhami.pdf (accessed 31 January 2009).

15 Annual Arab Public Opinion Survey 2006: 25.

16 'Sondage sur l'Europe et le partenariat' 2005. The poll was carried out by Ipsos Stat with 612 interviewees aged between 18 and 55, from the middle and upper classes, between 13 April and 9 May 2005.

17 Here we did not attempt to advance a comprehensive understanding of what civil society entails in Lebanon, but we tried to unpack this concept into analytical building blocks, such as NGOs, thus far given little consideration.

18 On the discussion in Iran about the definition of civil society, also see the article by Abbas Nasr in *E'temad-e Melli*, 7 May 2006.

19 Most NGOs in Iran are united under a Coordination Committee. We gathered the information discussed in this part of the chapter through a series of interviews and a workshop organized at the UN Development Programme headquarters in Tehran in June 2008.

20 This element is, however, recognized by many world leaders. This is the case of former EU Commission President Romano Prodi, who during a visit to Iran (October 2008) to attend a conference organized to celebrate Khatami's 'Dialogue among Civilizations' declared to an audience at the Italian Embassy that Iran had become an unavoidably relevant regional and world actor, expressing his hope that it would soon make positive use of its strong influence towards constructive participation in the international community. Prodi confirmed having stated this opinion to both Khatami and Ahmadinejad.

21 We considered a two-year time span a sufficient sample for pointing both at some underlying tendencies and potential changes in the orientation and stances taken towards foreign policy actors.

22 An example of such a stance is represented by the same Ahmadinejad, who affirmed: 'All independent nations should have the right to the know-how of peaceful nuclear energy.... Today using this know-how for agriculture, industry, energy and medicine is truly needed and serves to the betterment and improvement of nations' (*Resalat*, 11 September 2007).

23 This element is particularly proved by the marked interest shown by this newspaper in the EU's rotating presidency, a factor linked to the strong belief that some EU members are much keener to understand Iranian rights than others that are more US oriented and have strong colonial legacies (France, Great Britain and Germany).

24 When asked, the Lebanese Information Ministry supplied us with the following circulation data as at December 2007: *As-Safir* sells around 50,000 issues daily, while *An-Nahar* around 45,000.

25 Since the nineteenth century, different waves of generations coming from Beirut, Sidon, Tripoli and Mount Lebanon have gone to Paris, London, Brussels, Frankfurt and Stockholm to study and work. In the last decades, the attraction of the Lebanese lower classes towards Europe has been challenged by their growing interest in the United States and Canada, while the pro-Western cultural elites of Beirut have remained attached to the 'European myth': Paris and London are still their favourite physical, or at least ideological, shelter. For other Lebanese people, Europe continues to represent a portion of the 'West', due to internal problems and violence.

26 The German Foreign Ministry, through its embassy in Tehran, for example, finances German courses of study in Iranian universities as well as student exchanges, and organized the performance of a play in Tehran during the Fadjr International Theatre Festival. Interview with German diplomat, Tehran, February 2008. See also online, available at: www.auswaertiges-amt.de/diplo/en/Laenderinformationen/01-Laender/Iran.html (accessed 31 January 2009).

27 This information has been confirmed by a source at the European Delegation in Beirut, May 2008.

28 Ali Fayyad, senior member of Hizbullah's executive committee and director of a research institute affiliated with Hizbullah, interviewed in Beirut, January 2008.
29 Such a proposal, however, is to be considered in the framework of the predictably negative reactions of the Iranian regime (Hiro 2001: 260).

# References

Afray, J. and Anderson, K.B. (2005) *Foucault and the Iranian Revolution: gender and the seductions of Islamism*, Chicago: University of Chicago Press.

Corm, G. (2005) *Le Liban contemporain, Histoire et société*, Paris: La Découverte, p. 71.

Dawahare, M.H. (2000) *Civil Society in Lebanon: toward a hermeneutic theory of the public spheres in comparative studies*, Boca Raton, FL: Brown Walking Press.

Digard, J.P., Hourcade, B. and Richard, Y. (2007) *L'Iran au XXe siècle entre nationalisme, islam et mondialisation*, new reviewed and updated edition, Paris: Fayard.

Djalili, M.R. (2005) *Géopolitique de l'Iran*, Paris: Editions Complexe, p. 113.

Foucault, M. (1994) *Dits et écrits*, 1954–1988, Paris: Gallimard (edited by D. Defert and F. Ewald).

Fuller, G.E. and Francke, R.R. (1999) *The Arab Shi'a: the forgotten Muslims*, New York: Palgrave.

Halliday, F. (2001) 'Iran and the Middle East: foreign policy and domestic change', *Middle East Report*, 220 (Fall): 42–47.

Härdig, C.A. (2008) 'Finding Unity in Fragmentation: the role of civil society in a factionalized state', paper presented at the Annual Meeting of the International Studies Association, San Francisco, CA, 26–29 March.

Hiro, D. (2001) *Neighbors, not Friends: Iraq and Iran after the Gulf wars*, London: Routledge.

Khalaf, S. (2004) *Civil and Uncivil Violence in Lebanon: a history of internationalization of communal conflict*, New York: Columbia University Press.

Mauriello, R. (2006) 'Identità sciita tra potere e democrazia', *Rivista di Intelligence*, II (3): 38–56.

Mokhtari, F. (2005) 'No One Will Scratch my Back: Iranian security perceptions in historical context', *Middle East Journal*, 59 (2): 209–230.

Nasr, V. (2006) *The Shia Revival*, New York: W.W. Norton.

Perthes, V. (2006) 'Risse im Reich der Ajatollahs', *Handelsblatt*, 4 July, p. 9.

Thränert, O. (2004) 'Stopping the Unstoppable? European efforts to prevent an Iranian bomb', in J. Reissner and E. Whitlock (eds) *Iran and its Neighbors: diverging views on a strategic region*', vol. II, *SWP Policy Paper*, Berlin.

Van Engeland-Nourai, A. (2005) 'Le rôle des droits de l'homme dans les relations entre l'Union Européenne et l'Iran', *Les cahiers de l'Orient*, 79: 117–28.

# 5 Between attraction and resistance

## Israeli views of the European Union

*Sharon Pardo*

## Introduction[1]

Despite its growing power and importance, the European Union (EU) has not obtained a central place in Israeli political and social discourse. One of the reasons for this lack of centrality has to do with Israeli images and perceptions of the EU. These images and perceptions have driven Israel to behave more as if it were an island in the Atlantic Ocean rather than a Mediterranean country neighbouring the EU.

Historically, geographically and even religiously, it has been argued that 'Israel is from Europe, but not in Europe' (Diner 2007), and indeed the Union is Israel's economic, cultural and, in many respects, political hinterland. In this regard, a public statement made by Israel's former Foreign Minister, Tzipi Livni, is rather useful in order to understand the close connection between Europe and Israel: 'I truly believe that the road should ultimately lead us to a significant participation of Israel in the European integration project. And here the sky is the limit' (Livni 2006: 4).

This chapter explores some of the main images and perceptions of the EU in Israel. By providing empirical findings concerning the attitudes of Israeli public opinion, political elites, organized civil society and the press, this chapter offers insights into the overall assessment on the part of the Israelis of the EU's global actorness. At the same time, it also serves as an important indicator 'of how well intentions have been translated into observable actions' (Rhodes 1998: 6). The underlying assumption of this chapter is that only by understanding the various EU images and perceptions – and, in some cases, misperceptions – will the EU and Israel be able to improve and upgrade their relations.

## A brief background

The EU and Israel first established diplomatic relations in 1959. In 1975 the then European Economic Community (EEC) and Israel signed their first cooperation agreement and, ever since, trade, economic, political and cultural cooperation have consolidated EU–Israel relations. The EU is Israel's most important trading partner. In 2007, 35 per cent of Israeli imports came from the EU, and 35 per cent of Israeli exports were directed to the European market (both percentages exclude trade in diamonds). The EU ranks number one in Israel's imports and two in its exports. On the other hand, Israel is one of the Union's biggest trading partners in the Euro-Mediterranean area.

Israel is a full partner in the Euro-Mediterranean Partnership (EMP)/Union for the Mediterranean (UfM) and participates in all its programmes. To intensify their political, economic and technological-scientific relations, Israel and the EU signed the 'EU–Israel Association Agreement' in 1995 within the framework of the EMP. The agreement entered into force in 2000 and forms the legal basis for Israel–EU relations.

The EU is Israel's second biggest source of research funding, after the Israel Science Foundation. Moreover, Israel is the first non-European country fully associated with the EU's Framework Programmes for Research and Technological Development.

Following the launch of the European Neighbourhood Policy (ENP) in December 2004, the EU and Israel adopted the EU–Israel Action Plan. According to the Action Plan, Israel and the EU are to intensify political and security cooperation, introduce a significant element of economic integration, boost socio-cultural and scientific cooperation and share responsibility in conflict prevention and resolution. The ENP has acted as a catalyst in boosting Euro-Israeli relations and the Action Plan has provided the platform for developing EU–Israeli cooperation across various fields (Commission 2008).

In June 2008 the EU–Israel Association Council vowed to intensify EU–Israeli relations within the framework of the ENP, and it agreed to develop and upgrade these relations in three main areas: diplomatic cooperation, Israeli participation in European agencies, working groups and programmes and Israel's integration into the European Single Market (General Secretariat of the Council 2008). In December 2008, the EU External Relations Council reaffirmed its determination to upgrade bilateral relations and issued guidelines for strengthening the political dialogue structures with Israel (Council of the EU 2008: 2). However, after the Gaza war in January 2009 the upgrading process was de facto suspended.

Finally, in spite of the successful bilateral instruments, political relations between Israel and the EU have never fully recovered since the 1980 Venice Declaration in which, as Israel sees it, Europe clearly signalled its sympathy with the Arab side.[2] Ever since, the EU has been regarded as an anti-Israeli group of nations with an anti-Jewish history and sentiments.

## An analysis of Israeli perceptions of the EU

### Public opinion

Generally speaking, the Union's attitude towards Israel has been perceived as being quite hostile to this country's goals and vindications. Indeed, although the EU and its member states repeatedly state their commitment to the existence and survival of Israel, they do not shy from criticizing Israel when it comes to its policies in the occupied territories. Arguably, these criticisms influence the way the EU is perceived in Israel, especially with regard to the peace process in the Middle East.

Public opinion polls seem to confirm this argument. In a 2007 national survey on the Israelis' attitudes towards the EU and its member states (Konrad-Adenauer-Stiftung (KAS) and Pardo 2007), we found that 75 per cent of the respondents were of the opinion that the United States of America (USA) or the EU should be part of the peace process. Yet, when respondents were asked which of the two actors they would rather have involved, 69 per cent replied the USA while only a meagre 14 per cent argued in favour of EU involvement. Even more astonishing was the fact that 59 per cent of the respondents to the national survey thought that EU involvement in the region in recent years had prevented progress in the peace process (KAS and Pardo 2007: 16–17).[3]

A recent national survey from July 2008, which was commissioned by the Geneva Initiative,[4] shows that 73 per cent of Israeli citizens support increasing US involvement in the Israeli–Palestinian conflict. At the same time, the survey also shows a dramatic rise in public support for European involvement in the conflict (58 per cent).[5] Interestingly, the Geneva survey employs the term 'European involvement' as opposed to 'EU involvement' (Geneva Initiative 2008).[6]

It is likely that Israelis understand that the Union's policies towards the conflict in the Middle East reflect the EU's increasing role in global affairs. In other words, Israelis recognize that the recent involvement of the EU in the Middle East and, in particular, the Union's contributions to finding a solution to the Israeli–Arab conflict mirror the EU's emerging standing in the international arena. Both the EU Border Assistance Mission (EUBAM), which monitored the operations of the Rafah border crossing point (until Hamas took over the Gaza Strip in June 2007), and member states' military involvement in the United Nations (UN) Interim Force in southern Lebanon (following the 2006 war between Israel and Hizbullah) are testimonies to the Union's growing involvement in the Middle East in the field of security. These two missions marked a significant step forwards for EU–Israeli relations, especially since they marked an important recognition by Israel that the EU will be given responsibility in the 'hard security' sphere.

The EU's standing with regard to the peace process cannot be understood without a deeper appreciation of the most dominant Israeli perceptions of the EU. Currently, three major perceptions, widely shared by both the general public and the political elites, affect Israeli attitudes towards the EU and influence Israeli policies vis-à-vis the Union.

The most fundamental Israeli perception of the EU is that the Union represents a hospitable framework for Israeli accession, and therefore that Israel could and should join the EU within the foreseeable future. This perception is driven by the Israelis' desires to join the Union.

In a 2004 Dahaf survey of the Israelis' perceptions of the EU, 70 per cent of those surveyed thought that joining the EU was either very important or important (Dahaf Institute 2004).[7] In the 2007 KAS and Pardo national survey, an overwhelming majority of 75 per cent of the Israeli public generally supported the possibility of Israel joining the EU. In addition, following the EU enlargement in January 2007, about 42 per cent of Israeli citizens are now eligible for EU citizenship (KAS and Pardo 2007: 20).

An additional perception, which might appear to contradict the first one, is that relations with the USA are by far more crucial than relations with the EU. In the 2004 survey, 68 per cent of respondents considered relations with the USA as more important than relations with the EU. Only 6 per cent considered relations with the EU as more important. About one-quarter thought that both relations were equally important (Dahaf Institute 2004: 24). Furthermore, 69 per cent of the respondents to the 2007 survey maintained that they had more in common with Americans than with Europeans, particularly in terms of culture. Only 20 per cent of the respondents felt they had more in common with Europeans than with Americans (KAS and Pardo 2007: 17).

The third fundamental perception follows from the second and accentuates the tension with the first: the EU harbours deep-rooted anti-Israeli attitudes and geo-strategic views that are detrimental to the security of this country. Underlying this perception are Israeli feelings that large parts of the EU are anti-Semitic. The 2007 KAS and Pardo survey revealed that 78 per cent of those surveyed thought that the EU was not doing enough to prevent anti-Semitism in Europe (KAS and Pardo 2007: 18).[8] Likewise, 64 per cent of the respondents to the 2004 Dahaf survey agreed with the claim that the EU positions towards Israel were anti-Semitism thinly disguised as moral principles (Dahaf Institute 2004: 41).

## Political elites and organized civil society

At the political level, a number of Israeli leaders agree with the citizens' opinion that Israel could and should join the EU within the foreseeable future. Thus, for instance, a group of Israeli parliamentarians, representing a broad spectrum of Israel's political parties, signed a manifesto in 2002 advocating Israeli membership of the EU (Transnational Radical Party 2002).[9] In November 2002, former Israeli Foreign Minister and current Prime Minister, Benjamin Netanyahu, declared that Israel favours joining the EU and asked Italy to help Israel achieve this goal.[10] Likewise, former Foreign Minister Silvan Shalom stated in May 2003 that the Israeli government was weighing up the possibility of applying for EU membership, adding that 'we will be glad to be accepted by the EU'.[11] In January 2007, Avigdor Liberman, current Deputy Prime Minister and Foreign Minister, declared that 'Israel's diplomatic and security goal ... must be clear: joining NATO and entering the EU'.[12]

A different approach is taken by Israel's President, Shimon Peres, who believes that once Israelis and Palestinians sign a peace agreement 'they should be accepted, together with Jordan, as members of a united Europe', in which the three countries could form a trading partnership or 'a modern Benelux'. According to Peres such a membership 'will give hope to the three parties'.[13]

It is worth noting that some leaders in the EU also support the idea of Israel becoming a member of the EU. For instance, Italian Prime Minister Silvio Berlusconi has been a vociferous advocate of Israel's accession to the EU, especially during the 2003 Italian Presidency of the EU. In 2004 Berlusconi declared that 'Italy will support Israeli membership of the EU ... As far as Italy is concerned, Israel is completely European in terms of standard of living, heritage and cultural values. Geography is not a determinant'.[14] Israel is a natural candidate for EU membership also for French President Nicolas Sarkozy – or at least more natural than Turkey. As Sarkozy wrote in his election campaign book, 'if Turkey entered the EU, I also wonder on what basis we could exclude Israel, so many of whose citizens are at home in France and in Europe, and vice versa' (Sarkozy 2007: 148). Support for Israeli accession to the EU can also be heard in the European Parliament. The Transnational Radical Party, for instance, has been running a campaign for full Israeli membership of the EU for several years (Transnational Radical Party 2002).

Although Israeli policy makers are aware of the importance of the EU to Israel, many of them share the public's perception that relations with the USA are by far more crucial than relations with the EU. In a statement that hyperbolically reflects the Israeli dismissal of the EU, former Prime Minister Ariel Sharon told a group of Israeli ambassadors to Europe they could disregard criticism of European governments since we in Israel 'do not owe anyone [i.e. the Europeans] anything. We are obligated only to God!'[15] For Sharon, as for others in the Israeli political elites, Israel can dismiss the EU mainly because of Israel's special relationship with the US.

Israeli political elites also share the general public's perception that EU policies towards Israel are deeply rooted in and marked by anti-Semitism. In the last eight years, European anti-Semitism has been discussed several times by the Israeli government in its weekly meetings. In press statements issued by Israeli politicians following meetings with European officials, the topic of European anti-Semitism is regularly on the Israeli political agenda. This is invariably the case when it comes to Israel's Prime Ministers and Foreign Ministers.

In November 2003 in an interview with EUpolitix.com, former Prime Minister Sharon said:

> an ever stronger Muslim presence in Europe is certainly endangering the life of Jewish people ... I would say.... EU governments are not doing enough to tackle anti-Semitism ... the majority of countries in Europe do not have a balanced policy towards Israel'.[16]

Later on in 2004 Prime Minister Sharon warned the Israeli Knesset that 'the anti-Semitism virus woke again [in Europe] and is beginning to infect large parts of the continent'.[17] In mid 2004, Prime Minister Sharon told a meeting of the American Jewish Association that Jews around the world, and especially French

Jews, should relocate to Israel as early as possible, because of 'the spread of the wildest [European] anti-Semitism'.[18] Also for former Foreign Minister Tzipi Livni, 'anti-Semitism is still very much alive [in Europe]'. In February 2007, Livni stated that 'modern anti-Semitism is spreading from fringes to the mainstream, in parallel with the growth of radical Islamic ideology in Europe. It poses a significant threat. We are witnessing new types of cooperation in Europe between the racist right, radical left and the Jihadist Muslims in this campaign.' (Livni 2007: 2).

The fight against anti-Semitism in Europe is also included in the EU–Israel Action Plan (AP) and is part of the December 2008 EU Council guidelines for strengthening political dialogue with Israel. While several chapters and sections of the AP include references to anti-Semitism, the AP's section on 'shared values' contains a special subsection on 'combating anti-Semitism' in which both parties commit themselves to the struggle against all forms of anti-Semitism in Europe. Moreover, the EU Council's guidelines replace the informal working group on human rights with a formal subcommittee, which will also examine 'the fight against racism and xenophobia – including islamphobia and antisemitism' (Council of the EU 2008: 5).

At the level of organized civil society, the images and perceptions of the EU are somewhat different. In analysing Israel's civil society, we conducted a study of 100 websites of major Israeli trade unions, academic institutions and non-governmental organizations (NGOs).[19] An additional component of this analysis consists of face-to-face interviews with 20 representatives of Israel's leading trade unions, academic institutions and NGOs.

A total of 30 per cent of the organizations surveyed made some kind of reference to the EU/Europe in their websites. Of these, 5 per cent of the organizations made a reference on their home page and 25 per cent of them referred to the EU/Europe on other pages of their websites. Two per cent of the organizations included a picture of the EU flag in their websites. In the sites mentioning the EU/Europe, we counted 134 items and links referring to the EU and 749 items and links referring to Europe. We then catalogued all items and links under 11 themes. The results are summarized in Table 5.1.

In terms of face value, an overall amount of 30 per cent of organizations making reference to the EU/Europe in their websites represents a quite significant quantitative measure. However, a qualitative analysis of these references highlights a far less central role for the EU/Europe than the merely quantitative figure suggests.[20]

That said, it is important to emphasize that the Israeli civil society is not unified in its approach to the EU. It is possible to divide Israeli civil society organizations into three categories: organizations that are not concerned with the EU and for whose work the Union has no direct relevance, organizations that know that the EU can assist them but are not part of the group of organizations that enjoy the Union's financial support and organizations that enjoy the EU's financial support. This third group includes leftist and liberal civil society organizations that see the EU as a potential political, ideological and financial partner.

*Table 5.1* Distribution of items and links to the EU/Europe by theme in 100 Israeli civil
society organizations' websites (March–April 2008)

| Theme | Percentage |
|---|---|
| Human rights | 25 |
| Professional cooperation | 12 |
| Social | 12 |
| Health | 9 |
| Education | 9 |
| Economy and trade | 9 |
| Financial support | 9 |
| Middle East peace process | 6 |
| EU–Israel political relations | 3 |
| Environment | 3 |
| Legal | 3 |
| *Total* | *100* |

Source: Pardo *et al.* 2008.

They believe the EU respects the work of civil society, even when the activities of these organizations might be at odds with the policies of the Israeli government. As the director of one Israeli NGO explained, the EU exemplifies 'how a democratic system should behave' (Pardo and Eskenazi 2008, Interview no. 7: 3). Not surprisingly, these organizations perceive the EU as the global defender of human rights and as an independent global power.

Most of Israeli civil society organizations are financially dependent on foreign financial sources. The USA is thought to be the largest financial supporter of Israel's organized civil society. Nevertheless, it is important to note that most of the financial support does not come directly from the US government but rather from the Jewish communities in North America. Echoing the implicit political fault lines between American and European interests, some civil society organizations funded by the EU (particularly, those working on Israeli–Palestinian/Arab issues) maintain they 'feel better with funds that come from the EU rather than from rightist organizations in America' (Pardo and Eskenazi 2008, Interview no. 14: 5).

Unlike other sectors in Israel, organized civil society does not perceive the EU as an anti-Semitic entity. Most organizations report they have never faced any anti-Semitic behaviour. Yet all organizations report that the issue is not on their agenda. Most organizations would like Israel to strengthen relations with the EU. Some of them would even like to see Israel as a full member of the EU. According to the director general of one of the largest Israeli civil society organizations:

> if Israel were to join the EU, Israel would finally be a member of a family of nations that believe in human rights and in equality; a family of nations that fight for the protection of the environment. It is not that Europe is a perfect

place, but the European society is an enlightened society. Israeli EU membership will release us from our historical siege.

(Pardo and Eskenazi 2008, Interview no. 16: 4)

### *Israeli media*

Although press circulation is currently in decline worldwide, leading newspapers are still considered a major source of information for the general public, as well as for the country's elite and opinion leaders. Newspapers play a decisive role in shaping collective perceptions and influencing the character of international relations (Schulz 2001: 4). Here, a study of the three leading national Hebrew newspapers, *Haaretz*, *Yedioth Ahronoth* and *Maariv*, is summarized. These three newspapers cover the Israeli ideological spectrum from left to right. While *Haaretz* targets a narrow readership mostly associated with the left, *Yedioth Ahronoth* and *Maariv* target a wider readership mostly associated with the centre and right of the Israeli ideological spectrum. They are the most widely read newspapers in Israel. The analysis spans all news items in the printed editions between 1 October 2007 and 31 March 2008.[21] We used a simple matrix to catalogue each news item according to the position it related and whether the context was positive, negative, neutral or a simple presentation of general information.[22] We also checked to see whether it concerned Israel, Jewish communities/the Holocaust/anti-Semitism, foreign affairs, the economy, security, culture, gossip or immigration. The results are summarized in Tables 5.2 to 5.4.

The number of news items relating to the EU and its member states varied greatly across Israel's three leading newspapers. *Haaretz* published 63.4 per cent of all news items, while *Maariv* published 25.4 per cent and *Yedioth Ahronoth* the remaining 11 per cent. In terms of the contents of the news, it is interesting to note that most items were covered selectively by one or the other newspapers. Only a minority of topics cut across the three newspapers, including the October 2007 general elections in Poland, the French proposal to appoint former British Prime Minister Tony Blair to the presidency of the European Council, the

*Table 5.2* Press coverage of the EU in Israel's three leading newspapers (October 2007 to March 2008)

| Month | Haaretz | Yedioth Ahronoth | Maariv | Total |
|-------|---------|------------------|--------|-------|
| October 2007 | 71 | 14 | 46 | *131* |
| November 2007 | 86 | 14 | 51 | *151* |
| December 2007 | 88 | 15 | 44 | *147* |
| January 2008 | 92 | 16 | 15 | *123* |
| February 2008 | 84 | 10 | 28 | *122* |
| March 2008 | 100 | 22 | 25 | *147* |
| *Total* | *521* | *91* | *209* | *821* |
| Average per month | 86 | 15 | 34 | |

Source: Pardo *et al.* 2008.

Table 5.3 Coverage of the EU/Europe and EU member states in Israel's three leading newspapers by theme (October 2007–March 2008)

| EU/Europe/member state | Theme | | | | | | | | |
|---|---|---|---|---|---|---|---|---|---|
| | Israel | Jewish communities, holocaust, anti-Semitism | External affairs (excluding Israel) | Internal affairs | Economy | Security | Culture | Immigration | Gossip |
| EU/Europe | 10 | 3 | 34 | 24 | 17 | 7 | 3 | 7 | 0 |
| France | 22 | 21 | 57 | 63 | 1 | 13 | 16 | 10 | 52 |
| Germany | 30 | 40 | 17 | 20 | 0 | 9 | 4 | 7 | 0 |
| UK | 10 | 10 | 17 | 39 | 2 | 4 | 8 | 2 | 12 |
| Italy | 1 | 2 | 1 | 44 | 1 | 1 | 5 | 3 | 0 |
| Poland | 2 | 10 | 4 | 15 | 0 | 3 | 0 | 0 | 0 |
| Other EU member states | 11 | 21 | 8 | 75 | 4 | 4 | 6 | 25 | 2 |
| Total | 86 | 107 | 138 | 280 | 25 | 41 | 42 | 54 | 66 |

Source: Pardo *et al.* 2008.

December 2007 visit of Muammar Gaddafi to Paris, the collapse of the Italian government in January 2008 and the Spanish general elections of March 2008. Although the Treaty of Lisbon was signed during the period examined, this event attracted little attention in the three newspapers.

Out of the 27 EU member states, France was mentioned the most often by the Israeli newspapers. One may think that the focus on France stems from rapprochement in French–Israeli relations. Be that as it may, the contents were less political than personal. While 36 per cent and 38 per cent of the news items published in *Yedioth Ahronoth* and *Maariv* (respectively) focused on France, the majority of them were dedicated to pure gossip regarding the personal life of President Sarkozy. *Haaretz*, too, focused on France more than on any other EU member state during the said period (25 per cent of the news items), but most of these items covered French foreign and domestic affairs (30.5 and 27.4 per cent, respectively).

Next to France, Germany received the most attention in Israel's three leading newspapers, with 14.7 per cent of all news items referring to Germany. In *Yedioth Ahronoth* 90 per cent of the news items on Germany also related to Israel, the European Jewish communities, the Holocaust or European anti-Semitism. In *Haaretz*, 57 per cent of the news items did so, and in *Maariv* 48 per cent mentioned Germany in one of these contexts.[23]

## The EU as a global power

In February to March 2008 we conducted a survey on the dominant powers of the twenty-first century and the most important goals of international politics. Survey respondents were selected among Israeli politicians, decision makers and opinion leaders; key representatives of Israel's leading trade unions, academic institutions and NGOs; and journalists from major Israeli newspapers, television channels and radio programmes.

The interviewees place both the EU and France together in fourth place on the list of global superpowers after the USA, China, Russia and Germany. Nevertheless, they expect the EU to move up to third place in the future (by 2020). According to the survey's respondents, among the greatest challenges facing the world's superpowers are climate change, international terrorism and poverty. Consequently, protection of the environment, peacekeeping and the eradication of poverty should be the top goals of any superpower.

About 50 per cent of our interviewees were of the opinion that the USA is the best country to maintain peace and stability in the world. On the other hand, 33 per cent believed that the EU is the best champion of world peace (as opposed to the USA).

## Understanding Israeli perceptions of the EU

### Public opinion and the political elites' perceptions

It is easy to understand the general public's perception that the EU represents a hospitable framework for Israeli accession, and therefore that Israel could and should join the EU within the foreseeable future. Yet, such a perception can best be explained by Israeli wishful thinking. What is surprising is the degree to which senior Israeli officials as well as European leaders, policy makers and others who are familiar with the EU cling on to this idea. For these views on Israeli accession to the EU ignore fundamental incongruities between Israel's self-definition as a Jewish state and the state of the Jewish People, on the one hand, and the guiding principle of the EU as an open and unified space without sharp distinctions between the citizens of member states in terms of 'insiders' and 'others', on the other hand. However democratic and liberal Israel might be, Israel's reality and aspirations as a Jewish state and the state of the Jewish People make it exceptional and radically different from other states. Needless to say, this difference would present great obstacles for Israeli accession to the EU even if Israel were invited to join the Union. Yet this difference would not be something that Israel could easily give up, since for many Israelis this distinction underscores their country's very *raison d'être*. At the EU level, indeed, public officials do not even seem to consider the possibility of Israel entering the EU. As explained by Commissioner Benita Ferrero-Waldner: 'In the context of the [ENP] we still have a lot of work to bring Israel and the EU closer ... As for the question of [Israel's] EU membership – this question is not on the agenda.'[24]

It is possible that fuelling the expectations that Israel might become a member of the EU will harm the future development of the relationship. Indeed, Israeli and European recognition that Israel cannot and should not try to become a member of the EU, in distinction from deep and comprehensive cooperation agreements,[25] is a basic starting point for strengthening, developing and upgrading EU–Israeli relations.

The second Israeli perception that relations with the USA are by far more crucial than relations with the EU is also likely to have a negative impact on the country, since political relations with the EU are indeed quite crucial for the future of Israel. Not only does the Israeli economy and significant parts of its research and technology depend on cooperation with the EU, but the EU standing in global affairs and security policies, not to mention its desire to be more involved in the Middle East, are likely to remain strong. As the EU's Security Strategy fully clarifies: '[The] resolution of the Arab/Israeli conflict is a strategic priority for Europe ... The [EU] must remain engaged and ready to commit resources to the problem until it is solved' (Council of the EU 2003: 8).

Furthermore, the different treatment Israel reserves for Washington as opposed to Brussels is itself problematic, mainly due to the fact that the USA and the EU are increasingly working together, especially on the Middle East. The Middle East Quartet made up of the USA, EU, Russia and the UN has become the principal international framework to deal with the Israeli–Palestinian conflict.

For a meaningful upgrade of EU–Israeli relations the Union must be recognized by Israel as a major global actor bordering on the Middle East that has a potentially constructive role to play in shaping the political–economic–cultural–strategic future of Israel. Europe would certainly like to assume a key role in the international arena, as was clearly declared by the EU's Security Strategy (Council of the EU 2003: 14). The role that the EU has chosen to play in the Lebanese crisis following the 2006 war and in defusing the Iranian nuclear crisis may prove that the EU is committed to its international role and may help Israel dispel its own perception with regard to the value of good political relations with Brussels.

The Israeli perception that EU policies towards Israel are deeply rooted and that large parts of the EU are anti-Semitic will not be easy to put to flight, especially when institutional voices within the EU approve such thinking, feeding this Israeli perception. A case in point is a speech given in 2008 by Franco Frattini, former Vice-President of the European Commission and the current Italian Foreign Minister, who admitted that in the past 'the EU has on some occasions taken an unbalanced stance towards Israel, even by making an unacceptable confusion between legitimate political criticism of Israel and intolerance against Jewish people that can become anti-Semitism'.[26]

All the respondents interviewed for this study identified Europe's Muslims as a main source of the current rise of anti-Semitism in Europe. For them, in combination with growing Islamic populations in EU member states and some features of globalization, the results were radical versions of European anti-Semitism fused with anti-Zionism, anti-Israelism and anti-Americanism. All interviewees concluded that these culminated in the manifestation of a 'new' European anti-Semitism superimposed on the traditional core of European anti-Semitism.

### *Media perceptions*

An initial assumption of this study was that the image of the Union in the Israeli media would be significantly dominated by Israeli, European Jewish communities/anti-Semitism and economic themes. Moreover, it was assumed that the Israeli media would frame the EU as an 'economic power', as 'a political power of weakness' and as an anti-Jewish entity. Yet the first two parts of this assumption proved to be wrong. The analysis found that the majority of EU representations in the press described the EU as 'a powerful political system', sometimes even 'a power of passive aggression' (Leonard 2005: 49–56), acting internally and externally. However, the Union was also framed as a marginal economic power with an anti-Jewish character.

It is interesting to point out that the EU's internal policies and the member states' domestic affairs received the largest share of media attention – 34 per cent of all news items (Table 5.3). The second most visible media framing of the

EU was around the Union's external affairs – 16.8 per cent of the sampled news items.

Our analysis also revealed that Israel's three leading newspapers took a neutral or positive stance on the Union. In 89 per cent of all sampled news items the media presented the Israeli readers with a neutral position and in 7 per cent of all sampled news items the media presented its readers with a positive position. In only 4 per cent of the items did the Israeli media clearly take a negative position (Table 5.4). In spite of the EU's global economic role and the well-developed economic relations between Israel and the EU, media coverage of the EU as an economic actor turned out to be marginal. During the period under scrutiny, only 3 per cent of the news items focused on this theme.

The most evident connection between the findings concerning public opinion and political elites and the results of the media analysis is the issue of anti-Semitism. Our study found that representations of the EU as an anti-Jewish and maybe even an anti-Semitic entity received the third largest share of media attention – 13 per cent of all news items. These figures are troubling, and go against a positive trend across the EU. As reports commissioned by the EU's Agency for Fundamental Rights on the issue of anti-Semitism in the EU since 2002 reveal, the number of violent anti-Semitic acts in the EU grew dramatically between 2002 and 2004, decreasing thereafter until the war in Gaza in 2009. Despite this downward trend, this study shows that Israel's three leading newspapers framed the Union as an entity with an anti-Jewish bias.

In an attempt to explain the frequency of news items regarding the Holocaust and European anti-Semitism, some foreign news editors interviewed for our research conceded that the decision to report extensively on anti-Semitic incidents in Europe and on the Holocaust was 'simply because anti-Semitism and the Holocaust sell newspapers in Israel' (Eskenazi and Pardo 2008, Interviews nos 1–2). And indeed quite often news items on anti-Semitism and the Holocaust reach the front pages of the Israeli dailies. Notwithstanding this anti-

*Table 5.4* Number of times the EU/Europe and EU member states are mentioned in Israel's three leading newspapers (October 2007 to March 2008)

| EU/Europe/Member State | Evaluation | | | | |
|---|---|---|---|---|---|
| | Positive | Negative | Neutral | Informative | Total |
| EU/Europe | 9 | 2 | 35 | 47 | 93 |
| France | 15 | 7 | 70 | 148 | 240 |
| Germany | 12 | 8 | 34 | 67 | 121 |
| UK | 6 | 0 | 38 | 69 | 113 |
| Italy | 3 | 4 | 28 | 22 | 57 |
| Poland | 7 | 2 | 10 | 17 | 36 |
| Other EU member states | 7 | 6 | 56 | 91 | 160 |
| Total | 59 | 29 | 271 | 461 | |

Source: Pardo *et al.* 2008.

Semitic image, the Union and its member states are also portrayed as possessing democratic values and as advocating human rights. The EU is also viewed as a leading donor of international aid and an active negotiator in the Iranian nuclear crisis.

## Conclusions and recommendations

This chapter identifies and analyses three major perceptions held by Israelis about the EU. First, that the Union represents a hospitable framework for Israeli accession, which makes people believe Israel could and should join the EU within the foreseeable future. This perception is mainly driven by the Israelis' desires to join the Union. Apparently at odds with the first perception is the belief that good political relations with the EU are by far less crucial than relations with the USA, particularly when it comes to the peace process in the Middle East. The third fundamental perception, which follows from the second and accentuates the tension with the first, is that anti-Israeli attitudes and geo-strategic views detrimental to the security of Israel are deeply rooted in the EU. Underlying this perception are Israeli feelings that large parts of the EU are anti-Semitic.

However problematic some of these perceptions and images might be, it is crucial to bear in mind that they are likely to affect relations between Israel and the EU and how the interaction between these two partners plays itself out. If Israel wants to continue developing and upgrading its relations with the EU, however, it should make much more of an effort to understand, and in some cases even dispel, its (mis-) perceptions and images of the EU. The same responsibility lies, of course, also on the European side. While this chapter did not examine European perceptions and images of Israel, there is no reason to think that they deserve any less attention. As François Duchêne has already cautioned us: 'Israel can never be wholly foreign to ... Europeans ... Jews are so much part of the fabric of European history and contemporary life that relations with Israel must, in some sense, be an extension of folk memories on both sides' (Duchêne 1988: 11). And without understanding these memories, it will be difficult to address the (mis-) perceptions and images on which the future of EU–Israeli relations ultimately lies.

There is little advantage in improving images and relations with actors who do not have assets that can benefit the EU. However, this is not the case for Israel in its relations with the EU. The main strategic assets of Israel are both positive, in the sense of benefiting the EU, and negative in the sense of being capable at least of somewhat harming the EU. These are outlined below (Dror and Pardo 2006: 24–8).

1 Israel's ability to influence the Union's role in Middle Eastern affairs, which in turn has an impact on the Union's global and regional standing.
2 Israel's ability to offer help and advice to EU decision makers to understand better the Middle East.

3 Israel's assistance with intelligence in coping with terror against targets in the EU.

4 Israel's hard-power spare capacity to help protect essential EU interests in the case of serious ruptures.

5 Israel's significant buying capacity.

6 Israel's possibility to direct scientific and technological cooperation either to the EU or to other partners.

7 Israel's capacity to influence the soft power of the US Jewish community and its actions with respect to EU–US relations.

8 Israel's potential ability, if pushed into a dangerous corner, to 'throw surprises at history' and cause changes in the Middle East, which might influence the EU.

In view of the analysis presented in this chapter, therefore, the following 12 recommendations are tentatively proposed (Dror and Pardo 2006: 43–4):

1   To realize the crucial importance of EU–Israeli relations.

2   To recognize and explicate shared long-term interests.

3   To recognize and officially declare that Israel shall not become a full member of the Union.

4   To give high priority to improving EU–Israeli relations, including investing larger resources and avoiding unessential acts.

5   To understand better Israeli values, interests and worldviews.

6   To move from a debate on current issues to a clarification of fundamental disagreements.

7   To examine and confront EU-based Israeli images and perceptions.

8   To strive to cooperate on global issues.

9   To map shared strategic interests and offer more cooperation in advancing mutual objectives.

10  To initiate shared professional discourse on the long-range future of the Middle East and on global geo-strategy as a whole.

11  To consult Israel formally on major local and regional initiatives.

12  To strengthen the socio-cultural policy dimension of EU–Israel relations.

## Notes

1 This chapter is a condensed version of a study conducted under the Network of Excellence *Global Governance, Regionalisation and Regulation: the Role of the EU – GARNET*. Some sections of this chapter draw on an article co-authored with Yehezkel Dror, which was published in the *European Foreign Affairs Review* (Dror and Pardo 2006). I am grateful to Sonia Lucarelli and Lorenzo Fioramonti for their constructive suggestions and comments at different stages of this study. I would also like to express my gratitude for the invaluable assistance of Michal Eskenazi and Ayal Kantz.

2 The central parts of the Venice Declaration discuss: (i) the 'Palestinian problem', (ii) the 'question of Jerusalem' and (iii) the Israeli settlements.

3 The KAS and Pardo survey was carried out in February 2007, by KEEVOON

Research, Strategy and Communications. A total of 511 people, providing a representative sample of Israel's adult population, responded to the survey. The survey had
a 4.5 per cent margin of error.
4  The Geneva Initiative is a joint Israeli–Palestinian effort that suggests a detailed
model for a peace agreement to end the Israeli–Palestinian conflict.
5  The GI survey was conducted by the Market Watch Research Institute in July 2008. A
total of 600 respondents were polled by phone and the survey had a margin of error of
around 4 per cent.
6  The GI is also supported by European funds, mainly from the Swiss government.
7  The 2004 Dahaf survey was commissioned by the European Commission's Delegation to Israel and conducted by the Dahaf Institute in December 2003 and February
2004. A total of 997 people, providing a representative sample of Israel's adult population, responded to the survey.
8  In addition, 64 per cent of Israelis thought that the EU is not doing enough to prevent
Islamophobia (KAS and Pardo 2007: 19).
9  Of course, this is not to suggest that, should there be a vote on EU membership, the
Israeli parliament would approve it.
10  'Israel Should Join the European Union', *Galatz-IDF Radio*, 9 November 2002.
11  'Analysis: Israel weighing EU membership', *United Press International*, 21 May 2003.
12  'Avigdor Liberman: Israel should press to join NATO, EU', *Haaretz*, 1 January 2007.
13  'EU Membership Touted for Israel, Palestine, Jordan', *CBC News*, 11 February 2004.
14  'Berlusconi: Italy will support Israeli EU membership', *Globes*, 3 October 2004.
15  'An Advocacy Lesson: at a Jerusalem conference Sharon demanded from the ambassadors to Europe: do not be afraid of anyone', *Yedioth Ahronoth*, 29 December 2004.
16  'European Report on Anti-Semitism Shelved due to "Political" Reasons', *Israel-
insider*, 24 November 2003.
17  'Sharon: anti-Semitism in Europe has reached new levels after the Holocaust', *Ynet*,
27 January 2004.
18  'French Jews Must Move to Israel', *BBC News*, 18 July 2004.
19  The following types of organizations were surveyed: eight professional organizations
and 92 academic, civil and communal organizations. The Internet search was conducted in March to April 2008 and was based on a search for the terms 'European
Union' and 'Europe'.
20  In most cases the websites contain a mere reference to the 'EU' or 'Europe'.
21  The analysis is based on all news items in which any of the names of the 27 EU member
states or the terms 'EU' and/or 'Europe' were mentioned in the headline or in the sub-
headline, either in a value-laden context or used in a descriptive, factual manner.
22  Note that some of the articles were checked twice as they both presented the reader
with general information and in a positive context for example.
23  The 2007 KAS and Pardo survey also reveals that Germany has a very favourable
image among Israelis, with 67 per cent of those surveyed expressing their wish to see
a more dominant Germany within the EU (KAS and Pardo 2007: 35).
24  'We Will Take Advantage of the Improvement of Relations with the US for a Deeper
Involvement of the EU in the Peace Process', *Haaretz*, 8 February 2005.
25  For a discussion on a new model for Euro-Israeli relations, see Pardo 2008.
26  'Italian FM: EU biased against Israel', *Haaretz*, 19 June 2008.

# References

Commission (2008) *Commission Staff Working Document. Accompanying the Communication from the Commission to the Council and the European Parliament. Implementation of the European Neighbourhood Policy in 2007. Progress Report Israel*, SEC
(2008) 394, Brussels, 3 April.

Council of the EU (2003) *A Secure Europe in a Better World: European security strategy*, Brussels European Council, 12 December.

Council of the EU (2008) *Council Conclusions: strengthening of the European Union's bilateral relations with its Mediterranean partners*, Brussels European Council, 8–9 December.

Dahaf Institute (2004) *Israeli's Attitudes towards the European Union*, Tel Aviv: Dahaf Institute.

Diner, D. (2007) *Europa-Israel*, Tel-Aviv: Heinrich Böll Stiftung.

Dror, Y. and Pardo, S. (2006) 'Approaches and Principles for an Israeli Grand Strategy towards the European Union', *European Foreign Affairs Review*, 11 (1): 17–44.

Duchêne, F. (1988) 'Israel in the Eyes of the Europeans: a speculative essay', in I. Greilsammer and J.H.H. Weiler (eds) *Europe and Israel: troubled neighbors*, New York: Walter de Gruyter.

General Secretariat of the Council (2008) *Eighth Meeting of the EU–Israel Association Council: statement of the European Union*, Luxembourg, 16 June.

Geneva Initiative (2008) *MarketWatch Israeli Public Opinion Poll*, Tel-Aviv: Geneva Initiative.

Konrad-Adenauer-Stiftung and Pardo, S. (2007) *Measuring the Attitudes of Israelis towards the European Union and its Member States*, Jerusalem: Konrad-Adenauer-Stiftung.

Leonard, M. (2005) *Why Europe Will Run the 21st Century*, New York: PublicAffairs.

Livni, T. (2006) 'Israeli European Relations', speech delivered at the KAS and CSEPS International Workshop, Jerusalem, 11 December.

Livni, T. (2007) 'Address by FM Tzipi Livni to the Global Forum for Combating Anti-Semitism', Jerusalem, 11 February.

Pardo, S. (2008) *Toward an Ever Closer Partnership: a model for a new Euro-Israeli partnership*, Lisbon: EuroMeSCo.

Pardo, S. and Eskenazi, M. (2008) 'Israeli Civil Society Perceptions of the European Union', unpublished research, Centre for the Study of European Politics and Society, Ben-Gurion University of the Negev, Israel.

Pardo, S., Eskenazi, M. and Kantz, A. (2008) 'Israeli Media Perceptions of the European Union', unpublished research, Centre for the Study of European Politics and Society, Ben-Gurion University of the Negev, Israel.

Rhodes, C. (1998) 'Introduction: the identity of the European Union in international affairs' in C. Rhodes (ed.) *The European Union in the World Community*, London: Lynne Rienner Publishers.

Sarkozy, N. (2007) *Testimony*, New York: Pantheon Books.

Schulz, W. (2001) 'Foreign News in Leading Newspapers of Western and Post-communist Countries', paper presented at the International Communication Association Annual Conference, Washington, DC, May.

Transnational Radical Party (2002) *For Israel in the European Union*. Online, available at: http://servizi.radicalparty.org/israel_ue/appeal/english.php (accessed 31 January 2009).

# 6 Conflict and hope

## The EU in the eyes of Palestine

*Simona Santoro and Rami Nasrallah*

Be sure that Europe does not forget you; we will never let you down. The agreement I just signed is a clear sign that we are and will be supporting Palestinian refugees. The EU has no other agenda than to help build sustainable peace and prosperity.[1]

(Louis Michel, Gaza, November 2005)

## Introduction

At the roots of EU–Palestinian relations is a clear-cut interest in cooperation. The EU has declared stability in the Middle East as one of its priorities and makes no secret of its desire for a more active role in the efforts to resolve the Israeli–Palestinian conflict (Solana 2003). The Palestinians are heavily dependent on the EU's financial assistance and would welcome an intensified diplomatic role for the Union, which is broadly considered more favourable to the Palestinian negotiating position than the United States of America (USA).[2]

However, despite this context, the Palestinian image of the EU is far from being straightforward. An analysis of the views held by Palestinian elites, public opinion and the media highlights a mixed picture. In the following pages, this chapter will provide a description of these perceptions and will attempt to identify key factors leading to them.

Before proceeding, it is important briefly to refer to the framework in which the Palestinian perceptions of the EU are developed. First, Palestinian politics and life have been absorbed almost completely by the conflict with Israel and the struggle to establish a state. Statelessness and hence statehood are existential issues.[3] Palestine is also a constitutive element of national identity for all Palestinians. In the last two decades, the focus has been on the Oslo Process and negotiations with Israel.[4] Embarking on the peace process meant abandoning a decades-long armed struggle and accepting a phased settlement aimed at establishing a Palestinian state.

Second, the establishment of the Oslo Process and the Palestinian Authority (PA) in the West Bank and Gaza at the beginning of the 1990s was followed by the demise of the 'political, institutional and security framework' (Sayigh 2002) of the peace process itself, the quasi-collapse of the PA, and the split between Hamas in Gaza and Fateh in the West Bank ten years later. As a consequence of these changes, the PA and the population of the West Bank and Gaza have been confronted with a very serious political and humanitarian crisis.

## Two angles: self-representations of the EU in the Middle East conflict

An analysis of Palestinian perceptions of the EU cannot be undertaken without considering the image that the EU projects on to the Palestinians. This is why our study focuses on the Palestinian perceptions of the EU on the basis of two main images, which correspond to two 'angles' of EU involvement with the Palestinians. The first is the bilateral relationship between the EU and the Palestinian people as part of the EU's external relations with non-member states. This is primarily the competence of the European Commission. More specifically, the Commission's relationship lies with the Palestinian population, the Palestine Liberation Organization (PLO) and the PA and is most active in the fields of economic and financial assistance, support for the development of democracy and promotion of the rule of law and human rights.[5] The second angle is that of the EU's involvement as third party in the Middle East peace process: in this sphere the EU efforts are aimed at supporting the parties in the achievement of a peace agreement. When the EU wears this hat, the main actors are the EU Presidency, the High Representative for Common Foreign and Security Policy (CFSP) and the EU Special Representative for the Middle East Peace Process.

It is important to underline that the term 'angle' has been explicitly chosen to highlight the fact that this division is not to be interpreted as too clear-cut: in the eyes of both actors, these areas overlap and complement each other. However, the distinction between EU–Palestinian bilateral relations and the EU's role in the diplomatic process is useful insofar as it helps distinguish the EU as a 'donor' as opposed to the EU as a 'mediator'.

In the next pages, a more detailed account of the EU's involvement with the Palestinians will be presented, which will be followed by an analysis of Palestinian perceptions of the EU focusing on the two angles. The analysis will be based on research on the attitudes of Palestinian elites and public opinions conducted through primary and secondary sources, including interviews with representatives of Palestinian elites and public opinion polls. In some instances, the perceptions of the EU will be compared to the ones on other relevant actors such as the USA and the United Nations (UN) or the international community as a whole.

### The bilateral context: the EU as a donor

In its role as bilateral partner, the EU has played an increasing role in providing financial and economic support to the Palestinian people. Begun in 1971 as a contribution to the United Nations Relief and Work Agency, the EU's financial assistance has grown to become the largest source of funds to the PA.[6] While during the Oslo Process the EU's assistance to the Palestinians was focused on development aid, in the post-Oslo phase the EU has shifted to humanitarian and emergency aid (Asseburg 2003; Peters 2000).[7] Since the suspension by Israel of the clearance system that transferred to the PA a certain number local taxes, the EU has started providing direct budget assistance to the PA to compensate this loss and cover its operational costs (almost €2 billion between 2000 and 2006).[8]

The EU also acquired a primary role in the administration of funds with the creation of the Temporary International Mechanism in 2006, a framework set up to administer the EU's and other donor's direct assistance to the population of the West Bank and Gaza (as opposed to the PA) after the international community, including the EU, severed its political and economic ties with the PA in the wake of Hamas's electoral victory and the establishment of a Hamas-led government.[9] In 2008, following the presentation by the Palestinian caretaker government of a Palestinian Reform and Development Plan at the Paris donor conference (December 2007), the EU renewed its financial support to the PA through the Pegase mechanism, supporting both the costs of the PA (salaries, pensions and fuel) and development projects.[10]

Signed in the framework of the bilateral track of the Barcelona Process in 1997, the Euro-Mediterranean Interim Association Agreement on Trade and Cooperation is considered the basis for the contractual relations between the EU and the PA. The agreement aims to liberalize trade and establish a comprehensive dialogue between the two actors. Moreover, the agreement is aimed at the economic and social development of the West Bank and Gaza and it encourages regional cooperation.

In 2005, the PA became part of the European Neighbourhood Policy (ENP). An action plan for the Palestinian participation in the ENP was adopted in 2005, which supports reforms in the area of democracy and good governance. Importantly, the action plan extended the scope of political dialogue between the EU and the PA to the facilitation of the peace process and the implementation of the Roadmap (EU–Palestinian Authority 2005).[11]

Also election observation falls under the scope of bilateral relations with the PA. The EU organized election observation missions in 1996, for the first political elections in the West Bank and Gaza, and then again in 2005 and 2006. According to the EU Election Observation Mission, the latest Palestinian elections were open and well administered and demonstrated political maturity.[12]

### *Multilateral arena: the EU as a mediator*

Reams of paper have been written on the EU's role in the Israeli–Palestinian conflict. Moving from the rationale that Europe has close historical, cultural and economic links with the Middle East and represents a model of integration, much of the literature on this topic portrays the EU as still in search of a political role (Peters 2000). While the EU has affirmed itself as a primary actor in the donor's sphere, it is still a secondary player in the Israeli–Palestinian peace process. The USA has until now retained a monopoly on power politics resulting in concrete peace initiatives (Quandt 2001; Tessler 1994), while the EU is often depicted as the normative or soft power, which complements the mediator role of the USA (Kriegsberg 2001).[13]

The EU started as a facilitator in the process and this role can be traced back to a document entitled *The Return of Peace in the Middle East* written for the European Commission by Palestinian politician Ahmad Qurie in the early 1990s. It is considered to have stimulated the interest of the then Israeli Foreign Minister Shimon Peres and Deputy Foreign Minister Yossi Beilin to establish direct contacts with the PLO, thus opening the way to the Oslo secret channel (Qurie 2006). However, once the agreement was concluded, both Israel and the PLO reverted to the USA as the guarantor of the agreements. In the early stages of the peace process, the EU remained on the sidelines of the bilateral track of negotiations and only played a more active role in the soon-to-end multilateral Arab–Israeli talks (Peters 2000).

The EU tried to enhance its involvement when the peace process started experiencing periods of stalemate after the assassination of Israeli Prime Minister Yitzhak Rabin, the election of conservative Benjamin Netanyahu and a series of terrorist attacks in Israel. In 1996, to acquire more visibility, the EU established the position of Special Representative for the Middle East Peace Process. The mandate of the Special Representative includes observing negotiations between the parties, contributing to the implementation of international agreements between the parties and engaging with the parties in case of non-compliance.[14]

The first Special Representative, Miguel Angel Moratinos, is considered to have played a behind-the-scenes role in specific instances during the peace process, such as in the case of the negotiations for the Hebron Protocol signed in January 1997, the first agreement to be signed between the PLO and the Likud-led government of Netanyahu (Peters 2000).[15] After the Hebron agreement, the EU also became involved in security cooperation between the Israelis and Palestinians although in a less overt fashion than the USA. An EU–Palestinian security committee was set up to provide guidance and advice to the PA on security cooperation with Israel, principally aimed at combating Hamas and its infrastructure. This platform became the springboard for further EU ad hoc mediation initiatives in the past years, one example often cited being the siege of the Church of the Nativity in Bethlehem in 2002.

Moreover, since the beginning of the Al Aqsa Intifada and the collapse of the Oslo Process, the EU has institutionalized its third-party role through the Quartet (Solana 2001).[16] Together with the Quartet, the EU has been the promoter of democratic reforms within the Palestinian camp, which included strengthening public institutions and rendering the political process more inclusive (Shikaki 2007). When Hamas was elected to power in January 2006, the Quartet conditioned its recognition of Hamas on three factors: Hamas's acceptance of Israel, compliance with previous agreements signed by the PA and the PLO and renunciation of violence (Tocci 2007).

The EU has also put in place CFSP police missions specifically formulated in support of implementation of the peace agreements: the EU Coordinating Office for Palestinian Police Support and the European Union Border Assistance Mission for the Rafah Crossing Point. At the recently held Berlin Conference in Support of Palestinian Civil Security and Rule of Law, more than €200 million were pledged for police training in the West Bank (Irin 2008).[17]

The EU has never presented its own practical peace initiative aimed at Israeli–Palestinian peace making. However, in 2001, in the wake of the Taba talks on final status negotiations, Moratinos compiled a non-paper based on interviews conducted with negotiators on both sides. The document has no official status but it has been considered by the parties a reasonable description of the outcome of the permanent status negotiations conducted for the continuation of the Camp David summit (Moratinos 2001).[18]

## Palestinian perceptions of the EU

The analysis of Palestinian perceptions is based mainly on the views of Palestinian political and intellectual elites and public opinion as analysed through primary and secondary sources.[19]

Our study shows that Palestinians across different segments of society view the EU mainly as a donor and provider of financial and humanitarian assistance rather than a mediator. Palestinians acknowledge that the EU has a more balanced approach to the Israeli–Palestinian conflict than the USA. While Palestinians would welcome an enhanced EU role in the Israeli–Palestinian conflict, most respondents seem to point towards the USA as a more effective actor to broker an agreement between the two conflicting parties.

As mentioned at the beginning of this chapter, these macro-perceptions are influenced by political and historical variables, the main one being the conflict with Israel at the core of which is land – Palestine or Eretz Israel. The establishment of a nation state on the disputed land has shaped Palestinian political identity in the past decades and despite different ideological stances on the resolution of the conflict, the overarching goal of reaching independence is a common denominator among different Palestinian political factions.

An additional variable to take into consideration is the perception of asymmetry. Palestinians perceive the conflict with Israel as asymmetric in that it involves dissimilar parties: a fully fledged state against a national liberation movement (Miall *et al.* 1999). Hence the importance of international actors that can correct this balance, including third parties such as the EU.

Historically, Brussels has a record of supporting Palestinian national aspirations and is considered to have a rights-based approach to the conflict. Since its first declaration on the conflict in 1980, the European position has been unambiguous regarding its support for Palestinian self-determination. The Venice Declaration of June 1980 clearly states that 'a just solution must be found to the Palestinian problem' and that 'the Palestinian people must be placed in a position by an appropriate process defined within the framework of the comprehensive peace settlement, to exercise fully its right to self-determination' (European Community 1980). Moreover, many European governments in the past decades have traditionally been seen as supportive of the Palestinian cause.

### The view of Palestinian elites

The perceptions of the EU held by Palestinian intellectual and political elites (fieldwork in Jerusalem and the West Bank in 2008) share an acknowledgement of the EU's role in the sphere of economic and financial assistance.[20] Nonetheless, Palestinian elites seem to hold clear-cut opinions regarding the marginal position of the EU as a third party in the Israeli–Palestinian conflict. In the words of the former Minister of Planning and Labour of the PA, Ghassan Khatib, 'Palestinian perception of the EU is very positive with respect to financial and development assistance, but it is a negative one when it comes to its political role which should be based on the international legitimacy and law.'[21]

It is interesting to note that the political role of the EU is considered mainly in relation to its efforts in the context of Israeli–Palestinian negotiations, while the political image of the EU as a model for democratic and civic values did not emerge as a determinant element in the discourse of our respondents.

Despite being aware of the different aspects of the EU–Palestinian relations in the framework of the Barcelona Process and the ENP, elites do not seem to give this involvement much importance. The arguments used by Palestinian elites to explain the secondary role played by the EU in the peace process are twofold. The first argument concerns EU internal policy making, which is perceived to hamper effectiveness in the area of the CFSP. This creates what they view as a lack European foreign policy in the Middle East.[22] The second argument concerns the subordinate position of the EU with regard the USA.[23] The EU is seen as merely supporting the American diplomatic efforts, even at the level of individual member states or within the context of the Quartet.[24] Some also see Israel's aversion to an increased EU role in negotiations as another impediment.[25] At the level of EU member states, some respondents highlight the role played France and the United Kingdom, which are often seen as being more influential than the EU itself. Yet, Palestinian elites lament that most EU member states (particularly France, Italy and the new members from Eastern Europe) have shifted their hitherto independent stances regarding the Middle East towards a general endorsement of the US strategy.

Our respondents agreed on the fact that the EU should have heralded an inclusive policy and put in place efforts to integrate Hamas within the Palestinian political system. However, the EU followed the wrong path by interrupting its relations with the PA when controlled by Hamas and later with the national unity government. The EU is seen as following a policy of double standards: on the one hand, it expects Hamas to recognize Israel; on the other hand, it refrains from pushing Israel to respect international law and the UNSC resolutions.[26]

When asked about their views on the EU Border Assistance Mission, the majority of the interviewees point out that this force is considered the only formula under which open borders with Egypt are possible. However, some see the EU mission as merely a humanitarian mechanism rather than a political arrangement under which a border control system can be developed.[27]

A discourse analysis of secondary sources reflects and complements what was outlined in the interviews. Four main themes characterize the language used by Palestinian elites to describe the EU. First of all, there is a recognition of the EU stance on the peace process as being more respectful of international standards and Palestinian rights; for example, on the issue of Israeli settlement activity (Sayigh 2001). In addition, the EU is portrayed as a promoter of human rights in the international context: 'Europe's strength lies in the uniformity of values it aims to promote – those of democracy, tolerance and adherence to human rights. It is these same values that we, Palestinians, also hope will underpin our future state' (Fayyad 2007).

The EU, however, attracts criticism as well. One of the reasons is related to what is interpreted as the EU's passive acceptance of Israel's violation of Palestinian rights (Eldar 2007) as well as its rhetorical rather than substantial pressure on Israel (Abdul Hadi 1999). PA Chairman Abbas has called the EU's policy in the Middle East 'discriminatory' and expressed dissatisfaction at the fact that Israel enjoys close ties with the EU notwithstanding its human rights violations (Eldar 2007). Moreover, in a recent letter to Brussels, PA Prime Minister Salam Fayyad is said to have urged the EU not to upgrade its ties with Israel in light of the latter's violation of basic commitments such as the halt to the construction of new settlements (Kershner 2008). The Palestinian leadership has also demanded that the EU substantiate its declarations with deeds: 'Europe has spoken in the past but a louder voice is needed.... It is now time to bolster the credibility of the peace process and preserve the viability and global acceptance of the two-state solution' (Fayyad 2007). The Palestinian Prime Minister has also referred to specific areas of intervention where the EU's role could be instrumental in influencing Israeli policies, such as the issue of Israeli settlement expansion and detention of Palestinian prisoners.

In general, though, the major issue of contrast between the EU and the Palestinians remains the former's decision not to maintain contacts with Hamas and suspend humanitarian and development aid to the Hamas-controlled PA (Shikaki 2007).

### The EU in the eyes of Palestinian public opinion

For the analysis of Palestinian public opinion, more than 300 online opinion polls by six Palestinian research institutes were consulted; and selected interviews were conducted with opinion pollsters.[28]

It is important to note that none of these centres has conducted a specific poll on the EU. Nonetheless, the existing polls provide enough data to draw conclusions on the Palestinian perceptions of the EU (see Figure 6.1). By looking at what type and how many questions have been asked on the EU, especially in comparison with other similar players such as the USA and the UN, we are given information on how relevant the EU is considered and what aspects of the EU

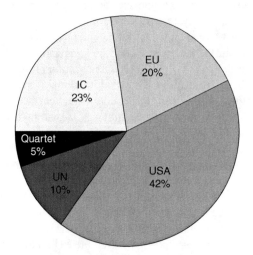

*Figure 6.1* Percentage of questions and answers on the EU, USA, UN, the Quartet and the international community (source: all polls).

role the polling institutes see as most important. A first analysis of the data shows a relatively low number of questions and answers on the EU throughout all polls.

Moreover, the EU is mentioned mainly for issues related to donor assistance; in questions on its role as third party in the conflict, the EU is often included under the category 'international community' or coupled with the USA; there are no questions on the EU Special Envoy; there are very few questions on Europe as a model for democracy; no questions are asked on the other component of the EU–Palestinian relations, such as the Association Agreement, the ENP, the Barcelona Process or election monitoring.

The answers given by Palestinians to questions on the EU broadly reflect the picture presented above. The EU definitely has a primary role in the eyes of the Palestinians in the sphere of donor assistance and international funding. Data in support of this statement can be found before as well as after the beginning of the Second Intifada, when the EU increased its presence in the Middle East. In 2000, the EU and some member states were seen as contributing the most to the Palestinian economy (25 per cent), compared to Japan (13 per cent) and the USA (11 per cent) (CPRS, Poll no. 47, February 2000). In 2005, overall, 79.5 per cent of Palestinians gave a positive assessment of the financial help provided by the EU; 74.2 per cent gave a positive evaluation of the support that the EU provides in infrastructure. The Arab countries only received a 55.6 approval rating for their financial support (Center for Opinion Polls and Survey Studies, Poll no. 10, January 2005). Similarly positive data emerged from an NEC poll conducted in April 2006, which indicated that nearly half (48 per cent) of the respondents believed the EU was the international donor that provided most humanitarian and developmental aid to the Palestinian people, followed by the Arab countries (27 per cent), the non-Arab Islamic countries (14 per cent), the USA (7 per cent) and Japan (4 per cent) (NEC, A Palestinian Perceptions Update, April 2006).

That this is the Palestinian outlook on EU funding has also been confirmed in interviews with academics and local researchers. Very positive data on the economic and financial assistance offered by the EU has come out also of polls on the specific issue of international assistance that are not available online. The EU is seen as the most important assistance provider, almost neck-and-neck with the UN.[29] More importantly, the EU is perceived as providing assistance for humanitarian reasons more than political reasons, as opposed to the USA.

As for the other component of the bilateral relationship, many research centres have also looked at the role of the EU and other international actors as an example to follow for Palestine. Some 72 per cent of Palestinians consider that their preferred system of government is a democratic system similar to the one in Europe or in Israel (CDS, Opinion Leader's Survey, February 2007). Europe also ranked second in a similar survey conducted in April 2006 (NEC, A Palestinian Perceptions Update, April 2006). However, this information should not be read in a vacuum: in a series of polls on the status of democracy in neighbouring countries, Israel and the USA ranked higher than the one European state chosen to represent Europe: France (CPRS, Poll no. 25, December 1996; CPRS Polls, Poll no. 47, February 2000). The USA is perceived as democratic and respectful of citizens (respectively 52.6 per cent and 66.5 per cent of the polled answered definitely yes to the question). Only 22 per cent of Palestinians considered the USA as promoting democracy around the world but 45 per cent would nonetheless like to see some features of American democracy applied in the Arab world (CDS, Poll no. 5, October 2001).

When analysing the public opinion's perceptions of the EU as a mediator in the conflict, two aspects will be taken into consideration: the reaction of the public opinion vis-à-vis specific instances of the EU's political role in the peace process and the level of trust in the EU as a credible/effective mediator.

As mentioned earlier, there are only a small number of questions in the polls regarding the role of the EU as a mediator in the peace process. The initiatives where the EU is considered to have played a role, such as the negotiations for the Hebron agreement in 1996–1997 or the Moratinos non-paper on the Taba talks of January 2001 do not appear in the polls. The EU Special Envoy for the Middle East Peace Process is never mentioned. Many of the polling institutes, as already argued, do not make a reference to the EU when mentioning the Roadmap or the Quartet. There are only a few instances where the EU is brought up in relation to a political initiative such as the EU–US request to the PA in May 1999 to continue permanent status negotiations and the proposal submitted by European personalities (OPSSC, Poll no. 25, January 2006). In addition, specific European countries are referred to, but only rarely.

One point that is important to highlight is the level of appreciation of the EU political role, at almost 27 per cent, compared to the approval rating for its financial assistance, which fares above 40 per cent (Table 6.1). This was also

*Table 6.1* Palestinian views of EU financial support to the PA (in per cent)

| Types of EU support | Good | Fair | Bad |
|---|---|---|---|
| Political | 26.9 | 42.5 | 26.7 |
| Financial | 41.8 | 37.7 | 16 |
| Infrastructural | 39.5 | 34.7 | 20.5 |

Source: OPSSC Opinion Poll No. 11.

confirmed in interviews, which portrayed the EU as not politically engaged enough in the peace process, while on the other hand also not reliable.

The second aspect is the level of trust that the public opinion has of the EU. The data does not present a uniform picture: the Europeans are considered to understand the Palestinian issues the most (34 per cent) if compared to other international actors, but the Americans are not ranked too far below (25 per cent). The Europeans are also considered to show more understanding of the issue than the Americans (36 per cent versus 10 per cent) (NEC, A Palestinian Perceptions Update, April 2006). More than 50 per cent did not see a difference between the EU and the USA in policies on the Israeli–Palestinian conflict (JMCC, Poll no. 51, June 2004). In a poll on which international actor was seen as possibly obstructing the national unity government, the EU was seen as potentially doing so – with 52 per cent (compared to 88 per cent for the USA). A total of 55 per cent, however, considered that internal Palestinian forces would represent one of these forces (CDS, Poll no. 30, February 2007). The negative assessment continues with more than 50 per cent believing that the EU is not really concerned with the success of the Hamas government. In the same question, the USA obtained a negative answer from 67.7 per cent and the Arab states from 35.3 per cent of the population (OPSSC, Poll. no. 19, March 2006). During the EU Presidency, 61.1 per cent saw Germany as biased towards the Israelis, while 21.5 per cent perceived Germany as neutral (JMCC, Poll no. 61, March 2007).

Finally, it is interesting to note that more than 82 per cent were against the attacks on the EU office in Gaza in the aftermath of the publication of the cartoons allegedly depicting Prophet Muhammad in Denmark. A total of 40 per cent continued to see Denmark as neutral with regard to the Israeli–Palestinian issue (NEC, Danish Cartoons Survey Results, February 2006). However, 49.3 per cent saw the USA and the Western countries as the external force responsible for the chaos in Gaza.

The third aspect relates to the international force in Gaza and the West Bank. In 2006, 56.2 per cent opposed and supported an international presence to a certain extent compared to 39.2 per cent who were strongly opposed to it (JMCC, Poll no. 60, September 2006). In May 2007, 67.9 per cent opposed an international force (NEC, Political Pulse, May 2007).

In case of the establishment of an international force, however, there seems to be a preference for a UN-led contingent. A large group of those polled would like the international presence to be invested with authority and power and the majority of the polled would prefer to have a UN-led force rather than an American–European one (JMCC, Poll no. 51, June 2004). The preferred international actor for a possible administration of Gaza after the Israeli withdrawal was the World Bank, followed by the Arab League, the United Nations and Egypt. The EU ranked ahead only of the USA (CDS, Poll no. 16, June 2004).

## A note on Hamas

Here, the views that Hamas and its supporters have of the EU are explored. As no interviews were conducted with Hamas officials, this part relies mainly on secondary sources as well as opinion polls, including disaggregated data on the political affiliation of those polled.

In its cabinet platform presented in March 2006, Hamas made reference to the EU and the international community, delineating an interest in sending out a message to these actors. Moreover, the platform commended the EU for its generous support of the Palestinian people and its 'serious positions' and criticisms of occupation policies, adding, however, that 'we expect it to play a bigger role in exercising pressure on the occupation forces to withdraw from the occupied Palestinian territories' (see Hroub 2006).

Hamas is very clear in condemning the US position in the peace process, the main reason being that the USA is not perceived as a neutral mediator (Abu Zuhri 2007).

Regarding the suspension of aid to the Palestinian population, Hamas officials condemn the international community's decision to interrupt dialogue with the PA after the establishment of the Hamas-led government. At the same time, though, the spokesperson for Mahmoud Zahar, the Foreign Minister of Hamas's government, seems to make a clear distinction between Europe and the USA:

> We also maintain contact with European countries and understand from them that they too want to see an end to the isolation imposed upon the government and our people. It is because of these friends that we have withstood the American–Israeli siege and maintained the struggle for the rights of our people.
>
> (al-Nuno 2007)

A look at the disaggregated data provided by public opinion polls shows a clear demarcation between Hamas and Fateh supporters on issues related to international engagement in the Israeli–Palestinian conflict.[30] Only 5 per cent of those who declared they were Hamas followers saw an international presence as beneficial; this figure stands in sharp contrast with the 50 per cent of Fateh supporters (NEC, Political Pulse, July 2007). A total of 90 per cent of Hamas supporters believed the appointment of Tony Blair as Special Representative for the Middle East peace process was negative, while only 58 per cent of Fateh supporters saw it as negative (NEC, Political Pulse, October 2007). Finally, 67 per cent of

Hamas supporters see Hamas's record of relations with the international community as positive (NEC, Political Pulse, December 2006).

## Conclusions and recommendations

While showing the complexity of Palestinian perceptions of the EU and the importance of further analysis on this topic, this chapter has also highlighted a few key elements that will be used to draw some conclusions and recommendations.

In the eyes of the Palestinians, the EU is perceived mainly as an aid donor rather than a credible mediator. Several additional aspects of the EU–Palestinian bilateral relationship such as the Interim Association Agreement, the ENP or the Palestinian participation in the Barcelona Process are quite marginal in Palestinian discourse on the EU. The image of the EU as an exporter of rights and fundamental liberties is important to the Palestinians because of its principled positions on the Israeli–Palestinian conflict (for instance, its position on Israeli settlements) rather than from the angle of these values being at the basis of an enhanced EU–Palestinian relationship in the future.

Furthermore, when it comes to the EU's role in the peace process, Palestinians seem to give more importance to the EU's statements and declarations on Israeli policies and the Israeli–Palestinian conflict rather than to specific EU programmes and policies. However, statements and declarations do not necessarily lead to great trust in the EU. Interestingly, the EU is not considered a credible option for a possible international presence in the West Bank and Gaza. For instance, the presence of the EU Special Envoy to the Middle East Peace Process is scarcely acknowledged. While the Quartet is seen as having raised the profile of the EU, its multilateral nature is put into question as this mechanism is seen as influenced by the USA.

The political context explaining these perceptions has already been presented earlier in this chapter, when the primacy of the goal of self-determination in the Palestinian political identity was highlighted. This provides a framework for elucidating on the pragmatic approach of the Palestinians vis-à-vis the role of mediators in the resolution of the conflict. However, other contingent variables have to be taken into consideration. One is related to the experience of interaction with the EU and the impact of the EU policies on the progress at the political level. In this case, there is a mixed experience. In some cases, the EU is considered as deeply involved in maintaining the PA but not in the long-term process of the national and state building of Palestinian society and institutions. The EU is sometimes seen as using its funding to pursue a specific agenda that reflects its interests. Additionally, on the EU policy vis-à-vis Hamas, there seems to be a perception that the EU should have heralded an inclusive policy and put in place efforts to integrate Hamas within the Palestinian political system. However, the EU followed the wrong path by interrupting its relations with the PA when controlled by Hamas and later with the national unity government. The EU is seen as following a policy of double standards; on the one hand it asks

Hamas to recognize Israel while on the other it does not request Israel to respect international law and the UNSC resolutions. Finally, some interviewees note for example that the EU has a scarce presence and visibility on the ground and that its outreach efforts need to be expanded.

Practical recommendations gathered through the field research conducted for this study include:

1   developing a more independent role and policy initiative for the EU within the Quartet (especially in relation to US positions),
2   enhancing the EU's contacts with Palestinian civil society actors and expanding its network of local institutions,
3   ensuring more transparency and open publicity for projects and programmes supported by the EU,
4   establishing exchange programmes between European and Palestinian universities, especially on topics such as the EU and European studies,
5   improving the public relations of the EU Office in the West Bank and Gaza, with the possibility of adopting an 'open door' policy,
6   keeping the Palestinian media more informed about different aspects related to the EU's role in the West Bank and Gaza. This would also include providing more user-friendly information on EU activities, institutions and policies.

## Notes

1 This statement was given by EU Commissioner for Development and Humanitarian Aid Louis Michel on the occasion of the signing of a €14 million fund to support the UNRWA food aid programme. For the quotation see online, available at: http://europa-eu-un.org/articles/en/article_5376_en.htm (accessed 31 January 2009).
2 According to Ghassan Khatib, former Palestinian Minister of Labour and Planning, Vice-President of Birzeit University, and co-editor of the online journal Bitterlemons. org:

> it is about time that other countries, particularly European countries, take a more proactive role. Europeans need to promote an alternative approach infused with European understanding to coordinate international efforts and base them on international legality to solve this conflict and potentially many more. It can only be hoped that such a rational approach will eventually win the full backing of the US.

(Khatib 2007)

3 See Sayigh 1995 for an analysis of Palestinian security issues and Sayigh 1997 for the history of the Palestinian national movement.
4 The term Oslo Process refers to the Declaration of Principles (DoP), negotiated in the capital of Norway and signed by the PLO and the State of Israel on 13 September 1993, and a package of subsequent agreements concluded between the two parties between 1993 and 2000. The DoP was negotiated by representatives of the PLO and the Israeli Labour-led government and based on a land-for-peace formula, and a step-by-step approach founded on the strategy of tackling the easiest problems first and subsequently engaging in the negotiation of the underlying causes of the conflict.
5 The EC's External Relations Directorate-General is responsible for the programming

of financial assistance. Information on this topic is available on the web page of the EC, online, available at: http://ec.europa.eu/external_relations/occupied_palestinian_territory/ec_assistance/index_en.htm (accessed 31 January 2009).

6 UNRWA was established after the 1948 Arab–Israeli conflict to provide assistance to Palestinian refugees. UNRWA is the main provider of basic services – education, health, relief and social services – to over 4.5 million registered Palestinian refugees in the Middle East.

7 Just before the signing of the DoP, the EU provided the PLO with a support package of ECU35 million to respond to emergency needs in the West Bank and Gaza. More funds were pledged after the launch of the Oslo agreements, in October 1993 and at key junctures throughout the Oslo Process. From 1993 to 1998 the EU is considered to have contributed to the process with ECU1.68 billion (Peters 2000: 162–3).

8 See online, available at: http://ec.europa.eu/external_relations/occupied_palestinian_territory/ec_assistance/eu_support_pa_2000_2006_en.pdf (accessed 31 January 2009). The Oslo agreements established a semi-customs union between Israel and the PA, which, except for specific products, basically shared the same import policies and regulations (Albin 1999; Elmusa and El Jaafari 1995; Fouet 1998). The Palestinians were also linked to Israeli taxation policies as these could not be more than two percentage points lower than Israeli taxes. For VAT and other indirect taxes, a special clearance mechanism based on the principle of destination was set up. According to this principle, indirect taxes on products bound for the West Bank and Gaza transiting via Israel were transferred to the PA. See Israeli–Palestinian Interim Agreement on the West Bank and the Gaza Strip 1995: art. 6b, annex V.

9 The TIM was a new financial mechanism established to make it possible to bypass the PA and provide assistance directly to the Palestinian people through support in education, social services, provision of electricity (fuel delivery to the power plant in Gaza), health care, sanitation and direct cash assistance to vulnerable segments of the Palestinian population. See TIM Overall Implementation Progress 2008.

10 See online, available at: http://ec.europa.eu/external_relations/occupied_palestinian_territory/tim/aid_2008_en.pdf (accessed 31 January 2009).

11 The EU–Palestinian Authority Action Plan is available on the website of the EC Technical Assistance Office, online, available at: http://ec.europa.eu/world/enp/pdf/action_plans/pa_enp_ap_final_en.pdf (accessed 31 January 2009).

12 The post-election press release of the EU EOM is online, available at: http://ec.europa.eu/external_relations/human_rights/eu_election_ass_observ/westbank/legislative/press_release_260106.pdf (accessed 31 January 2009).

13 A 'facilitator' has a more neutral role and instead of aiming to change the positions of the parties, it acts as a guarantor and confidence builder. A 'mediator' is able to influence the preferences of the parties through threats and concessions, utilizing its position of power. See Kriegsberg 2001. See also Asseberg 2003 and Moratinos 1998. For Silvestri, it is now clear that the European 'civilian power' is not effective when dealing with Middle Eastern crises (Silvestri 2003).

14 See Peters 2000.

15 The Hebron Protocol provided for the Israeli redeployment to one part of the city and defined the terms for the step-by-step continuation of the Oslo Process.

16 The Quartet is a diplomatic and mediation mechanism comprising the EU, the USA, the UN and the Russian Federation and established in April 2002 to coordinate conflict resolution efforts on the Israeli–Palestinian issue.

17 A similar plan coordinated by the USA put forward plans to establish five major security bodies in the West Bank (Abdul Hadi 2007).

18 The Moratinos Non-Paper was published by the Israeli newspaper *Ha'aretz* for the first time on 14 February 2002.

19 The Palestinian political spectrum can be roughly divided into three categories, according to the stance on negotiations with Israel. First, the pro-peace camp of Fateh,

the party of the late Chairman Yasser Arafat and current Chairman Mahmoud Abbas, which, as explained, has been involved in negotiations and signing agreements and the establishment of the PA. Second, the national opposition of the Popular Front for the Liberation of Palestine (PFLP) and the Democratic Front for the Liberation of Palestine (DFLP), two political parties based in Syria. The leftist opposition's criticism stemmed from the consideration that the Oslo agreement neglected the fundamental elements of the Palestinian struggle for independence and that Arafat had negotiated and signed agreements without a consensus within the PLO (Lindholm Schulz 1995). Third, the Islamist opposition of Hamas, Islamic Jihad, other Islamist parties and independent Islamists (Shikaki 1996). The Hamas–Fateh split became the determinant of Palestinian domestic politics after the January 2006 Hamas victory in Palestinian elections, and the Hamas takeover of Gaza in June 2007. This research attempts to take into consideration the different political dimensions of Palestinian perceptions. However, in light of security concerns, interviews with Palestinian elites did not include representatives of Hamas. Moreover, opinion polls are often disaggregated according to the Gaza–West Bank division but not necessarily along the Hamas–Fateh split.

20 A list of interviews is included in the References. In light of security concerns, the interviews did not include representatives of Hamas.
21 Interview, 21 June 2008.
22 Interview with Roger Heacock, 4 June 2008.
23 Interview with Gadah Araft, 16 June 2008.
24 Interview with Lily Habash, 6 June 2008.
25 Interview with Lily Habash, 6 June 2008.
26 Interview with Ghassan Khatib, 21 June 2008.
27 Interviews with Roger Heacock, 4 June 2008, and Eyad Muhammad, 18 June 2008.
28 Six main institutes located in the West Bank and Gaza conducted opinion polls in Gaza and the West Bank, including East Jerusalem, in roughly the past two decades. The Jerusalem Media and Communication Center (JMCC) and the Ramallah-based Palestinian Center for Policy and Survey Research (PCPSR/PSR) started their polling in 1993 and have released regular surveys since. The Center for Development Studies (CDS) and the Opinion Polls and Survey Studies Center (OPSSC) are university research centres located respectively at Birzeit University in Ramallah and Najah University in Nablus. Polls from Birzeit University are available from the year 2000 onwards, whilst the first survey of Najah University dates back to 2003. Additionally, the new institute Near East Consulting (NEC), also located in Ramallah, began conducting its research in 2006; and the website of the Palestinian Center for Public Opinion (PCPO) in Beit Sahour, a predominantly Christian town near Bethlehem, offers polls starting from 2005.
29 Interview with Jamil Rabah, 8 May 2008.
30 Interview with Hussein Ahmad, 9 May 2008.

# References

Abdul Hadi, M. (1999) 'The Prospects for Peace: a Palestinian view'. Passia Paper, Jerusalem. Online, available at: www.passia.org/about_us/MahdiPapers/7-Prospects.doc (accessed 31 January 2009).

Abdul Hadi, M. (2007) *The Gaza–West Bank Split. A Palestinian State without Territorial Unity*, Jerusalem: Passia Publications.

Abu Zuhri, S. (2007) 'A Complete Failure' (an interview with Sami Abu Zuhri), in *After Annapolis*, Bitterlemons, Edition 44, 3 December. Online, available at: www.bitterlemons.org/previous/bl031207ed44.html (accessed 31 January 2009)

Albin, C. (1999) 'When the Weak Confront the Strong: justice, fairness, and power in the Israel–PLO interim talks', *International Negotiation*, 4 (2): 327–67.

al-Nuno, T. (2007) 'Still Going Strong', (an interview with Taher al-Nuno), in *Hamas and the World, One Year Later*, Bitterlemons, Edition 5, 5 February. Online, available at: www.bitterlemons.org/previous/bl050207ed5.html (accessed 31 January 2009).

Asseburg, M. (2003) 'From Declarations to Implementation? The three dimensions of European policy towards the conflict', *Chaillot Paper* no. 62: *The European Union and the Crisis in the Middle East*, July, Paris: Institute for Security Studies.

Eldar, A. (2007) 'Abbas Accuses EU of Discriminating Against PA, Being Pro-Israel', *Ha'aretz English Edition*, 6 March. Online, available at: www.haaretz.com/hasen/spages/833150.html (accessed 31 January 2009).

Elmusa, S.S. and El Jaafari, M. (1995) 'Power and Trade: the Israeli–Palestinian economic protocol', *Journal of Palestine Studies*, 24 (94): 14–32.

EU–Palestinian Authority (2005) *Action Plan 2005*. Online, available at: http://ec.europa.eu/world/enp/pdf/action_plans/pa_enp_ap_final_en.pdf (accessed 31 January 2009).

European Community (1980) *Venice Declaration on the Middle East*, Venice European Council, 12–13 June. Online, available at: www.ec.europa.eu/external_relations/mepp/decl/index.htm#10 (accessed 31 January 2009).

Fayyad, S. (2007) Remarks at the PASSIA/FES Conference Europe and the Middle East, Ramallah, November. Online, available at: www.passia.org/conferences/2007/Salam-FayadPaper.pdf (accessed 31 January 2009).

Fouet, S. (1998) 'Le Contrôle des Mouvements comme Enjeu de Pouvoir', *Monde Arabe Maghreb Machrek*, no. 161, July–September: 28–42.

Hroub, K. (2006) 'A "New Hamas" thought its Documents', *Journal of Palestine Studies*, 35 (4), issue 140, summer.

Kershner, I. (2008) 'Palestinian Leader Urges Talks with Hamas', *New York Times*, 5 June.

Kriegsberg, L. (2001) 'Mediation and the Transformation of the Israeli–Palestinian Conflict', *Journal of Peace Research*, 38 (3): 373–92.

Irin (2008) 'Israel–OPT: donors pledge aid to Palestinian police, judiciary', 27 June. Online, available at: www.irinnews.org/Report.aspx?ReportId=78968 (accessed 31 January 2009).

Lindholm Schulz, H. (1995) *One Year into Self-Government: perceptions of the Palestinian political elite*, Jerusalem: Passia Publications.

Moratinos, M.A. (1998) 'Europe and the Peace Process', *Ha'aretz English Edition*, 12 February.

Moratinos, M.A (2001) The Moratinos Non-Paper 2001, January. Online, available at: www.bitterlemons.org/docs/moratinos.html (accessed 31 January 2009).

Miall, H., Ramsbotham, O. and Woodhouse, T. (1999) *Contemporary Conflict Resolution: the prevention, management and transformation of deadly conflicts*, Cambridge: Polity Press.

Peters, J. (2000) 'Europe and the Arab–Israeli Peace Process', in S. Behrendt, C.-P. Hanelt (eds) *Bound to Cooperate: Europe and the Middle East*, Bielefeld: Bertelsmann Foundation Publishers.

Quandt, W.B. (2001) *Peace Process*, Washington, DC: The Brookings Institution.

Qurie, A. (2006) *From Oslo to Jerusalem: the Palestinian story of secret negotiations*, London: I.B. Tauris.

Sayigh, Y. (1995) 'Redefining the Basics: sovereignty and security of the Palestinian state', *Journal of Palestine Studies*, 24 (96): 5–19.

Sayigh, Y. (1997) *Armed Struggle and the Search for State: the Palestinian national movement, 1949–1993*, Oxford: Clarendon.

Sayigh, Y. (2001) 'Arafat and the Anatomy of a Revolt', *Survival*, 43 (3): 47–58.

Sayigh, Y. (2002) 'The Palestinian Strategic Impasse', *Survival*, 44 (4): 7–21.

Shikaki, K. (1996) 'The Peace Process, National Reconstruction and the Transition to Democracy in Palestine', *Journal of Palestine Studies*, 25 (98): 5–20.

Shikaki, K. (2007) Paper presented at the Islam and Contemporary Palestine conference. PASSIA, Ramallah, 20 May. Online, available at: www.passia.org/meetings/Shikaki_Transcription%20rev%20.pdf (accessed 31 January 2009).

Silvestri, S. (2003) 'The European Union, the United States and the Middle East: some scenarios', *Chaillot Paper* no. 62: *The European Union and the Crisis in the Middle East*, Paris: Institute for Security Studies.

Solana, J. (2001) 'The European Vision for the Middle East', *Jordan Times*, 24 October.

Solana, J. (2003) *European Security Strategy. A Secure Europe in a Better World*, 20 June. Online, available at: http://ue.eu.int/ueDocs/cms_Data/docs/pressdata/en/reports/76255.pdf (accessed 31 January 2009).

Tessler, M. (1994) *A History of the Israeli–Palestinian Conflict*, Bloomington and Indianapolis, IN: Indiana University Press.

Tocci, N. (2007) *What Went Wrong? The impact of Western Policies towards Hamas and Hizbollah*, Brussels: Center for European Policy Studies. Online, available at: http://shop.ceps.eu/BookDetail.php?item_id=1523 (accessed 31 January 2009).

## *Opinion polls*

More than 300 opinion polls were consulted. They can be found at the following websites:

Center for Development Studies (CDS): http://home.birzeit.edu/cds.

Jerusalem Media and Communication Center (JMCC): www.jmcc.org.

Near East Consulting (NEC): www.neareastconsulting.com.

Opinion Polls and Survey Studies Center (OPSSC): www.najah.edu/nnu_portal/index.php?page=178&lang=en.

Palestinian Center for Public Opinion (PCPO): www.pcpo.ps.

Palestinian Center for Policy and Survey Research (PCPSR/PSR): www.pcpsr.org.

## *List of interviews*

Dr Hussein Ahmad, Director of the Opinion Polls and Survey Studies Center, al-Najah University, phone interview, 9 May 2008.

Ms Gadah Araft, Head of the EU Department at the PA Foreign Ministry, Ramallah, 16 June 2008.

Abed Arnaout, *al-Ayyam* newspaper, Jerusalem, 4 March 2008.

Khalil Assali, media expert, Jerusalem, 2 July 2008

Talab Awad, activist working with international solidarity groups against the wall, Jerusalem, 12 June 2008.

Alistair Crooke, security adviser to Miguel Angel Moratinos, Tel Aviv, 10 May 2001.

Mr Nasseif al-Deek, Al Mubadara – Palestinian national initiative, Jerusalem, 11 June 2008.

Ms Lily Habash, PA Prime Minister's Office, Ramallah, 6 March 2008.

Dr Roger Heacock, Ibrahim Abu Lughod Institute of International Studies, Ramallah, 4 June 2008.

Dr Ghassan Khatib, former Palestinian Minister of Labour and Planning, Vice-President of Birzeit University, and co-editor of the online journal Bitterlemons.org, Jerusalem, 21 June 2008.

Eyad Muhammad, Head of the International Affairs Department of the PLC, Ramallah 18 June 2008.

Mr Jamil Rabah, Director of Near East Consulting, phone interview, 8 May 2008.

Adeeb Salem, German-Palestinian young political leadership exchange programme, Willy Brandt Center, Jerusalem, 30 June 2008.

# 7 The emerging 'global south'

## The EU in the eyes of India, Brazil and South Africa

*Gerrit Olivier and Lorenzo Fioramonti*

### Introduction[1]

As explained at the outset of this volume, the European Union (EU) represents itself as a *qualitatively* unique actor in world politics. This self-representation is based on the assumption that the EU's foreign policy follows principles and values, based primarily on multilateralism and soft power, that are fundamentally different from nation states, which by contrast define their foreign policy objectives according to the overarching doctrine of 'national interest'.

For many years this assumption of 'uniqueness' has gone largely untested. More recently, some analysts have begun to scrutinize EU policies in a range of sectors and, although highlighting some inconsistencies and contradictions, have reaffirmed the notion of the EU as a 'unique' and 'better' global power (see Manners 2002; Telò 2006; Lucarelli and Manners 2006).

Interestingly, most of this research has been conducted in Europe itself, with an inevitable 'northern' bias, although the most distinctive EU policies, ranging from development aid to multilateralism and peace promotion, have a stronger impact on developing and poor countries. Since the turn of the millennium, these countries (which encompass least developed, middle-income and emerging countries) have often been described under the label of the 'global south'. The aim of this chapter is to test the EU 'uniqueness' theory by looking at how it is perceived by three leading nations of the 'global south', namely India, Brazil and South Africa (collectively known as IBSA).

In the next part of the chapter, we provide a background description of the relationship between the EU and the IBSA countries as representatives of the 'global south'. The analysis of the findings is concentrated in the central parts of the chapter, while the final part is dedicated to some concluding remarks and general policy advice for the EU.

### The EU and the 'global south'

India, Brazil and South Africa have seen their importance in world affairs grow in the past few years, together with China and Russia. In some key multilateral settings (since the World Trade Organization meeting in 2003), the IBSA countries have set their sights on representing the interests of the emerging markets as well as the least developed countries. They have contributed to creating the G20 and, more recently, have played an important role in the reform projects concerning the United Nations (UN) system. Brazil and India have joined the Group of 4, with Germany and Japan, to ask for a seat at the UN Security Council, while South Africa has continued lobbying for a collective 'African' seat.

India, Brazil and South Africa are also key partners of the EU, in terms of trade and foreign investments. Between 2004 and 2007, the EU signed strategic partnerships with each of these countries with a view to strengthening the bilateral relationships and normalizing political dialogue on a number of issues, including regional integration. Indeed, these countries are also characterized by both symbolic and geostrategic importance, with Brazil and India being the largest democracies in Latin America and Asia, and South Africa the most successful example of democratic and economic success in Africa. In geostrategic terms, these nations are prominent leaders in their respective regions of influence (South America, sub-Saharan Africa and South-East Asia). All these reasons, coupled with their global ambitions, make the IBSA countries a good test bed for the EU's 'distinctiveness' thesis, especially insofar as soft power and multilateralism are concerned.

Obviously, each of the IBSA countries operates at the international level primarily as an individual player. India has experienced significant economic growth, which makes it one of the most promising engines for the future of the global economy. At the economic level, its relationship with the EU has mainly been characterized by growing trade volumes (with an 80 per cent increase between 2000 and 2006) and deepening financial relations, in addition to close technological cooperation (sealed by the joint venture on the Galileo project). At the political level, India suffered a significant blow after the United States of America (USA) turned to Pakistan to seek support for the 'War on Terror'. While this created a window of opportunity for the EU to expand its political ties with New Delhi, India's refusal to join the non-proliferation treaty has reduced the extent of this collaboration. In general, it seems as if the EU has not been able to grasp fully Indian security concerns, which span from its relationship with nuclear Pakistan to the growing number of terrorist groups operating within the country and around its borders.

Relationships between Brazil and the EU have been stable over the past couple of years. At the subregional level, Brazil is the leading economy in Mercosur, the common market of the southern cone established in 1991 with Argentina, Paraguay and Uruguay. Until 2004, the EU and Mercosur made significant steps forward in the direction of a free trade agreement. Ever since, negotiations have stalled mainly due to disagreements over agricultural products and geographical denominations. In July 2007, the EU–Brazil strategic partnership was launched on the occasion of the first ever visit by President Lula to the Commission's headquarters. Besides trade reforms, a number of new issues were put on the table to strengthen the bilateral partnership, including energy security and biofuels (of which Brazil is a major producer), climate change and sustainable development as well as regional integration.

Similarly to Brazil, the relationship between the EU and South Africa has been influenced by the 'gatekeeper' role played by the latter in sub-Saharan Africa. Not possessing the same economic might as its IBSA counterparts, South Africa has projected itself on the global scene mainly as the leading emerging power of the African continent. Since the establishment of the African Union in 2002, continental issues have influenced the relationship between the EU and South Africa, which, in spite of the strategic partnership adopted in 2006, has been marked by several setbacks. A first issue of concern was raised by the deteriorating political and economic situation in Zimbabwe, which saw South Africa under former President Thabo Mbeki adopting a rather conciliatory approach in contrast to the EU sanctions against Mugabe's regime. A second reason for tension was generated by the reform of trade relations between the EU and the African, Caribbean and Pacific (ACP) countries, which saw South Africa playing a leading role in the African opposition to the signing of the Economic Partnership Agreements (EPA).[2]

This analysis is structured around four different groups of stakeholders in each country: public opinion, political elites, civil society and the media. Our research focused exclusively on existing information such as press releases, newspaper articles, institutional documents and additional information available on key websites.[3] This approach undoubtedly affected the 'comparability' of our data, since available information varied across the three countries. For instance, opinion polls regarding the EU were only available in Brazil and South Africa; furthermore the questionnaires were slightly different. It is also important to acknowledge that public documents, articles and press releases are not as neutral as face-to-face anonymous interviews. An additional factor such as 'rhetoric' therefore plays a potentially distorting role that is worth bearing in mind when reading the remainder of the chapter.

## What do *they* think of the EU? Public opinion, political elites, civil society and the media in India, Brazil and South Africa

At the global level, India, Brazil and South Africa cooperate on a number of policies, particularly in trade and development. At the same time, though, their foreign policies are also dominated by unique domestic and regional priorities. Obviously, these contextual differences are likely to impact on the public's perceptions of foreign actors. Yet an important dimension of the unique quality of the EU, neither a conventional state actor nor in competition with existing power configurations, is that it is generally perceived uniformly by public opinion, elites and the media in IBSA countries. Relations with the EU are generally framed in a fairly neutral policy matrix. The EU is still largely perceived as a 'technocratic' entity with few political ambitions, despite being characterized by huge economic power. It should also be noted that, in all three countries, foreign relations are not a common issue for public opinion and, therefore, the EU must compete for greater relevance with nation-state role players, which use different styles, strategies and methodologies to advance their objectives.

### Public opinion: the great unknown

Although the EU's starry flag is omnipresent on thousands of booklets, brochures and annual reports, opinion surveys reveal that only a minority of people have ever heard about the EU. That is, only a minority of people have an overall opinion about it.

The public opinion surveys available from Brazil and South Africa confirm this general trend, as does qualitative information on knowledge of the EU in India. In the 2002 Afrobarometer, it was found that only a minority of South African citizens had an opinion about the EU (42 per cent), while most respondents had never heard of it (Table 7.1). Interestingly, the same survey found that the EU was the least known international organization in the country, faring not only below international institutions such as the UN and the World Trade Organization (WTO), but also sectoral organizations such as the World Bank, the International Monetary Fund (IMF) and regional organizations like the African Union (AU) and the Southern African Development Community (SADC).

According to the *Latinobarómetro* 2004, among Brazilian citizens the awareness of the existence of the EU (43 per cent) equals the level of their South African counterparts. On the other hand, their knowledge of other international and regional organizations is even lower: 36 per cent have heard of the WTO and 34 per cent of the North American Free Trade Agreement (NAFTA). Both surveys confirm that there exists a positive correlation between educational levels and knowledge of the EU (which is probably explained by the complexity of the EU as a supra-national entity). Moreover, the higher the level of education the more positive the respondent's opinion of the EU tends to be.

Although quantitative data on the Indians' knowledge of the EU is not available, there is significant qualitative information to argue that India is no different from the other two countries. According to various Indian analysts, there is an enormous information deficit about the EU in India and the average Indian has considerable difficulty in understanding what kind of political and economic 'animal' the EU is. In the words of Rajendra K. Jain, Director of the Centre for European Studies at

*Table 7.1* Brazilian and South African citizens who have heard of the EU

|  | UN (%) | World Trade Organization (%) | NAFTA/SADC (%) | EU (%) | EU (university educated) (%) |
|---|---|---|---|---|---|
| Brazil | 70 | 36 | 34 | 43 | 68 |
| South Africa | 55 | 44 | 49 | 42 | 61 |

Source: Afrobarometer 2002 and Latinobarometro 2004.

Jawaharlal Nehru University, 'the EC stands for the *election commission* and if the EU Delegation is said to be an embassy, the usual query is: which country does it issue visas for?' (Jain 2008). Indian perceptions of the EU are essentially conditioned by the Anglo-Saxon media, which precludes a more nuanced understanding of the intricacies and complexity of the EU project. Although cultural relations between India and Europe date back to four centuries ago, 'there continues to be a gap between peoples, partly as a result of mutual indifference and an information deficit, despite growing civil society dialogue' (Jain 2005).

The picture gets more complex when we analyse the assessment of the EU as a global actor. In South Africa, the EU is viewed as a rather ineffective actor, especially when compared to other international institutions (Table 7.2). Again, when looking at the most educated group among respondents, the percentage of those who believe the EU is effective goes up to 20 per cent from 15 per cent.

According to the *Latinobarómetro*, more than half of Brazilian citizens (55 per cent) had a positive perception of the EU in 2004, up from 42 per cent in 1998. In addition, similar patterns emerge when it comes to evaluating the relationship between Brazil and the EU: 56 per cent of respondents declare that they have either a 'good' or 'very good' opinion of the state of the EU–Brazil relationship. In comparison, though, many more citizens believe that Brazil entertains a good or very good relationship with other Latin American countries (64 per cent) or even with global powers such as Japan (63 per cent) and, probably even more interestingly, the USA (69 per cent). The same downward trend is also reflected in the Latin American average: the EU comes in last when compared to the other countries included in the survey (Table 7.3).

Perhaps surprisingly, most Brazilian citizens believe that the USA is the best promoter of democracy, development and free trade (Table 7.4). The only exception is peace, where the EU ranks higher (22 per cent). However, when looking at the Latin American average, the USA fares better than the EU in all sectors. Once again, however, education appears to be an important factor: if we only consider respondents with the highest level of education (university level), the EU jumps to the top in all four policy fields.

Despite having adopted a strategic partnership in 2005, India and the EU are still far apart when it comes to cultural linkages. As acknowledged by a British

*Table 7.2* Effectiveness of international institutions for South African citizens

|  | EU (%) | AU (%) | UN (%) | WTO (%) | IMF (%) | World Bank (%) | SADC (%) |
|---|---|---|---|---|---|---|---|
| Totally or rather ineffective | 39 | 36 | 31 | 31 | 37 | 35 | 29 |
| Somewhat effective | 46 | 46 | 46 | 49 | 46 | 48 | 46 |
| Effective | 15 | 18 | 23 | 20 | 17 | 17 | 25 |

Source: Afrobarometer 2002.

*Table 7.3* How would you define relations between your country and…

|  | USA (good/very good) (%) | Japan (good/ very good) (%) | Other countries in Latin America (good/ very good) (%) | EU (good/very good) (%) |
|---|---|---|---|---|
| Brazil | 69 | 63 | 64 | 56 |
| Latin America | 71 | 64 | 68 | 58 |

Source: Latinobarometro 2004.

*Table 7.4* Which power contributes most to…

|  | USA | | EU | |
|---|---|---|---|---|
|  | Average (%) | University educated (%) | Average (%) | University educated (%) |
| …democracy | 25 | 21 | 22 | 53 |
| …free trade | 18 | 13 | 13 | 30 |
| …world peace | 17 | 7 | 22 | 48 |
| …development | 17 | 15 | 12 | 29 |

Source: Latinobarometro 2004.

member of the European Parliament, Neena Gill, in an interview with the *Hindustan Times* on 13 August 2006, 'a vast majority of the people [in India] is not aware of [the] EU or its activities'.[4] Various Indian commentators also point to the limited social links between Europe and India. With the exception of Britain (and to some extent also Portugal and the Netherlands), there are more Indians in the state of New Jersey than in the rest of the EU (Lisbonne de Vergeron 2006).

### The elites' views: policy makers, business and civil society

In their public statements, the IBSA political elites describe the EU as a contradictory global power: on the one hand, it is viewed as an important partner for fostering development and economic growth; on the other hand, it is accused of stifling developing economies through its protectionist policies. The first image is mainly due to the fact that the EU is these countries' largest trading partner. Moreover, the political elites are aware of the magnitude of the European market and see it as a key opportunity to boost their economic growth. Additionally, the EU is also appreciated for being the most significant source of foreign direct investment. By contrast, the second image derives mainly from issues concerning agricultural subsidies (principally in Brazil and South Africa) and other non-tariff barriers (mainly India). For all the IBSA countries, international trade has become a key opportunity to reassert their standing in global affairs. All these countries have registered sustained rates of economic growth. Brazilian agricultural production and natural resources are now able to compete with European produce, while Indian manufactured commodities are very competitive on the global market. Thus, in their eyes, it is unfair of the EU, while trying to protect its domestic markets, either to subsidize domestic producers or impose a number of non-tariff trade barriers (such as packaging requirements, health and environmental standards), which contribute to moderating the inflow of produce exported by emerging markets.

Double standards, inconsistencies and contradictions are at the core of their criticisms of the EU's external policies in the fields of international trade and social development. It has been noted elsewhere that South African political elites dramatically changed their perceptions of the EU after the end of apartheid, when harsh trade negotiations revealed the 'self-interest' of EU policies as opposed to the 'altruistic' reputation it had gained through its support for the liberation movements (Olivier 2006). In 2007, the dire negotiations concerning the so-called EPAs proved to be another significant stumbling block in the South Africa–EU relationship.[5] After the collapse of the Doha Round, also caused by the IBSA countries' opposition to a deal 'made in the US and EU', the EPA negotiations confirmed the self-interested attitude of the EU in its dealings with Africa. According to Rob Davies, South African Deputy Minister for Trade and Industry, the EU acted to defend its interests 'against preferences for domestic producers' with a view to exerting 'significant influence on our economic governance in a highly partisan and non-developmental manner'.[6] Furthermore, the EPA process also dented the hitherto impeccable reputation of the EU as a genuine promoter of regional integration in Africa insofar as the negotiations with the EU contributed to dividing 'the members of the Southern African Development Community into five different negotiating configurations' with the risk of hampering its ambitions to realize a uniform customs union by 2010.[7]

The way these negotiations were carried out by Brussels projected an image of the EU as being guided by its own narrow trade interests regardless of the price it exacted from its negotiating partners. Like its trade policy (and its agricultural policy in particular), the EPA episode starkly contradicted the preferred image of the EU as a developmental agent and benefactor to the poor and disadvantaged countries of Southern Africa. Officially, the EU goals in South Africa are similarly clothed in the ubiquitous and altruistic terms of 'what is good for the country', emphasizing qualities such as sustainability, capacity building, socio-economic development, poverty relief, support for democratization and promotion of human rights. Yet a number of local observers and political elites find it astonishing that the EU follows two simultaneous policies that clearly contradict one another. This adds to the general image problem of the EU in the public mind: what it really is and what it stands for (Olivier 2006: 9).

In many regards, the Indian political elites do not differ from their South African counterparts. Both the previous government and the current Congress-controlled executive have used caustic expressions against the EU's trade policies, especially in terms of non-tariff barriers. At the sixth EU–Indian summit held in 2005, Indian Prime Minister Manmohan Singh remarked that 'as tariff barriers disintegrate, non-tariff barriers suddenly come up' to hamper exports from developing economies.[8] At the Hong Kong meeting of the WTO in December 2005, the then Minister of Trade Kamal Math defined the EU export subsidies as 'the most trade distorting measure', perpetuating the inequalities between the developed nations and poor countries.[9]

During high-level summits, the EU has often been portrayed as an opportunity for the economic growth and a stronger global status for India. Since early 2000, the discourse on the India–EU partnership has focused mainly on 'common values' such as democracy and tolerance, which make the two parties inherent allies in areas such as sustainable development, security and world peace. The EU's proclaimed focus on multilateralism and democratic governance is endorsed by the Indian political elites, who stress the significance of their country since it is not only the biggest democracy in the world, but also the only consolidated democracy in a region dominated by authoritarian regimes. Yet the discourse around 'common values' should not be overemphasized. Similarly to Brazil and South Africa, India is actively committed to a 'multipolar' world led by sovereign powers rather than a multilateral global governance system. In part this might explain the Indian policy makers' long-standing attraction towards the USA, something that is likely to strengthen in the post-Bush era.

A qualitative study of the Indian elites' views of the EU maintains that political and business leaders are quite pessimistic about the future significance of the EU in a globalized world: Europe is seen as in 'economic decline', 'too small, divided, and backward-looking' and a 'niche player providing luxury goods and services' (Lisbonne de Vergeron 2006: 24).

In this regard, a number of analysts have highlighted that the widely heralded strategic partnership between the EU and India has fallen short of expectations, further contributing towards growing disillusionment among Indian elites of what can actually be gained from a stronger relationship with the EU (Jaffrelot 2006). By and large, Indian business continues to perceive the EU as a conglomerate of sovereign states, characterized by different strategies and economic objectives. In part, this explains why the bulk of financial relations between the two partners still takes place at member state level.

In the past few years, the Brazilian elites have seen trade relations with the EU as an opportunity to achieve its developmental goals and reaffirm the leading role of their country's economy in the South American region (Biato 2004). Until 2005, relations with the EU in the context of the Mercosur contributed to shaping positive perceptions among the Brazilian political elites: stronger commercial ties with the EU were seen as a viable alternative to the US-sponsored Free Trade Agreement of the Americas, widely opposed by all left-leaning governments of the region (De Almeida 2004). At that time, President Lula described the EU as the only trade interlocutor of Mercosur that 'putting on the table offers in all the relevant areas, signals a positive disposition towards negotiations'. More recently, though, this perception of the EU as an 'opportunity' has gradually shifted towards a more negative depiction of the EU as a 'fortress'. In May 2008, the Brazilian government echoed African countries in expressing serious concerns as to the effects EPAs would have on poor economies and, particularly, on south–south trade arrangements.[10] At a bilateral level, immigration issues have also become a source of contrast between the two parties. In September 2008, the Brazilian Ministry of Foreign Affairs attacked the decision by the EU Ministers of Justice to adopt a European Pact on Immigration and Asylum restraining migrants' access to Europe. In a critical statement, the Ministry reminded the EU that Brazil has traditionally 'hosted millions of foreigners, mainly from Europe, with generosity and without discrimination' and underlined the:

> worrying escalation of measures adopted within the European framework which, by purportedly fighting illegal immigration and encouraging regularization, reinforce a negative predisposition toward migration, generalize selection criteria and allow forms of control that, when applied, may prove arbitrary or contrary to human rights.[11]

Most of the issues raised by civil society organizations operating in the IBSA countries overlap with those highlighted by their political elites, although the tone is often more critical. The harshest criticisms target EU free trade proposals and protectionist policies. Interestingly, the special partnerships signed between the EU and the IBSA countries did not generate any public debate within IBSA civil societies.

In South Africa, the trade unions and some leading non-governmental organizations (NGOs) accuse the EU of double standards and hypocrisy in its dealings with the African continent. South African civil society was unanimous in opposing the EU-sponsored EPAs in 2007, echoing the negative sentiments of the Indian and Brazilian social movements with respect to the EU's stance in the Doha Round. On 16 August 2008, the Southern African People's Solidarity Network took part in a street protest in Sandton, the richest area in Johannesburg and economic heart of Africa, carrying banners saying 'Stop EPAs Now'.[12] According to the Cape Town-based Alternative Information Development Centre, the EPAs are a new ploy by European countries to 're-colonize' Africa through subtle economic coercion and 'arm-twisting tactics', leaving countries receiving aid from Europe in a vulnerable position.[13]

Traditionally, trade liberalization has been at the core of Brazilian civil society's critique of the EU's global agenda. In a 2004 common declaration spearheaded by Brazilian social movements and subscribed to by a number of civil society organizations operating in Latin America, it is possible to read a clear criticism of the EU's initiative to establish a free trade agreement with Mercosur. According to the signatories, the:

> EU itself has given the world a lesson of patience and moderation in taking no less than fifty years to construct an agreement amongst the European

nations, but now they want to impose on us a very comprehensive and far reaching agreement in less than no time.[14]

Like their Brazilian and South African counterparts, Indian civil society organizations have long stigmatized EU policies concerning agricultural subsidies. For them, the distortion caused by unfair competition in the global market has become a matter of social justice and human rights. The opening of the Indian market to global competition has further exacerbated social unrest and poverty in the country, especially in the poorest segments of the population, while the wave of suicides among Indian farmers not able to compete with subsidized produce from Europe and America became a matter of national security after 2003.[15] By contrast, Indian ecological associations have praised EU opposition to genetically modified organisms and its leading role in the adoption of the Kyoto Protocol. Nevertheless, the image of the EU as an 'environmental leader' has been tainted with inconsistencies, mainly due to its incapacity to rein in European companies that do not apply the same environmental standards to their offshore plants in India.

## The media

The analysis of the media in Brazil (the press), India (the press) and in South Africa (both press and TV) confirms most of the points raised above (Table 7.5).[16]

As already anticipated above in 'public opinion', the EU is not really a 'hot' topic in the public domain. Across the three countries, the EU is more accurately covered in financial newspapers and is mainly portrayed as an economic actor. The political component of the EU, such as its internal policies and hard-core foreign policies (from peace operations to diplomatic missions), is far less common in the media.

The Brazilian press focused primarily on the EU's role in international trade, with specific emphasis on the trade negotiations with Mercosur and the Doha

*Table 7.5* Main issues associated with media coverage of the EU in Brazil, India and South Africa

| Brazilian press | Indian press | South African TV and press |
|---|---|---|
| International trade | Trade issues | Trade controversies (EPAs) |
| EU economic policies | Peace and security | Crisis in Zimbabwe |
| Agricultural subsidies | Agricultural subsidies | Agricultural subsidies |
| EU political developments | Cultural and scientific cooperation | European sporting events |

Note
Themes are organized in descending order in terms of volume of coverage.

Round. Within this sector of policies, a number of articles also discuss the controversies around agricultural subsidies, highlighting their damaging effects on the Brazilian economy. Since the media review was conducted in 2005–2006, the internal policies of the EU gained some coverage mainly due to the failed French and Dutch referenda on the European constitutional treaty. Although a lot fewer than the items covering the EU's economic policies, the articles dealing with the 'political nature' of the EU often underlined the unmet aspirations and contradictions of the European integration process.

Whereas the Brazilian press looked primarily at trade issues through the perspective of international negotiations, the Indian newspapers reviewed for this research focused mainly on the bilateral components of trade. In particular, the press covered the various developments of India–EU trade exchanges, including the controversies around agricultural subsidies and non-tariff trade barriers. Besides the trade component, a number of EU peace and security initiatives were also registered. In this regard, the main issues concerned Indian–EU cooperation in the fight against terrorism, a growing concern for India especially after the weakening of the institutional apparatus in Pakistan. Although this closer cooperation between the EU and India on security issues is likely to fall short of expectations (mainly due to the limited capacity of the EU in the sector of military operations and its critical stance on India's nuclear arsenal), it is interesting to note that Indian security concerns have also shaped the public debate on the EU. This happened at a time when the relationship between India and the former US administration was under strain. As explained in an op-ed featured in the *Asian Times* in 2006:

> India is not interested in a 'US' Europe […] The US, as the greatest champion of democracy, has been drawn close to two non-democracies – the military dictatorship of Pakistan and communist China. For India, these new relationships of the US have a direct bearing on its perceptions in world politics, since India sees its security threats emanating only from these two non-democratic countries. […] To the extent that India is able to perceive an independent EU policy particularly involving India's critical security concerns, India would look to the EU for enhanced levels of cooperation in different fields.[17]

A certain prominence is also given to cultural and scientific cooperation between India and the EU, although cultural ties, diaspora communities and language commonalities still push most Indian students towards the USA to further their studies. In general, though, the Indian media shows very limited interest in the EU. As one Delhi media executive put it, 'Indians are not interested any more in European history, or art, or society. We want our own history and our own art and to develop our own social models' (quoted in Lisbonne de Vergeron 2006: 34). As discussed above, most Indian media coverage of Europe comes through London-based journalists who are likely to have a rather different perspective on the European integration process, generally filtered through the British political and social debate.

Similarly, the South African media is largely influenced by British news-papers and magazines, particularly *The Economist*, which is widely read by the South African political and business elite. Overall, the South African mass media tends to portray the EU as an organization of restrictions rather than assistance. Over time, the focus on development aid to Africa, for instance, has become vir-tually absent from the main newspapers and TV news and more space is occu-pied by issues relating to the economic ties and trade conflicts between South Africa and Europe. This shift is particularly considerable, given that the EU has not only been the most important donor to the newly democratic South Africa since the mid 1990s but also a significant ally in restructuring the South African social fabric. Expectedly, the EPAs and the EU–Africa trade negotiations took centre stage in the media coverage of the EU during most of 2006 and 2007. At a more political level, the political and economic crisis was another important topic in which the EU featured quite prominently. Although accused by a number of policy makers of patronizing attitudes due to the travel ban imposed on Zimbabwean President Robert Mugabe (which sparked a vitriolic debate before the EU–Africa summit in December 2007), the South African media has looked quite favourably at the European stance against the Zimbabwean regime, mainly due to the very poor approval rating Mugabe enjoys within South Afri-ca's public opinion. Finally, it is worth emphasizing that South Africa is the only IBSA country in which European social and cultural news receives a compara-tively greater level of coverage in the media. Mostly due to the upcoming World Cup in 2010, some articles have begun to focus more specifically on European sporting events and the role of EU legislation in that sector. In a way, this con-firms the potential of European mass phenomena to project a more popular image of the EU around the world.

## What next? Some concluding remarks

Given the power of orthodoxy in international relations, the EU as a non-state actor appears to struggle as far as image building is concerned. While the pol-icies and actions of the EU are generally better understood by elites, this does not automatically translate into a more favourable assessment of the EU as a global player. Both its effectiveness and public profile remain widely questioned in the IBSA countries. In spite of the European Commission's ambitious plans to promote the EU's image in the global arena, there is still a long way to go before significant results are achieved. The EU will need to make bold decisions with regard to pending trade imbalances if it wishes to shrug off the neo-colonial stigma. Moreover, it will need to show serious leadership on a number of critical issues pertaining to global governance, from effective multilateralism to energy policies and climate change, if it intends to respond to the 'ineffectiveness' accu-sation and re-establish itself as a credible counterpart to the IBSA countries.

Although public opinion, political elites, civil society and the media stress different aspects of the EU's international role, there is a high degree of consist-ency across the various groups within and among the three countries. By and large, trade emerges as the key lens through which the EU is evaluated as a global player. And the picture coming out of this research is not rosy. Agricultural subsidies, non-tariff barriers and other protectionist measures against emerging economies of the 'global south' contribute to reinforcing the perception of the EU as a neo-colonial power. Moreover, recent legislation curtailing migration flows to Europe has given new currency to the image of the EU as a 'fortress' trying to protect itself against the threats deriving from economic and social globalization.

In this regard, the short-sightedness shown by the EU when embarking on the EPA process without due preparation has further damaged its credibility within the 'global south', triggering acrimonious reactions from the IBSA countries (particularly South Africa). In this case, long-term factors (such as the colonial history affecting all three IBSA countries) and new policy developments (such as the quest for a stronger voice in global affairs) have coalesced to the detriment of the EU's external image and credibility. As underlined by Kumi Naidoo, spokesperson of the South Africa-based Global Call to Action Against Poverty:

> the countries of the 'global south' have come to know the EU all too well. In spite of their rhetoric, we know that their trade subsidies are also harming European peasants because they pour money into the pockets of big commercial farmers. Thus, it is also in the interest of common European citizens to change this unjust system.[18]

Generally, the views of the 'global south' represented by leading countries such as India, Brazil and South Africa deeply question the consistency and credibility of the EU as a 'different' global actor. If it is true that the EU is seriously concerned with issues such as social justice and sustainable development, then it should pay particular attention to the views of those societies that suffer most from social injustices and underdevelopment. This is particularly true in the economic sphere, where the impact of EU policies can be quite dramatic. By contrast, the overall image of the EU in the global 'political' sphere is much closer to its self-representation. For instance, political elites in the IBSA countries widely acknowledge the qualitative difference between the EU and the USA with respect to issues such as strengthening global democratic governance mechanisms, multilateralism and a more balanced distribution of power at the global level. Thus, while the image of the EU as an economic power is very much tainted by self-interest and selfishness (which results in the EU's resemblance to any conventional global power), its political character is perceived to be much more in line with the principles and values at the basis of the European integration project.

Although the IBSA countries are regarded as important elements in EU foreign policy aspirations, our analysis seems to point to the fact that the so-called 'strategic partnerships' are not really relevant in public debate in any of the IBSA countries. Perhaps, the importance of these bilateral agreements is much more emphasized in Brussels than it is in Brasilia, Delhi or Pretoria. The perceptions analysed in this chapter seem to point towards a paradigmatic shift in the relationship between the EU and IBSA. Due to their economic growth and regional influence, these countries have become increasingly powerful in the global arena. Besides declarations of intent and summits, they are increasingly asking for concrete action. What used to be gentle pleas to the 'global north' have now become firm requests. Will an 'unconventional' global player like the EU be able to respond effectively? Or will it miss this opportunity to the advantage of more traditional global powers such as the USA and China?

## Notes

1 The authors would like to thank Arlo Poletti, who compiled a research report on the image of the EU in Brazil, and the National Centre for Research on Europe at the University of Canterbury (New Zealand), which supported the research in South Africa. A special recognition to Sonia Lucarelli for providing insightful comments on the early drafts of this chapter.

2 See Chapters 9 and 12 for more details.

3 A preliminary account of this research was published in Fioramonti and Poletti (2008).

4 India E-News, 'For India–Pakistan Peace, Terrorism Has to Go: EU', 13 August 2006. Online, available at: www.indiaenews.com/nri/20060813/18330.htm (accessed 31 January 2009).

5 See Chapters 9 and 12 for more details.

6 See the speech given by the South African Deputy Minister for Trade and Industry, Rob Davies, to the budget vote on 29 May 2008. Online, available at: www.money-web.co.za/mw/view/mw/en/page87?oid=208901&sn=Detail (accessed 31 January 2009).

7 See Davies's speech, op. cit.

8 The speech is online, available at: www.saag.org/%5Cpapers16%5Cpaper1536.html (accessed 31 January 2009).

9 The speech is online, available at: www.twnside.org.sg/title2/twninfo323.htm (accessed 31 January 2009).

10 'African Ministers and CSOs in Scathing Attack on EPAs', *SUNS-South North Development Monitor*, 24 April 2008. Online, available at: www.twnside.org.sg/title2/wto.info/twninfo20080507.htm (accessed 31 January 2009).

11 Brazilian Ministry of External Affairs, press release no. 520, 26 September 2008. Online, available at: www.mre.gov.br/ingles/imprensa/nota_detalhe3.asp?ID_RELEASE=5873 (accessed 31 January 2009).

12 'An Injury to One Market is an Injury to All', *Inter Press Service*, 18 August 2008. Online, available at: http://allafrica.com/stories/printable/200808181466.html (accessed 31 January 2009).

13 'An Injury to One Market is an Injury to All', op. cit.

14 'EU Mercosur Free Trade Agreement. Profits for a Few: threats for the majority of our people', Declaration by the Social Movements and Civil Society Organisations from the Mercosur, 22 October 2004. Online, available at: www.tni.org/detail_page.phtml?page=altreg-docs_mercosurdecl (accessed 31 January 2009).

15 'On India's Despairing Farms, a Plague of Suicides', *New York Times*, 19 September 2006.

16 This part of the chapter is based on an analysis of news items mentioning the EU. In the case of Brazil, the media review focused on *O Globo*, *Jornal do Brasil*, *O Estado de Sao Paulo* and *Folha de Sao Paulo* (time span May 2004 to February 2006). In India, the following newspapers were reviewed: *Hindustan Times* and *New Statesman*

(time span January 2005 to October 2006). In South Africa, we relied on the results of an extensive media analysis by Media Tenor (time span July 2001 to September 2002), updated with a review of two newspapers: *Business Day* and *The Star* (time span July 2007 to June 2008).

17 'India Is Not Interested in a US Europe', *Asian Times*, 26 June 2006.

18 Face-to-face interview, Johannesburg, 3 October 2007.

# References

Biato, M.F. (2004) 'Brazil. The EU: a rising global power?' in M. Ortega (ed.) *Global Views on the EU*, Institute for Security Studies Chaillot Paper, no. 72: 43–54.

De Almeida, P.R. (2004) 'Una Política Externa Engajada: a diplomacia do governo Lula', *Revista Brasileira de Política Internacional*, 47 (1): 163–84.

Fioramonti, L. and Poletti, A. (2008) 'Facing the Giant: southern perspectives on the European Union', *Third World Quarterly*, 29 (1): 167–80.

Jaffrelot, C. (2006) *India and the European Union: the charade of a strategic partnership*, Paris: CERI-Sciences Po.

Jain, R.K. (2005) 'How They See Us', *E!Sharp*, March–April 2005, XX.

Jain, R.K. (2008) 'EU and India: past, present and future', paper presented at the conference 'Europe in a Changing World: challenges, priorities and research collaboration', organized by the EUC Network of New Zealand, Christchurch, 25–27 September.

Lisbonne-de Vergeron, K. (2006) *Contemporary Indian Views of Europe*, London: Chatham House.

Lucarelli, S. and Manners, I. (eds) (2006) *Values and Principles in European Union Foreign Policy*, London: Routledge.

Manners, I. (2002) 'Normative Power Europe: a contradiction in terms?' *Journal of Common Market Studies*, 40 (2): 235–58.

Olivier, G. (2006) *South Africa and the European Union: self-interest, ideology and altruism*, Pretoria: Protea Book House.

Telò, M. (2006) *Europe, a Civilian Power? European Union, global governance, world order*, Basingstoke: Palgrave Macmillan.

# 8 So far, so close?

## Mexico's views of the EU

*Alejandro Chanona*

## Introduction

The relationship between Europe and Mexico has always been very important for historic, political, economic and cultural reasons. Beyond the historical ties of the colonial period, Europe has remained significant in the collective imagination of the Mexican people since the early years of the country's independence: from the assimilation of the ideas of liberty and equality emanating from the French Revolution that fuelled the fight for independence, passing through the late nineteenth-century notions of progress, up to the twentieth-century process of regional integration and the European social model.

The Mexican government in particular has promoted an image of the European Union (EU) as a key trade partner that is indispensable for the diversification of Mexico's economic dependency on the United States of America (USA). Over time, a series of perceptions of the EU have gained currency, ranging from strategic economic partner to 'civilian power' and political ally, with a stronger focus on its international role.

It is possible to identify a mosaic of perceptions held by the Mexicans about the EU. The main objective of this chapter is to analyse these images. First, the analysis will examine the historical account of this bilateral relation. Second, it will present the most relevant perceptions by dividing them into different sections and actors in Mexican society: public opinion, political and economic elites, civil society and the media. Finally, the chapter presents a series of recommendations for the Union's strategy towards my country.

## Mexico and the EU in historical perspective

The contemporary relations between Mexico and EU can be divided into three general stages: (a) the political dialogue of the earliest contacts between Mexico and the then European Economic Community (EEC) in the 1960s and 1980s, (b) the impulse to the economic trade agenda of the 1990s, whose main result was the signing of the Global Agreement and (c) the 'strategic partnership' based on the Global Agreement and the European Union-Latin America and Caribbean summits (EU-LAC).

Formalization of Mexico's relations with the European Community began in 1960 when Mexico opened its mission in Brussels. This first stage was centred in the political dialogue initiated within the framework of relations between the European Community and Latin America after the 1970 Buenos Aires Declaration. The first Economic Cooperation and Trade Agreement between Mexico and the EEC in 1975 established the basis for stronger economic relations. This first stage culminated in 1989 when the European Commission set up an office in Mexico and economic issues took centre stage.

In the framework of the liberalization policy of Carlos Salinas's administration (1988–1994), relations with Europe became a priority, centred on the economic agenda and the foreign relations' diversification policy. This resulted in a number of important steps: Mexico entered the European Bank of Reconstruction and Development, mechanisms for high-level bilateral political consultations were established and an EC–Mexico Framework Cooperation Agreement was signed, as well as a number of additional agreements on reciprocal promotion and the protection of investments (Chanona 2003: 277–92).

The signing of a free trade agreement with the EU became an objective of the Zedillo government's foreign policy. In May 1995, Mexico and the EU announced their willingness to create a framework for strengthening the political dialogue, establishing a free trade zone and intensifying cooperation. However, the negotiations were not easy. Mexico wagered on a trade liberalization agreement under its market diversification policy, while the EU countries were interested in the Mexican government's commitment to democracy and respect for human rights through the inclusion in the text of the so-called 'democracy clause'.

On 8 December 1997, the negotiations for the Economic Partnership, Political Coordination and Cooperation Agreement – also known as the Global Agreement – were concluded. It should be noted that, despite the Mexican government's efforts to strengthen economic relations with the EU, during the 1990s bilateral commerce had fallen by 43 per cent: from representing 11.4 per cent of Mexico's foreign trade in 1990 to 6.6 per cent in 2001. For this reason, the signing of the EU–Mexico Free Trade Agreement (EUMFTA) on 23 March 2000 generated great expectations in both the government and the country's business sectors.

The coming into force of the EU-LAC marked the beginning of the strategic partnership stage, built on the pillars of economic relations, political dialogue and cooperation.

Although the EU holds a consolidated position as the country's second most important trade partner and investor and bilateral trade grew by 33 per cent between the years 2000 and 2008, for Mexico the trade balance with the EU continues to be negative, without mentioning that the country occupies a marginal place among the European bloc's major partners and the fact that they have not managed to regain the same trade levels as at the beginning of the 1990s.

For this reason, in recent years political dialogue and cooperation have become crucial issues in the strategic relationship, whose potential for development is considerable. Mexico and the EU share a set of values such as democracy, respect for the rule of law, human rights and individual freedoms, and a common vision of international order based on multilateralism.

In terms of political dialogue there are two key themes: (1) the strengthening of multilateralism and the multidimensional vision of security in the international system and (2) cooperation focused on democratic governance and human rights in Mexico, particularly in the framework of the Global Agreement.

From the EU perspective, Mexico is able to contribute to the reconfiguration of the international system as a leading country in the LAC region, while Mexico views the EU a strategic partner with which to share some key principles of its foreign policy.

With regard to the relations within the EU-LAC summits, in particular the third one concerning the adoption on the agenda of the social inclusion issue, they have had a positive impact on the EU–Mexico bilateral agenda, especially in terms of cooperation, an area which in May 2007 counted 47 projects between the two partners, both bilaterally and regionally.

However, from the Mexican perspective, in addition to focusing on specific issues in the integration process, such as enlargement and the Treaty of Lisbon process, over the past few years the EU has focused its efforts and attention on relations outside its geographical neighbourhood and has, consequently, neglected Mexico and Latin America. Likewise, in recent times, Mexico has been most concerned about the European Parliament's approbation of the directive on the return of illegal immigrants, which could affect Mexican migrants in the EU. Each of the historic and economic elements analysed in this first part have influenced the Mexicans' perceptions of the EU. The following parts of this chapter present the various images of the EU gathered through a detailed survey of public opinion data, documents and declarations by political and economic elites as well as organized civil society.

## Mexican public opinion's views of the EU

In order to have a long-term perspective of Mexico's public opinion, this part of the chapter presents data from the *Latinobarómetro* in the decade from 1995 to 2005. This time span provides the context for the analysis of more detailed data generated by the 'Mexico and the World' surveys of 2004 and 2006, which were carried out by the Centre for Economic Research and Teaching and the Mexican Council on Foreign Relations.[1] A specific survey by the Institute of Marketing Opinion, concerning Mexican perceptions of the 2004 Third EU-LAC Summit in Guadalajara, has also been included in the analysis.

In Mexico, it is not common to survey public opinion's perceptions regarding issues of foreign policy and international relations. Moreover, the few existing surveys focus almost exclusively on relations with the USA, a result of geographical proximity and interdependence, especially on issues such as the economy, migration and security.

The 1995–2005 *Latinobarómetro* data show a positive trend regarding

Mexican perceptions of the EU, primarily concerning knowledge of the EU and its policies.

In 1995, only 12 per cent of Mexicans had a 'good' opinion of the EU. Yet, ten years later, this view was held by almost 60 per cent. It is in 1999, the year of the First EU-LAC Summit, that the first significant increase in favourable public opinion can be found, doubling the preferences of previous years. Since the turn of the millennium, favourable opinions of the EU continued to rise incrementally.

This trend can be explained by two specific factors: first, the signing of the Global Agreement increased Mexicans' interest in and awareness of the EU; second, there was a convergence of values between the Mexican and the European society, especially around democracy and human rights.

The Global Agreement and the EUMFTA generated great expectations in the Mexican public opinion. For some, the strengthening of EU–Mexican ties was seen as the only possible counterweight to the asymmetric interdependence between Mexico and the USA. For others, the focus was rather on the EU as an ally in the promotion of democratization and the struggle for the defence and promotion of human rights in the country.

However, during the same period of time, unfavourable opinions towards the EU also rose: in 1995, for instance, less than 1 per cent of Mexicans held a 'very bad' opinion of the EU, while this had gone up to about 6 per cent in 1999. Similarly, the number of people with a 'bad' opinion of the EU also grew over the years, reaching its peak in 2004.

In all likelihood, the reasons for the growing criticism are to be found in public debates on the agreement's so-called 'democracy clause', which, according to the most conservative and protectionist segments of society, equated to EU interference in Mexican political life. At the same time, Mexican civil society became also quite critical of the neoliberal model that, in their view,

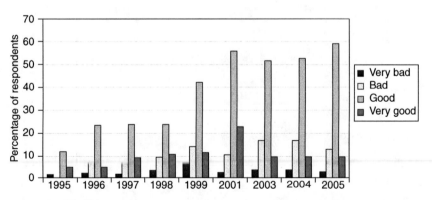

*Figure 8.1* Public opinion's perceptions of the EU (1995–2005) (source: *Latino-barómetro* 1995–2005).

Note
'No opinions' are not included in the graph.

disqualified the Global Agreement as an economic model focused primarily on free trade and market liberalization, with no promotion of social welfare.

The Mexican public opinion's interest in the EU can be explained by the fact that most Mexicans feel an affinity for Europe and view it as an international counterweight to the USA. In this regard, the IMO survey on Mexican opinions about the relationship between Latin American and the EU allows us to compare the Mexicans' different perceptions towards the EU and the United States.[2]

According to the data from this survey, the vast majority of respondents (63 per cent) considered the strategic partnership with the EU as a counterweight to the USA's influence in the country. The international agenda dominated the survey: 51 per cent of Mexicans would prefer a stronger relationship with the EU in world affairs, compared to 40 per cent who chose the USA (IMO 2004).

However, the survey also revealed that the Mexicans still hold a preference towards the USA with 51 per cent of the respondents claiming to feel culturally closer to the USA, compared to 32 per cent who chose the EU. Also, concerning economic relations, Mexicans seem to give preference to relations with the USA over the EU (IMO 2004).

Continuing on the theme of economic relations, the 'Mexico and the World' surveys allow us to compare the Mexicans' preferences for the EU and Latin America as options for diversification in the country's relations. Due to geographical proximity as well as historical and cultural identification, Mexicans consider Latin America as their privileged partner for the diversification of their own economic relations, offering the EU a second place.

Nonetheless, the survey revealed differences between social sectors in the country. As Figure 8.3 shows, in 2004 political elites were comparatively more favourable towards the EU than the general population (CIDE-COMEXI 2004: 36). In 2006, the survey revealed a further increase in the number of Mexicans

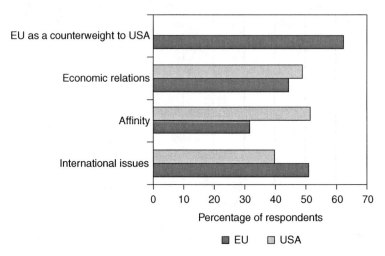

*Figure 8.2* Mexicans believing the EU is a counterweight to the USA and preferences for either actor according to policy sector (2004) (source: IMO 2004).

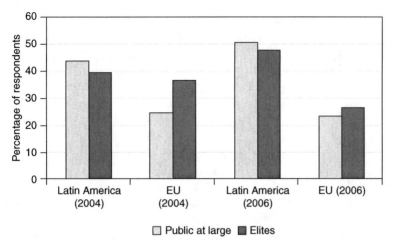

*Figure 8.3* Mexico's preferences for Latin America and EU (from 2004 to 2006) (source: CIDE-COMEXI 2004, 2006).

who prefer the Latin American region, while the EU experienced a slight decrease in overall favour, including political elites, down to 27 from 37 per cent in 2004 (CIDE-COMEXI 2006: 20).

Two situations help to explain the decline in preferences for the EU and the conviction that Latin America is the privileged option for Mexicans. In the Mexican case, rapprochement and solidarity with Latin America were motivated by a general critique of the regional foreign policy of former president Vicente Fox, which led to isolation mainly due to ideological conflict with Cuba and Venezuela and differences about the Free Trade Agreement of the Americas with Argentina and Brazil. On a more global level, political leaders also highlight the importance of strengthening relations also with Asian countries, perhaps in direct competition with the preferences given to the EU.

Regarding free trade, it is important to note that, despite the strong preferences for Latin America over the EU as a priority partner in foreign trade, 79 per cent of Mexicans believed EUMFTA represented the most favourable trade agreement for Mexico, followed by the Free Trade Agreement with Chile (70 per cent) and the North American Free Trade Agreement (64 per cent).

## Mexican political elites' perceptions of the EU

In the case of the Mexican political elites' perceptions of the EU, we analysed two actors: (a) the executive branch, represented by the president's office, with the examination based on the last three administrations' national development plans and (b) the political parties, by studying their basic documents and electoral platforms in order to find out whether ideological differences among Mexico's political forces translated into differences towards their perceptions of the EU.

### Governmental elites

Since Carlos Salinas de Gortari's administration (1988–1994), the economic agenda has taken on a central role in Mexico's foreign policy towards the EU. Considered a priority for Mexico's trade diversification policy and in its efforts to attract foreign investment, the EU de facto displaced Latin America as the priority region for diversification.

This tendency was fortified by Presidents Zedillo (1994–2000) and Fox (2000–2006), even though they belonged to different political parties. Their objectives in this regard were practically the same: to establish trade agreements and attract investment through a new marketing strategy for Mexico based on the success of its democracy and market modernization.

The Mexican government has traditionally pointed towards the EU as an important ally for the promotion of an international system that respects the principles of international law, human rights, the strengthening of democracy and other topics such as the multilateral vision of security and international cooperation for development.

However, at the bilateral level, issues such as democracy and the respect of human rights have also generated controversy, a case in point being the Global Agreement negotiations during President Zedillo's administration: while the Mexican government was impelled to prioritize the topic of free trade with the European bloc, an important number of EU members showed their concern about democratic standards and human rights' violations in the country, especially due to the conflict with the Zapatista army.

The former Minister of Foreign Affairs, José Angel Gurría, declared that 'nobody could teach Mexico how to be democratic', while other parliamentarians went so far as to indicate that the democratic clause constituted interference in the country's internal affairs.

Nevertheless, Mexico and the EU finally reached an agreement on the incorporation of the clause into the Global Agreement, particularly as a result of increasing European pressure after the Matanza de Acteal.[3] The Foreign Affairs Ministry changed its tone by affirming that 'of course we were always in favour of the democratic clause', while at the time the presidency had remarked that in any form the clause was a transgression to national sovereignty and that the state was already engaged with democracy and the respect for human rights.

In 2000, the EU considered the election of Vicente Fox as a big democratic step forward, and in recent years it has recognized Mexico's efforts to protect and promote human rights. But it is true that these efforts have had more impact abroad (thanks to a foreign policy that promotes human rights) than domestically, because of the weaknesses in Mexico's institutions and the remaining legacies of its authoritarian culture.

The current administration led by Felipe Calderón continues along the lines of its predecessors, pointing to the EU as a priority region for the establishment of a strategic alliance and the diversification of the country's economic relations, as reported in the 2007–2012 national development plan. Specifically, the document indicates that the EU offers a 'great leeway for increasing trade, investment and capital flows and cooperation for social development and strengthening the Mexican population's capabilities through the transfer of investments, techno-logy and know-how' (Presidencia de la República 2007).

The bilateral relationship is also assessed in terms of its impact on a multire-gional dialogue that:

> offers the country the opportunity to participate as a global actor and con-tribute to responding to transnational challenges like market access and trade liberalization, climate change, the development of Africa, energy security and management, and the treatment, control and eradication of infectious diseases
>
> (Presidencia de la República 2007)

The Mexican President confirmed this approach when he first visited its Euro-pean counterparts, although Mexican presidents have traditionally paid their first visits to their American neighbours. Thus, Felipe Calderón's visit was viewed as a clear sign of the desire to strengthen relations between Mexico and the EU, with a strong focus on the consolidation of cultural, political and economic ties (Notimex 2006).

Some months later, a second trip by the Mexican government to the European region further confirmed this strategy.[4] It also emphasized new topics for the future of bilateral relations, making public security and the fight against organ-ized crime central issues on the agenda (AFP 2007).[5] It is important to mention that emphasis on cooperation on the issues of security, the fight against drug traf-ficking, and more recently the fight against terrorism, is set against a particularly delicate context in Mexico. Mexican drug cartels have responded to the federal government's military offensive through systematic violent attacks, such as exe-cutions and the intimidation of government officials and common citizens.

The EU could play a fundamental role to support the Mexican government in its fight against terrorism. Even more so, if one considers that the EU has been able to marry the 'securitization' of its territory with the respect of its citizens' individual liberties, which would be an important best practice for Mexico.

### Political parties

Despite ideological diversities, Mexican political parties agree on their percep-tion of the EU: they all recognize the EU's central role in the international system, admit that Mexico has not taken advantage of the benefits of the Global Agreement and propose the strengthening of bilateral relations.[6]

All parties pay special attention to the economic agenda, despite different points of view: while for the right-wing parties trade and investment issues are the essence of the relationship, the left-wing parties centre their attention on the European social model and the cooperation mechanism in order to support the development of the Mexican society.

It is also important to note that traditionally the left-wing parties have long seen the EU as a fundamental partner for the democratization and defence of human rights in Mexico. Clear evidence of this perception was provided by the senate's debate on the ratification of the Global Agreement, which saw left-wing senators supporting the inclusion of the 'democratic clause' as an incentive to take Mexican democratization further (Calderón 2005).

From the perspective of the National Action Party, cooperation with the EU should improve the role of Mexico as a bridge between both continents. From this point of view, Mexico must capitalize on the Global Agreement in order to improve trade and promote economic opportunities. With regard to the political agenda, the National Action Party states that Mexico's participation in certain European institutions (as an observer in the Council of Europe) should be taken as an opportunity to intensify links and work on issues of common interest (Partido Acción Nacional 2004 and 2006).

In the eyes of the Institutional Revolutionary Party, Europe has played a central role in Mexican efforts to diversify its foreign relations; however, the strategic partnership has still not resulted in tangible outcomes. As a consequence, the party proposes intensifying relations with the EU in order to strengthen economic, political and cultural ties. This perspective is shared by the centre-right Mexican Ecological Green Party, which participated in the 2006 elections as part of the Alliance for Mexico, in coalition with the Institutional Revolutionary Party (Partido Revolucionario Institucional 2007; Alianza por Mexico 2006).

According to the Convergencia party, Mexico should enforce its relations with the EU and optimize the Global Agreement in order to reduce dependence on trade with only one country, in clear reference to its relations with the United States. This party is also interested in studying the European social model as a reference for Mexico in order to improve the cooperation agenda (Convergencia 2004). Likewise, in their electoral platform, the Coalition for the Welfare of All (PRD-PT-Convergencia) stated that the diversification strategy required stronger relations with the EU and a reversal of the trend to decrease bilateral exchange (Coalición por el Bien de Todos 2006).

Finally, for the Social Democratic Party, Mexico should seek out closer relations with Europe and make an additional effort in order to gain better assets from this relationship. For that reason, the Social Democrats consider it important to deepen and follow up the achievements of the EU–Mexico Agreement.

### The EU viewed by Mexican business and civil society

The perceptions of business elites and civil society were analysed using basic sources, such as the documents presented by these organizations in the 2005 sessions of the Social Dialogue for a State Foreign Policy and at the Second Forum of Dialogue among Civil Societies and Institutions between the Mexican government and the European Union at Mexico's Foreign Ministry.

The most important Mexican business associations, like the Mexican Businessmen's Foreign Trade, Investment and Technology Council, the National

Chamber of Industry, the National Association of Mexican Importers and Exporters, the Businessmen's Coordinating Council and the National Confedera-tion of Industrial Chambers, recognize the opportunities given by the EUMFTA.

Nevertheless, factors like language, geographical distance and the ongoing lack of familiarity with the European market contribute to creating common per-ceptions of the EU as an inaccessible market. Therefore, most business groups believe that the free trade agreement has provided significant advantages to European companies, while benefiting Mexican corporations only marginally to the lack of national development policies and coherent information on support programmes for small and medium enterprises.[7]

As a consequence, the Mexican business community is quite critical towards the EUMFTA. They list a number of reasons: (a) increasing trade deficit with the EU, (b) Mexican products' high levels of dependence on the US market[8] and (c) control of more than 50 per cent of the country's bank by Europeans, which in the eyes of small and medium enterprises inevitably endangers the Mexican government's ability to lead national development (SRE, UNAM, CELARE, 2006).

Thus, according to the Mexican business community, the EUMFTA poses a number of challenges to Mexican industries: they have to become more interna-tionally competitive, they have to develop experience and financial capability to attract European investments and, finally, they must acquire the necessary skills to place their products within the European market.

In the case of civil society organizations, two main positions with regard to the EU can be identified. On the one hand, some organizations recognize the importance of the Union as an important political actor in the international system, a social model of reference and a leader par excellence on issues related to the defence of human rights and promotion of democratic governance. Indeed most civil society groups hoped that the leadership of the EU would provide incentives for the Mexican government to take social demands and respect human rights more seriously.

On the other hand, numerous movements have roundly criticized the Global Agreement, in particular because it does not establish a central body to monitor compliance with the clauses on democracy, human rights and protection of the environment (Döler and Castro 2004). Moreover, some organizations and civic groups have attacked the Mexican government for not having a citizens' obser-atory and demanded the establishment of a joint consultative council to monitor the detrimental impact of the EUMFTA in different social fields.

Some social movements, such as the Mexican Network against Free Trade, assess the EUMFTA as a de facto copy of the North American Free Trade Agreement in so far as it privileges trade issues over the social agenda. In the same way, some organizations have directly attacked various European com-panies for failing to comply with Mexican labour legislation.

Finally, it must be recognized that the pressure of these civil society organiza-tions on the Mexican government made it possible to establish a dialogue process during the Fox administration. This dialogue contributed to furthering the participation of civil society in bilateral meetings held with European social organizations in the framework of the EU–Mexico social dialogue.

## Conclusions and recommendations

For Mexico, the EU is a point of reference from an economic, political and social perspective. Particularly, we have observed that all the sectors of Mexican society believe in the importance of a strategic relationship with the EU, although there exist differences in how this relationship is perceived.

These sectors agree that the Union is a strategic ally of Mexico and a fundamental actor in the defence of human rights, democracy and multilateral institutions. Likewise, they clearly converge in accepting the 'moral' leadership of the EU on the international scene.

In spite of being perceived as a strategic partner and a potential counterweight to the USA, there are significant differences between the public opinion's views and the elites' perceptions of the importance of the EU as a target for the diversification of Mexico's political and economist interests. For political leaders, Latin America and the EU have practically the same importance, whereas Mexican citizens give uncontested primacy to Latin America.

During Felipe Calderón's government, there have been a number of steps taken towards reinforcing the relationship with the EU. Diplomatic relations have taken on a new importance, as also demonstrated by the Mexican President's official visits to a number of European countries. Nevertheless, it must be underscored that this is by no means evidence of a new Mexican predisposition towards forging alliances with the EU in a common vision of a shared international responsibility, the defence of human rights, the fight against terrorism or a new dialogue on international security. More pragmatically, Calderón's government needs the EU buy-in to strengthen its national security strategy (especially against organized crime and drug trafficking).

Therefore, it should not be interpreted as a strategy to counterweight to US unilateralism and its narrow vision of national and international security. It is rather an attempt at building international consensus around the Mexican government's political agenda.

In the economic field, the government has further invested in the diversification of economic and commercial relations. In this context, the EU continues to be a priority. If, on the one hand, the government recognizes that the strategy has its limitations, on the other hand, it continues to encourage exports to the European market. More realistically, though, Mexican business groups still consider Europe as a distant market, with little viability that is at times hostile against Mexican exports. In turn, this contributes to continued focusing on the USA as the most attractive market for Mexican commodities.

The most vocal critics of the EU continue to be some organizations within civil society. They believe the Global Agreement has overwhelmingly focused on commercial aspects while neglecting the social agenda, in spite of the political and human rights clauses. Nonetheless, most of these critics would like the

EU to be more involved in supporting human rights and social well-being in Mexico, since they perceive the former to be a point of reference in these sectors. In this regard, a positive element is the creation and consolidation of frames for dialogue between Mexican and European civil society organizations.

On the basis of this analysis, we can sketch some general recommendations. The strategy of the EU in its relations with Mexico must be clear and forged on the basis of economic exchange, democracy and human rights, and social inclusion. At the same time, the EU must support the Mexican government in the fight against organized crime, drug trafficking and terrorism, which is part and parcel of a wider approach to respecting human rights and individual liberties. In this regard, the creation of a civil joint observatory would be very useful in order to check that human rights and citizen guarantees are fully respected.

At the same time, the EU should also encourage schemes to support the training and education of Mexican students in Europe in order to promote a deeper cultural understanding of the EU and build knowledge of the EU–Mexican schemes of economic exchange and cooperation. This process can be strengthened by creating centres of information and orientation on the cultural cooperation schemes financed by the EU, similarly to the information centres already established to boost Mexican exports to Europe. Such a process would also contribute to consolidating research networks and scientific cooperation between the two partners, thus bridging the cultural divide that still exists between Mexico and the EU.

## Notes

1 The 2004 and 2006 'Mexico and the World: public opinion and foreign policy in Mexico' surveys were the result of a long-term research project that these two centres began in 2004, 'with the aim of periodically filling in gaps in information and knowledge about how Mexicans, including the country's foreign affairs leaders, understand and respond to changing world realities'. The project comprised two mirror surveys: (a) house-to-house visits to a representative sample of the adult population (general public opinion survey) and (b) telephone interviews with political, economic and social leaders in foreign affairs (leaders survey). The 2004 general public opinion survey was carried out from 9–19 July 2004. The survey consisted of 1,500 face-to-face interviews based on a probabilistic sample design.
2 The objective of the survey was to study the Spanish and Mexican visions of regional integration in social, cultural and economic matters. It was carried out in May 2004, and consisted of 440 telephone interviews selected on the basis of stratified random sampling (IMO 2004).
3 The murder of 45 native *tzotziles* from the civil organization *Las Abejas* (The Bees) linked to the Zapatista National Liberation Army is known as the *Matanza de Acteal* (the Acteal Killings). The people were found praying in a chapel. The incident occurred on 22 December 1997 at the hand of a paramilitary group opposed to the Zapatistas in the community of Acteal, located in *Los Altos* of Chiapas.
4 This second tour of Europe included Italy, the Vatican, France, Belgium, Germany and Denmark.
5 Mexico's President met the Italian Prime Minister Romano Prodi, the National Anti-Mafia Attorney General and the heads of the Rome, Milan, Naples and Palermo district anti-Mafia offices to familiarize himself with Italy's successful experience in the battle

against organized crime. Calderón's meeting with French President Nicolas Sarkozy centred on the possibilities of cooperation on issues of public security and the justice system.

6   Currently, eight parties of different ideological persuasions and membership are registered with Mexico's Federal Electoral Institute. From right to left, the parties are: the National Action Party, the New Alliance Party, the Green Ecologist Party, the Institutional Revolutionary Party, the Convergence Party (Convergencia), the Social Democratic Party, the Party of the Democratic Revolution and the Labour Party. The only party that made no explicit reference of the EU in its basic documents and electoral platform was the National Action Party, whose 2006 platform referred to the need to diversify the country's trade without specifying which countries or regions would be the targets of that policy. Seven of the country's eight political forces mentioned the EU in their basic documents or electoral platforms to a greater or lesser degree. Only the Institutional Revolutionary Party and the Convergencia referred to it in their action programmes. The only party that made no explicit mention of the EU in any document was a centre-right party, the New Alliance.

7   One of the sectors that has received the most attention in government speeches and statements and in EUMFTA development programmes are small and medium-sized companies. Given this, the Ministry of the Economy, through the Mexico–EU Business Center, promotes and supports small and medium-sized companies so they can participate in strategic sectors and place their products on the European market. Another government mechanism is the Project to Facilitate the Free Trade Agreement between Mexico and the EU, developed by the Ministry of the Economy and the European Community to promote bilateral trade cooperation and facilitate government and business administrative processes in order to simplify some of the activities included in the EUMFTA.

8   Between 2000 and 2003, imports of European products, particularly intermediate and capital goods, grew by 9 per cent a year, reaching USD17.8619 billion in 2003. On the other hand, between 2004 and 2006, European imports amounted to an average of 11.32 per cent of all Mexican imports. Thus, by January 2007, Mexico's trade deficit with the EU amounted to USD1,952,674,290.

## References

AFP (2007) 'Calderón lleva a Europa su desvelo por la seguridad', *Noticias Vanguardia*, 31 May. Online, available at: http://noticias.vanguardia.com.mx/ (accessed 31 January 2009).

Alianza por México (2006) *Plataforma Electoral 2006*, Mexico City.

Calderón, J. (2005) 'Evaluación del Acuerdo de Asociación Económica, Concertación Política y Cooperación México y la Unión Europea', paper delivered at the Second Forum of Dialogue between the EU and Mexico Civil Societies, SRE, 13 March.

Chanona, A. (2003) 'La política exterior de México hacia Europa', in R. Gómez, R. Vargas and J. Castro (eds), *Las políticas exteriores de Estados Unidos, Canadá y México en el umbral del siglo XXI*, Mexico City: CISAN, UNAM.

CIDE-COMEXI (2004) *México y el mundo. Visiones globales 2004: opinión pública y política exterior en México*, Mexico City.

CIDE-COMEXI (2006) *México y el mundo. Visiones globales 2006*, Mexico City.

Coalición por el Bien de Todos (2006) *Plataforma Electoral 2006*, Mexico City.

Convergencia (2004) *Programa de acción. Política exterior, degnidad nacional y desarrollo*, Mexico City.

Döler, J. and Castro, G. (2004) *México y la Unión Europea*. Online, available at: www.ecoportal.net/contenido/temas_especiales/economia/mexico_y_la_union_europea (accessed 31 January 2009).

Instituto de Mercadotecnia y Opinión IMO (2004) *The Mexican and Spanish Societies Express their Opinion on Latin America–European Union Relationships*, Mexico: Instituto de Mercadotecnia y Opinión.

Notimex (2006) 'Primer viaje de Calderón como presidente será a Europa', *El Universal*, Mexico City, 6 October. Online, available at: www.eluniversal.com.mx/noticias.html (accessed 31 January 2009).

Partido Acción Nacional (2004) *Programa de Acción*, Mexico City.

Partido Acción Nacional (2006) *Plataforma Electoral 2006*, Mexico City.

Partido Revolucionario Institucional (2007) 'Por un orden internacional justo: soberanía y prosperidad en la globalización', *Programa de Acción*, Mexico City.

Presidencia de la República (2007) *Plan Nacional de Desarrollo 2007–2012*, Mexico City.

SRE, UNAM, CELARE (2006) *2do Foro de diálogo social, México y la Unión Europea: Sociedad civil y gobierno*. Marco del Acuerdo de Asociación económica, concertación política y cooperación entre la Unión Europea y México (Acuerdo Global), Mexico City.

# Part II

# International organizations, regional institutions and the media

# 9 Partnership in peril?

## Images and strategies in EU–ACP economic partnership agreement negotiations[1]

*Ole Elgström*

## Introduction

Relations between the European Union (EU) and the African, Caribbean and Pacific (ACP) countries – today numbering 76 nations, mostly former European colonies – have generally by both parties been described in terms of partnership, friendship and equality. Since the 1970s, the ACP states have enjoyed preferential treatment in trade and been a privileged recipient of EU assistance, as enshrined in first the Lomé agreements (1975–2000), and then in the Cotonou Agreement, signed in 2000. These agreements have been heralded as unique and groundbreaking in their design, reflecting a 'true partnership' that is to the benefit of both parties. These ideals were, as agreed upon in Cotonou, to be developed and solidified by the conclusion of Economic Partnership Agreements (EPAs) between the EU and six regional groupings of ACP countries.

The climate of debate has been quite different since the signing of interim EPAs in November to December 2007. While the EU praises the agreements as 'moving beyond a relationship of dependency to one of genuine partnership' (Mandelson 2008a), many ACP commentators are much more hesitant and uncertain in their substantive evaluation of the final deal. Their most noteworthy reaction is, however, the severe criticism raised by many against the process leading up to the final deal. Both official and unofficial ACP sources complain about the EU's negotiation tactics and behaviour. EU negotiators are claimed to have exerted undue pressure, using hard bargaining tactics, including threats, manipulation and other coercive instruments. This of course stands in sharp contrast to the type of diplomacy expected in a 'partnership' between 'long-time friends'. Why on earth – if these allegations are true – should a friendly actor resort to hard bargaining (Dür and Mateo 2008; Elgström and Jönsson 2000) against its partner? This is the puzzle that underlies this chapter.

The aim of the chapter is to document ACP criticism against the EU's negotiation behaviour, to analyse to what extent the EU actually made use of hard bargaining tactics with coercive elements in EPA negotiations, especially during their final phases, and to explain why such instruments were used and/or why ACP participants interpret the negotiation process in these terms. To this end, I shall make reference to the actors' beliefs, images and perceptions.

My analysis of the negotiations is based on documents and interviews. Most documents (official declarations, newspaper articles, statements by non-governmental organizations, etc.) have been retrieved from the extremely useful *ACP-EU News Weekly E-alert* (available at www.ecdpm.org/news), which gives all kinds of information on the EPA process. Interviews were carried out with seven ACP ambassadors/ministers in Brussels, as well as with two other ACP representatives. The approximately hour-long interviews were semi-structured, using more or less the same set of questions in each, but letting the interviewees talk freely. Interviews were given under the promise of anonymity.

I will start by giving a background to and overview of the EPA negotiations, emphasizing the main bones of contention between the parties. I shall then systematically document the ACP criticism raised against the EU both during and after the negotiations and link this account to EU arguments and bargaining tactics. I end by giving an explanation of this behaviour, and of the ACP reactions thereto, in terms of beliefs, images and perceptions.

## The EPA negotiation process: background and key themes

For 25 years, relationships between the ACP countries and the EU were guided by the Lomé trade and aid regime. The Lomé agreements were often heralded by EU spokespersons as positive models of development assistance. The trade components were developed as tools to promote growth and development, not least by granting the ACP group non-reciprocal preferential access for most goods (excluding, however, some important agricultural products) to the EU market. Efforts were also made to stabilize export revenue earnings for those Least Developed Countries (LDCs) producing raw materials. The size of the aid component, which basically aimed at improving the living conditions in the recipient states, was determined by intergovernmental negotiations between the EU member states. The budget (the European Development Fund, which lies outside the regular EU budget) amounted to €13.1 billion for 1995–2000. This meant that the EU is one of the biggest multilateral donors. Many ACP member states were and continue to be heavily dependent upon EU assistance for their development efforts.

Already at the time of Lomé I in 1975, a European *partner identity* had developed (Grilli 1993: 93; Ravenhill 1992) that consisted of beliefs in a special responsibility for the EU, in special ties between the EU and Africa, in the possibility of mutual benefits and in interdependence between rich and poor. The result was a rhetorical emphasis on Lomé as a contractual relationship between equal entities – a partnership – and a specific conception of strong EU interest in maintaining lasting relations with the ACP countries. The partnership spirit translated into non-reciprocity in trade (contrary to the principles of the General Agreement on Tariffs and Trade, GATT) and into little conditionality in aid. These were the elements that formed the normative basis for EU policy towards the ACP until the mid 1990s.

In the early 1990s, several factors came together to put mounting pressure on the existing regime (Elgström 2005). First, questions started to be raised about the effectiveness of the Lomé arrangements. Despite two decades of preferential market access and substantial flows of foreign assistance, growth figures as well as development indicators remained unimpressive. The existing regime did not seem to deliver the results that the parties had hoped for. Second, contextual developments served to undermine the relative importance of the ACP countries. The fall of the Soviet empire and the resulting 'need' for EU assistance in Central and Eastern Europe constituted a direct threat to traditional aid recipients as they competed over the same scarce resources (Lister 1997: 138–43). Also, the trend towards lower global tariffs as a result of GATT negotiations further undermined the relative advantage of preferences within the Lomé system.

Third, the spread of new transnational norms eroded the traditional ideals and thoroughly changed the ideological basis for the EU's approach to development. The EU as a donor became more demanding: conditional aid for structural adjustment and links between giving aid and human rights were introduced in 1990. These steps constituted an adaptation to prevailing international norms and reflected a 'virtual international consensus in favour of aid conditionality' (Lister 1998: 31). Fourth, the Lomé Conventions were *ipso facto* a contravention of the principles of the World Trade Organization (WTO), in that they discriminated between developing countries. These tensions accentuated the dilemmas of EU trade policy. Under the leadership of Directorate-General (DG) Trade, the EU had positioned itself as a champion of the WTO, but the EU could hardly assume a leading role in the new organization by disregarding its rulings or by perpetuating a waiver from the core principles of the trade system (Ravenhill 2002: 2; Dickson 2004: 47).

Taken together, these four trends created fertile ground for a transformation in regime. When the Fourth Lomé Convention (1990–2000) was up for revision, the time was ripe for EU reform initiatives. The actual negotiations between the EU and ACP were a highly unequal affair. The ACP states had little influence on the course of the negotiations, and the EU's negotiation mandate was more or less transcribed into the final agreement (Ravenhill 2002: 17; Elgström 2005; Holland 2002: 186ff.). The resulting Cotonou Agreement basically laid down the form of future negotiations. It stipulated that a six-year negotiation period was to be initiated in 2002, the aim being to finalize regional agreements (that is, the EPAs) by 2008. The agreement was in essence a timetable for moving from a regime of non-reciprocal trade preferences to a free trade system aimed at liberalizing all bilateral trade on a reciprocal basis. The most innovative part was the emphasis on trade and investments as agents of development, replacing the Lomé agreements' reliance on trade preferences and aid (Holland 2002: 208). The agreement carried over much of the traditionalist jargon from Lomé, but the gist of the agreement and especially the provisions on trade cooperation were altered substantially. According to Anna Dickson, '[t]he introduction of the principle of reciprocity signalled the beginning of the end of the preferences that made Lomé unique' (2004: 49).

EPA negotiations between the EU, represented by DG Trade, and the ACP started in September 2002. After general talks between the two blocs, the ACP countries divided into six groupings (the Caribbean, the Pacific and four African regions) in 2004 and negotiations were from then on conducted on an interregional level. Nothing much happened, however, during the first years. Many ACP governments were sceptical of trade liberalization, while most EU member states gave little priority to these negotiations that seemed to promise them limited economic advantages. It was not until well into 2006 that negotiations began in earnest. Under the shadow of the looming deadline – the end of the WTO waiver on 1 January 2008 – the negotiations became extremely intensive. DG Trade tried to drive the talks forward at a hectic pace. The result was what I have elsewhere (Elgström 2009) described as 'crisis negotiations', as they involved perceptions of time pressure, great uncertainty and high values at stake.

Negotiations focused on market access, on the role of development aspects in these free trade agreements (FTA), and on services and trade-related issues. As regards access for trade in goods, there existed different interpretations of the WTO rule that requires 'substantially all' trade to be covered in an FTA. To begin with, the EU demanded zero tariffs on products that account for 90 per cent of the current trade between the parties. The ACP, on their part, wanted to exempt at least 40 per cent of products – so-called 'sensitive products' – from tariff liberalization. The length of transition periods was another bone of contention, with DG Trade considering ten years a reasonable implementation period, and the ACP asking for up to 20–25 years to adapt to the world market. The EU also preferred EPAs in which all countries in a region committed to the same obligations, while the ACP wanted rules that acknowledged regional diversity. Finally, and related to the development dimension of the agreements, the ACP saw little prospect for increased exports to the EU if they were not granted substantial additional development support to help them alleviate supply-side constraints. DG Trade was against including explicit development aid provisions in the EPA legal framework, as assistance was already covered by the Cotonou Agreement and handled in other forums. For the ACP, increased assistance was the main objective and a *sine qua non* to be able to benefit from the new trade regime. The EU insisted on including provisions on the liberalization of trade in services and on introducing binding commitments in trade-related areas (the 'Singapore issues'), such as investment and competition policy, arguing that rules in these areas were needed to ensure economic growth and development. At first, the ACP regions refused to negotiate most of these issues, both because they preferred to handle these questions in a WTO context and because they wanted to retain their policy space.

In November to December 2007, 35 ACP countries initialled EPAs with the EU. Except for the agreement with the Caribbean countries, which was a comprehensive EPA, all the other agreements were partial, mostly covering provisions related to the liberalization of trade in goods. DG Trade, in mid 2007, realized that full agreements were unlikely to be reached in time and instead proposed interim EPAs, to be transformed into comprehensive agreements in 2008 or even later. Still, 41 ACP states did not initial any agreement. Most of these were LDCs, eligible for the EU's Everything But Arms preferences. The trade of the non-LDCs that chose not to be part of the EPAs is now framed under the less advantageous Generalized System of Preferences (GSP).

The agreements included a decision to remove all remaining tariffs and quotas to the EU for all exports from the ACP, with transition periods for sugar and rice; a gradual liberalization in ACP countries, with phase-in schedules of around 15 years; and an exclusion of sensitive products from liberalization. Most agreements will eventually result in about 80 per cent trade liberalization on the ACP side. They also included chapters on development that endorse a range of development-supporting measures. These sections typically commit the EU to supporting the implementation of interim EPAs through the European Development Fund. Commitments on assistance in specified forms, quantities and time frames are, however, not part of the agreements (cf. Southcentre 2008). However, the EU has unilaterally made a firm commitment to increase its funding of trade-related assistance ('Aid for Trade') to €2 billion per year by 2010. The Singapore issues were among those postponed for later debate.

## EU negotiation tactics and ACP criticism

The interim EPAs have evoked considerable criticism from ACP governments. Their negative comments have concerned both the substance of the agreements and the process leading to them. The focus in this chapter is on evaluations of the *process*, rather than on the assumed effects on goals, such as development and regional integration. It should also be noted that evaluations have varied from region to region: while many (but far from all) official commentators from the Caribbean region tend to be relatively positive both towards the outcome and process (Camilo 2008; Humphrey 2008; Stabroek 2008), voices from Africa have been more likely to express apprehension about the consequences of EPAs and disappointment in the EU's negotiation behaviour. Here I will focus on the critique, mainly from African and Pacific sources.

In December 2007, just after the agreements had been initialled, the ACP Council of Ministers collectively 'deplore[d] the enormous pressure [...] brought to bear on the ACP States by the European Commission ... contrary to the spirit of the ACP–EU partnership' (ACP 2007). Similar statements, echoing disquiet and frustration over 'undue pressure' from the EU and a 'rushed process', are frequent in the material (interviews 4–7; ECOWAS official in *Daily Graphic* 2008; former Guyana Foreign Minister Ramphal in Bilaterals 2008; AU Commissioner Tankeu 2008; cf. Stevens *et al.* 2008: 70–85). Malawi's President Mutharika accused the EU of 'imperialism', saying it was punishing countries that resisted the EPAs by threatening to withhold aid from the European Development Fund (EDF), reportedly adding: 'if the agreement is so good, why do they have to force people to sign?' (AllAfrica 2008).

The EU's, or rather the Commission's, intentions and official goals are repeatedly questioned. In the eyes of ACP officials, the EU is clearly driven by commercial concerns and its main goal is to safeguard (against notably Chinese competition) and open up ACP markets (interviews 2, 6, 7). DG Trade is claimed to have carried out EPA negotiations with a narrow trade approach, treating the EPAs as 'any other free trade agreement', in the process giving scant attention to the ACP's development agenda (interviews 1, 2, 8). The EU is thus seen as a self-interested actor that utilizes its superior power to further its own 'mercantilist interests' (ACP 2007). The partnership ideal is fine, but there cannot be a partnership 'between a horse and a horse rider' (interview 4).

Much criticism is raised against the Commission's negotiation tactics and behaviour. This critique targets the EU's alleged refusal to consider any alternatives to EPAs, its use of the deadline and the dependence of ACP countries on EU trade, its insistence on bringing new issues into the negotiations, its use of 'divide-and-rule tactics' and its refusal to listen to ACP demands and concerns. First, the Commission is claimed to have shown little interest in alternative solutions to the problem of WTO compatibility. According to the Commission, there was 'no Plan B' (Mandelson 2007a) and a failure to reach agreement by the end of 2007 would not spur the EU to engage in an alternative strategy. The wishes of the ACP to get more time to consider alternatives, or to obtain an extension of the waiver or the granting of GSP+ preferences to all ACP countries were flatly refused (Stevens *et al.* 2008: 77; Agbadome 2007; interviews 2, 3, 4, 7). The Commission was – despite its protests to the contrary (Commission 2008) – perceived to be insensitive to ACP pleas for alternative solutions.

Second, many ACP representatives insist that EPAs were signed 'under huge duress and with little enthusiasm' (South Africa's Deputy Trade Minister in *Ipsnews* 2008; cf. the Guyana President in the *Jamaica Gleaner* 2008). The reason interim EPAs were initialled was, in this view, that the alternative – GSP status for non-LDCs – was far worse (interviews 2–7); many ACP countries had no alternative but to initial. The EU repeatedly referred to the looming deadline (interview 5) and thereby put enormous pressure on ACPs, which, at the same time, faced intense lobbying from domestic producers foreseeing disaster if the preferential exports to the EU were stopped. The economies of many ACPs were so reliant on the EU that the EPAs were 'a must', especially as no alternative was acceptable to Union negotiators. Under 'the shadow of GSP' (interview 3), they felt that they were presented with a 'take it or leave it' proposal (interviews 4, 5), which they were 'forced to initial' (interview 7): 'Under pressure and the threat of disruption of their trade with the EU and of losing their preferential access to the EU market if they reject the proposal … 18 African countries have had to initial [EPA] agreements' (AU Commissioner Tankeu 2008). What the Commission regarded as an explanation of objective consequences if the EPAs were not signed (that is, as a warning) was by many ACP representatives interpreted as a threat.

Third, the Commission has consistently insisted on the inclusion of provisions on services and trade-related issues in the EPAs, issues that the ACPs are not required to negotiate according to WTO rules and that were not prioritized by ACP negotiators. Despite the Commission's efforts to explain the link between, for example, investment rules and development, the stubborn insistence of the EU to include the Singapore issues was seen an attempt to force upon the

ACPs rules that would favour EU interests (interviews 3, 4, 7). Fourth, because of its willingness to sign interim EPAs with individual countries, and not just with entire regions, and also because it allowed different provisions and rules in different agreements, the EU was accused of a 'divide-and-rule' strategy (interviews 1, 7; Pacific Trade Ministers in Bilaterals 2008). Extremely sensitive about the group's internal cohesion and regional harmonization (AU 2008; AU Commissioner Tankeu 2008; Ethiopian Trade Minister Birru 2008), many ACP spokespersons rejected every move by the EU that could be interpreted as creating divisions within the group. Furthermore, the Commission has been accused of withholding information on developments in parallel negotiations, of claiming progress in a contentious area in one region to convince others to agree to the same and of not honouring commitments (interviews 1, 4; Stevens *et al.* 2008: 81).

Fifth, the EU is considered insensitive to ACP needs and demands and unwilling to integrate seriously the main interests of the ACP into the agreements. According to ACP sources, the Commission 'didn't seem to listen to [our] development concerns' (interview 2; cf. 5) and an African Union representative complained about 'the failure of the EC to address issues of major interest and concern to Africa' (Tankeu 2008). For the ACPs, development was the main interest at all times. In their thinking, large amounts of additional assistance were necessary to enable them to take advantage of any increased access to EU markets. Therefore, their focus in the negotiations was often on the inclusion of an explicit 'development dimension' in the EPAs and, more concretely, on promises of 'more money' (interviews 5, 8). DG Trade, seeing the EPAs as trade agreements, for a long time rejected the demand to include a development chapter, arguing that the aid dimension was taken care of in the Cotonou Agreement and was to be handled in other forums (and by DG Development) (Southcentre 2008). In the end, development chapters were made part of the interim EPAs, but did not include any concrete details regarding sources and volumes of funds. There is widespread agreement – despite frequent EU assertions to the contrary – among the interviewees that in reality no additional funding is provided to cover the huge expenditure needed to overcome the ACP countries' trade capacity problems and to meet their adjustment costs (interviews 2, 6, 7, 9; cf. AU 2008: 8).

In addition to the questioning of EU *motives* and the critique of EU negotiation *behaviour*, complaints are widespread about the *attitudes* demonstrated by EU officials during the negotiations. The Commission negotiators' behaviour and attitudes are described by my interviewees as 'patronizing', 'paternalistic', 'condescending and very rude', 'over-aggressive', 'intimidating' and as 'showing disrespect' (interviews 7, 8, 3, 5, 9, 7). In a letter leaked to NGOs, the Minister of Foreign Affairs for the Cook Islands Rasmussen described former Trade Commissioner Mandelson as being 'insensitive to our protocols and issues' and his attitudes to Pacific Ministers as 'harsh and unnecessarily dominating' (Bilaterals 2008). One interviewee claimed that the good relationship between the EU and ACP countries that had been built up over the years was now hurt because of the 'ill will and bad political feelings' generated by EU behaviour during the EPA process (interview 7). Likewise, Stevens *et al.* (2008: 84) conclude that 'too much pressure in an asymmetric relationship like that between the EU and the ACP, can lead to a lot of suspicion and a lack of owner- ship of the final result … not conducive to a harmonious relationship'.

In brief, there are in the EU's approach to the EPA negotiations a number of elements that are typical of 'hard bargaining' (for a list of hard bargaining tactics, see Dür and Mateo 2008), at least in the interpretation of its behaviour given by ACP observers. Its strong insistence on EPAs as the only available alternative, its equally strong commitment to certain issues that were not priori- tized by the ACP, its use of warnings (by many ACP representatives seen as threats) and deadlines to put pressure on its opponent, and an alleged manipula- tion of private information all belong to this category. Furthermore, ACP render- ings of EU attitudes reinforce this picture. Commission negotiators are characterized as patronizing and showing little understanding and sympathy towards ACP needs. Thus, the EU's negotiation behaviour seems to stand in sharp contrast to what should be expected from a 'partner'.

## An explanatory sketch

In my explanation of this puzzle, I refer to the cognitive constructs of the parties, to their beliefs, images and perceptions (cf. Jervis 1976; Jönsson 1990; Vertz- berger 1990). I argue that both parties were guided by strong principled and causal beliefs (Goldstein and Keohane 1993) and by their images of 'the other', and that these constructs informed their perceptions and interpretations of the behaviour. My explanation is a 'sketch' in the sense that it is an interpretation of my material in terms of a specific theoretical perspective, rather than an attempt to prove the correctness of my diagnosis.

At the bottom of the EU–ACP tension seems to lie a fundamental divergence in terms of beliefs concerning and approaches towards development (cf. Stevens *et al.* 2008: 71–2; Agbadome 2007; interviews 2, 3, 5, 8, 9). The goals stated by the EU in the EPA process are to encourage a process of 'economic reform, regional integration and progressive trade opening' (Mandelson 2007b). Behind these goals lie a number of overarching principles that seem to guide DG Trade: a belief in the developmental potential of free trade and liberalism, combined with an equally strong belief in the benefits of regional integration, stemming from the EU's own experience. According to former Trade Commissioner Man- delson, 'My overall philosophy is simple: I believe in progressive trade liberali- sation. I believe that the opening of markets can deliver growth and the reduction of poverty' (2005a). Regional integration, meanwhile, can build markets where economies of scale and enhanced competition stimulate employment and devel- opment (Mandelson 2005b). The EPAs will become the norm among the ACPs, 'not because the EU is forcing them … but because their development rationale is so powerful' (Mandelson 2008b). Many ACPs are, however, not convinced. Their main focus is on development assistance. Free trade is dangerous and may lead to disaster, as many of their producers are not competitive on an open market. Before markets are opened, the ACPs need substantial assistance to strengthen their competitiveness and to take away supply-side constraints (interviews 2–5). Hence, the demands for additional aid and long transition periods.

Commission officials were committed to EPAs as the only – as they saw it – available realistic, WTO-compatible solution (Mandelson 2007a). As an ardent, principled supporter of multilateralism and the WTO trade regime, the Commission was adamant that the deadline of the WTO waiver be met. This was a major factor behind the hectic pace of final negotiations and the reluctance to discuss alternative solutions. Totally convinced that their free trade approach was correct, Commission officials considered it necessary to put pressure on unprepared (interviews 1, 2, 3, 4, 6) and hesitant ACP negotiators. On the ACP side, the perceived unwillingness on the EU's part to discuss their main concern, development aid, created frustration. A situation characterized by high uncertainty, both concerning the substantive effects and the domestic consequences of initialling the agreements, strengthened their frustration. At the same time, they saw themselves as facing an ultimatum, and, having a very bad BATNA (best alternative to a negotiated agreement), they felt pressured and cornered. Many of them saw no alternative but to sign the agreement.

Existing images may also have influenced the interpretations of the bargaining behaviour. ACP negotiators realized that the bargaining situation was highly asymmetric and were therefore mentally prepared for pressure from the stronger party. Believing that their 'opponent' was seeking to further its own commercial interests (interviews 2, 6, 7), it was easy to interpret the EU proposals and moves as part of a sinister plan to exploit their relative weakness. The patronizing *besserwisser* EU attitude that many ACP negotiators have described may be due to a high degree of sensitivity among ACP representatives to signs of unfairness from their former colonial masters, but also to lingering images of superiority among the EU negotiators. Anyhow, perceptions of disrespectful behaviour evidently strengthened ACP suspicions of EU manipulation.

## Concluding remarks: the EPAs in the light of the explanatory framework

In this chapter, I have argued that the EU negotiators – mainly DG Trade officials – were preoccupied by what they saw as an absolute deadline, in the form of the end of a WTO waiver, and therefore were determined to finish negotiations before that time. They were also convinced that the EPAs in the form proposed by DG Trade were actually in the best interests of the ACPs, and therefore devoted little effort to potential alternatives. Against this background, they felt that the EU had to put some pressure on the ACPs in order to finalize the negotiations, while perceived time pressure made them pay scant attention to ACP concerns. At the same time, ACP negotiators were from the beginning sensitive to ulterior motives behind EU proposals and wanted to prioritize their development concerns, which they felt were downplayed by DG Trade officials. This meant that the Union's attempts to hasten an agreement were interpreted as coercive and illegitimate. In brief, a clash of expectations and beliefs created an atmosphere of distrust and led to misunderstandings and negative interpretations.

The images held by the parties – and consequently also their strategies and behaviour – can convincingly be explained by the collective impact of the framework and contingent variables detailed in the explanatory framework elaborated in the Introduction to this volume. The colonial history and lingering memories of a long-standing patron–client relationship make us understand both the extreme sensitivity of the ACP to any trace of colonial attitudes and their fear of underlying imperialist motives behind EU behaviour. ACP attitudes were also shaped by a conception of world order that emphasizes the inequalities and inherent injustice of the present global economic system and makes them see preferential treatment and aid transfers as natural components of any agreement with the former colonial powers. The common political identity of the group, forged during consecutive Lomé negotiations, made them resent any perceived attempt by the EU to 'divide and rule'. At the same time, the regional integration preference of the EU, which is part and parcel of the Union's own experiences, made it natural for the EU to pursue the idea of regional free trade groupings among their ACP counterparts. Similarly, the EU's preference for multilateralism led its representatives to perceive WTO conformity as inevitable. Thus, fundamental, long-term framework variables worked to produce a situation of contrary expectations and strategies.

Contingent factors were also at play. The crucial power asymmetry between the parties was translated respectively into perceptions of weakness and strength that fuelled fears of exploitation among the ACP states and attitudes of superiority among the EU negotiators. It also strengthened the perceived need for unity within the ACP group. The feelings of surprise and anger that hit ACP negotiators in the early phases of the EPA negotiations when they encountered unexpectedly tough bargaining tactics from the Commission can be explained with reference to interaction variables: used to a partnership spirit and relatively soft negotiation tactics from DG Development during the Lomé rounds, the businesslike attitude of DG Trade came as an unpleasant shock. On the other hand, the EU negotiators probably entered the negotiations expecting to strike a deal with a relatively unprepared and weak negotiation partner, making it necessary for them to take a leading role in the negotiations. Finally, the social role of DG Trade as a 'promoter of free trade', developed during 'ordinary' trade negotiations with a number of other actors over the years, arguably contributed to the tactics and strategies chosen by its representatives. This role was quite different from the one enacted by DG Development, namely the role of a 'partner in development'.

## Note

1 This chapter, in a slightly different version and under another title, also appears in Aggestam, K. and Jerneck, M. (2009) *Diplomacy in Theory and Practice*, Malmö: Liber Publishing Company.

# References

ACP (2007) Declaration of the ACP Council of Ministers at its 86th Session, ACP/25/013/07, 13 December. Online, available at: www.acp.int/en/com/86/ACP2501307_declaration_e.pdf (accessed 31 January 2009).

Agbadome (2007) Interview with A.S. Agbadome, Conseiller Régional en Négociations Commerciales à la CEDEAO, *acp-eu-trade newsletter*, 8.

AllAfrica (2008) 'If EPAs Are So Good, Why Force Us to Sign?' by P. Semu-Banda, 23 April. Online, available at: http://allafrica.com/stories/printable/200804230768.html (accessed 31 January 2009).

AU (2008) Addis Ababa Declaration on EPA Negotiations, African Union Conference of Ministers of Trade and Finance, 1–3 April, AU/EXP/CAMTF/Decl. (1).

Bilaterals (2008) 'Pacific Trade Ministers Slam EU Trade Commissioner Mandelson', 18 April. Online, available at: www.bilaterals.org/article-print.php3?id_article=11848 (accessed 31 January 2009).

Birru, A.G. (2008) Statement by His Excellency Ato Girma Birru, Minister of Trade & Industry for the Federal Democratic Republic of Ethiopia, at the African Trade and Finance Ministers Meeting, Addis Ababa, 1–3 April.

Camilo, F. (2008) 'The CARIFORUM-EC EPA: the first development-enhancing agreement in history', presentation to a workshop organized by DG Trade in Brussels by the Ambassador of the Dominican Republic to the EC, 13 February.

Commission (2008) Interim Economic Partnership Agreements: questions and answers, DG External Trade, 27 March.

*Daily Graphic* (2008) 'EU Support Not Enough – Ecowas Commission', 10 June. Online, available at: www.modernghana.com/news2/169190/1/eu-support-not-enough-ecowas-commission.html (accessed 31 January 2009).

Dickson, A. (2004) 'The Unimportance of Trade Preferences', in K. Arts and A. Dickson (eds) *EU Development Cooperation: from model to symbol*, Manchester: Manchester University Press.

Dür, A. and Mateo, G. (2008) 'Bargaining Power and Negotiation Tactics: the negotiations on the EU's financial perspective, 2007–13', paper presented at the 58th Political Studies Annual Conference, Swansea, 1–3 April.

Elgström, O. (2005) 'The Cotonou Agreement: asymmetric negotiations and the impact of norms', in O. Elgström and C. Jönsson (eds) *European Union Negotiations*, London: Routledge.

Elgström, O. (2009) 'From Cotonou to EPA Light: a troubled negotiating process', in G. Faber and J. Orbie (eds) *Beyond Market Access for Economic Development: EU–Africa relations in transition*, London: Routledge.

Elgström, O. and Jönsson, C. (2000) 'Negotiation in the European Union: bargaining or problem-solving?' *Journal of European Public Policy*, 7 (5), 684–704.

Goldstein, J. and Keohane, R.O. (1993) *Ideas and Foreign Policy: beliefs, institutions and political change*, Ithaca: Cornell University Press.

Grilli, E.Z. (1993) *The European Community and the Developing Countries*, Cambridge: Cambridge University Press.

Holland, M. (2002) *The European Union and the Third World*, Houndmills: Palgrave.

Humphrey, E. (2008) 'CARIFORUM EPA Negotiations: initial reflections on the outcome', presentation to a workshop organized by DG Trade in Brussels by the Ambassador of Barbados to the EC, 13 February.

*Ipsnews* (2008) 'TRADE: Barroso's EPA intervention to be "more than symbolic"', by

D. Cronin, 31 January. Online, available at: www.ipsnews.net/news.asp?idnews=41015 (accessed 31 January 2009).

*Jamaica Gleaner* (2008) 'Golding Slams EPA Critics', by John Myers, 1 February. Online, available at: www.jamaica-gleaner.com/gleaner/20080201/business/business6.html (accessed 31 January 2009).

Jervis, R. (1976) *Perception and Misperception in International Politics*, Princeton: Princeton University Press.

Jönsson, C. (1990) *Communication in International Bargaining*, London: Pinter.

Lister, M. (1997) *The European Union and the South*, London: Routledge.

Lister, M. (1998) 'Europe's New Development Policy', in M. Lister (ed.) *European Union Development Policy*, London: Macmillan.

Mandelson, P. (2005a) Statement to the Development Committee of the European Parliament, 17 March. Online, available at: http://ec.europa.eu/commission_barroso/mandelson/speeches_articles/ (accessed 31 January 2009).

Mandelson, P. (2005b) Address at the ACP–EU Joint Parliamentary Assembly, 19 April. Online, available at: http://ec.europa.eu/commission_barroso/mandelson/speeches_articles/ (accessed 31.1.2009).

Mandelson, P. (2007a) 'There is no Plan B', *Trade Negotiations Insights*, 6 (5), September. Online, available at: www.acp-eu-trade.org/tni (accessed 31 January 2009).

Mandelson, P. (2007b) Comments at the INTA Committee, European Parliament, 22 October. Online, available at: http://trade.ec.europa.eu/doclib/docs/2007/october/tradoc_136542.pdf (accessed 31 January 2009).

Mandelson, P. (2008a) Conference speech, EC–ESA Trade Ministerial Meeting, 3 March. Online, available at: http://Mandelson_EN_030308_EC_press-conference-speech-Lusaka.pdf (accessed 31 January 2009).

Mandelson, P. (2008b) Commission seminar on Economic Partnership Agreements, European Parliament, 17 April. Online, available at: http://ec.europa.eu/commission_barroso/mandelson/speeches_articles/sppm200_en.htm (accessed 31 January 2009).

Ravenhill, J. (1992) 'When Weakness is Strength', in I.W. Zartman (ed.) *Europe and Africa: the new phase*, Boulder, CO: Lynne Rienner.

Ravenhill, J. (2002) 'Back to the Nest? Europe's relations with the African, Caribbean and Pacific group of countries', *Working Paper PEIF-9*, Edinburgh: University of Edinburgh.

Southcentre (2008) 'EPA Negotiations: state of play and strategic considerations for the way forward', Analytical note SC/AN/TDP/EPA/13. Online, available at: www.southcentre.org (accessed 31 January 2009).

Stabroek (2008) 'EC Pact Allows Access to 460M High-income Consumers – Bernal – Cariforum heads expected to sign deal by mid-April', 21 February. Online, available at: www.stabroeknews.com/index.pl/print?id=56539492 (accessed 31 January 2009).

Stevens, C., Meyn, M., Kennan, J., Bilal, S., Braun-Munzinger, C., Jerosch, F., Makhan, D. and Rampa, F. (2008) *The New EPAs: comparative analysis of their content and the challenges for 2008*, London and Maastricht: ODI and ECDPM.

Tankeu (2008) Statement by Mrs Elisabeth Tankeu, AU Commissioner for Trade and Industry, at the Conference of AU Ministers of Trade and Finance, Addis Ababa, 1–3 April.

Vertzberger, Y.Y. (1990) *The World in Their Minds: information processing, cognition and perceptions in foreign policy decisionmaking*, Stanford: Stanford University Press.

## Interviews

1 Ambassador, African initialling country, 12 June 2007
2 Ambassador and First Secretary, African non-initialling country, 23 June 2008
3 Councillor, Pacific initialling country, 23 June 2008
4 Minister, African non-initialling country, 24 June 2008
5 Minister Plenipotentiary, African initialling country, 24 June 2008
6 Ambassador, African initialling country, 25 June 2008
7 Ambassador, African non-initialling country, 25 June 2008
8 Representative of the Caribbean Regional Negotiating Machinery, 6 March 2007
9 Official at the ACP Secretariat in Brussels, 6 March 2007

# 10 Aid, trade and development

## World Bank views on the EU's role in the global political economy

*Eugenia Baroncelli*

## Introduction[1]

With its contributions of over €45 billion, the European Union (EU) is by far the largest development aid donor in the world. Since the launch of the EU Consensus on Development in 2005, the EU has also stressed its renewed support towards the achievement of the Millennium Development Goals (MDG) (Commission of the EU 2008). Furthermore, as estimated by the Organization for Economic Cooperation and Development, most of the aid increase (90 per cent) pledged in the MDG-focused policies is expected to come from European countries (Commission of the EU 2008: 5). The emphasis put on aid effectiveness in global negotiations has highlighted the need, at the EU level, to work towards increased policy coherence. This effort has added a further dimension to the original importance of boosting aid in the global challenge to eradicate poverty. The ensuing redefinition of EU development policy making has entailed a search for horizontal coherence across different policy domains, prompting a drive towards increased policy consistency for the sake of both the EU's internal cohesion and the effectiveness of its external action. The Union's historical prominence in the area of trade, as well as its sustained effort to improve the quality of its action in the fields of migration, security and the environment require that the EU places greater attention on attaining such coherence through the pursuit of development objectives.

This chapter explores how the EU is viewed at present by one of the biggest international financial institutions in the world, as well as a key actor in the context of multilateral development policies: the International Bank for Reconstruction and Development, also popularly known as the World Bank (WB). The EU's weight in development policy making, coupled with its search for increased policy coherence, suggests that an analysis of the EU's external action through the eyes of one of the major development institutions is perhaps a crucial step towards providing elements for a constructive redefinition of the EU's role in world politics.[2]

While sharing a number of goals and cooperating in several thematic and regional areas in the pursuit of their respective missions, the EU and the Bank are however different in kind, and have different missions and agendas on multiple counts. The former is a political–economic supranational union, to which member states have delegated authority in the making of important internal and external policies. The latter is an international lending organization, composed of sovereign states, which works through intergovernmental procedures and is largely influenced by technical standards. Taken as a bloc, the member states of the EU are the largest shareholders in the WB, with their combined shares accounting for around 30 per cent of the Bank's resources. In 2006 the European Commission contributed on its part with more than USD 5 billion to the World Bank trust funds (World Bank Brussels Office 2007b). In their capacity as shareholders, EU member states have had an opportunity to influence the Bank's policies even though to date there is no joint European seat on the Bank's executive board. On the ground (i.e. in partner/client countries), the EU and the Bank often work side by side in multidonor projects, either through individual bilateral agencies or through the disbursement of EU (mostly Commission) funds. The Bank mainly works with EU member states and their development agencies, either by receiving funds that are then allocated according to global development priorities, or through trust funds that are tied to countries or policy areas.

As a result of both the sheer size of the resources devoted to the cause of development, and the importance of their joint effort in coordinating aid policy design and delivery, I have chosen to focus this chapter on the World Bank as the most significant multilateral source of images on the EU's developmental policies. The Bank's perceptions of the EU have been reconstructed based on a two-level methodology. First, I conducted a review of official and non-official World Bank documents on development and trade topics that make explicit reference to the EU's action in these two fields.[3] Second, I put together two questionnaires, targeted at the executive directors and vice-presidents, to gather their views on the EU. Washington and Brussels-based World Bank technical and political staff were then given interviews at both the headquarters of the World Bank in Washington, DC, and by phone.[4] Although the methodology relies on the tenets of qualitative social research, it is to be underlined that the overall number of the Bank's top political and technical management is approximately twice the number of interviewees, which somehow supports the 'quantitative' significance of these findings.[5]

The chapter is organized as follows. The first part sketches the main findings of the study, against the background of global dynamics affecting development policies. The subsequent parts deal with the Bank's perceptions of the EU in the global arena (from a foreign policy perspective), in regional political developments and in development policies and other related issues, while also analysing what, according to the World Bank, are the EU's strengths and weaknesses. The final part of the chapter puts forward some recommendations to improve the EU's action in the area of development and to develop expand the existing synergy with the World Bank at the different policy stages.

## The EU in the eyes of the World Bank

### *How important is the EU to the World Bank?*

Institutional and organizational aspects, such as the role of the EU member states as donors to the Bank and in the wider development community, were deemed to be important in allowing the Bank to pursue its developmental mission. An additional element of significance was the similarity between the EU and the Bank's respective approaches to development policies, especially compared to the US approach, often viewed as being too prone to the vagaries of different administrations.

When asked to give their opinion on the importance of the EU in the Bank's current action and policies, a strong majority of respondents (almost 78 per cent) rated it between important, very important or essential. A total of 17 per cent of the respondents judged the EU's importance as negligible for the Bank, on the premise that they did not consider the EU as a unified actor, either on the Board or in the wider arena of development policies (see Table 10.1). However, when asked to give an opinion on the weight of EU countries considered collectively, they stressed their crucial role for the Bank. Owing to the Bank's intergovernmental nature, most respondents voiced their uneasiness with having to evaluate the importance of the Union on the basis of the two terms 'EU' and 'EU member states'.

*Table 10.1* The EU in the eyes of the World Bank (in % of respondents)

| | |
|---|---:|
| **Current importance of the EU** | |
| Essential | 5.56 |
| Close to essential | 5.56 |
| Very important | 38.89 |
| Important | 27.78 |
| Somewhat important | 5.56 |
| Not important at all | 16.67 |
| **Future importance** | |
| Higher importance in the future | 38.89 |
| Same importance as now | 44.44 |
| Lower importance in the future | 16.67 |
| **The EU as an international power** | |
| Yes | 77.78 |
| No | 22.22 |
| **Coverage of EU-related issues in WB publications\*** | |
| Extensive | 13 |
| Adequate | 40 |
| Insufficient | 47 |

Source: Baroncelli 2008b.

Notes
Sample: $n = 18$, top political and technical World Bank management staff.
\* Sample: $n = 15$.

Relative to the evolving importance of the EU for the Bank in the past 15 years, all answers unequivocally pointed to its increased relevance, due to both EU enlargement (perceived as a pro-development choice) and its augmented financial effort to sustain growth and poverty reduction in developing countries.

As shown in Table 10.1, when projecting the importance of the EU for the Bank into future scenarios, a relative majority of respondents (44 per cent) foresee a rather stable situation, which appears to be linked in several answers to the exhaustion of the push for enlargement. However, a number of respondents (39 per cent) suggest that the EU may grow in its importance for the Bank in the future, due both to increased emphasis on multilateral aid policies and to possible changes in the criteria for attaining a representative role in internal Bank governance. A minority (17 per cent) believe that the EU will become less important, as a result of the relative growth of some of the emerging countries, notably China, Brazil, India and Russia (BRICs), in terms of their development support effort.

All respondents unequivocally rate the EU, or its major member states, such as Germany, France and the UK, as key actors within the Bank. Along with the EU as a group, the Bank regards a number of actors as important partners, including the European Commission, the European Investment Bank, the European Parliament (as well as the various national parliaments), a number of European NGOs and civil society at large, though in different respects. Client countries (partners) are also seen as main allies for the Bank, especially due to emerging markets such as the BRICs. While most respondents acknowledge that large bilateral donors are still the Bank's main partners (in addition to the EU also US/USAID and Japan), private sector actors such as foundations and private funds also appear to be gaining more importance.

Finally, the findings point to a general perception at the Bank of the EU as an international power (78 per cent). Some respondents note the exceptional nature of the EU, which is seen as the first and sole example of regional integration that aims to improve both the well-being of its citizens and that of other countries by increasing the provision of aid and strengthening fundamental freedoms. In addition, the EU is also perceived as a powerful counterbalance to the USA and Russia. Those who do not see it as an international power refer to, among other things, the absence of a credible alternative to the North Atlantic Treaty Organization (NATO) in security and military policies (due to both the lack of financial capacities and the imperfectly overlapping memberships of the EU and NATO), the multiplicity of foreign policy objectives and the lesser influence of the Commission in foreign affairs, compared to the weight of the member states.

## *Is the EU an international power? Strengths and weaknesses*

A cursory look at some of the 'non-rational images' associated with the idea of the 'European Union' suggests that some degree of polarization exists between positive and negative elements, with the latter prevailing in relation to EU foreign economic policy. The 'blue flag' and the Commission's office in Brussels rank at the top of the most recurrent visual images that respondents associate with the EU. Equally frequent are images such as 'large bureaucracy' and 'huge and intricate buildings'. Words such as 'chaos' and 'confusion' follow suit, accompanied by images such as 'big success story', 'US of Europe', 'soft power', 'joy', 'Monnet', 'Waldner' and 'Lamy'. Among the clearly negative images one can find 'slowness', 'centralization', 'pretentiousness', 'preaching' and 'simple collection of European countries', indicating how respondents are also concerned about the EU's lack of internal cohesion and its impact on external effectiveness. When analysing the EU's economic policies and their impact on other countries, the images tend to become particularly negative: 'protectionism', 'absurd agricultural policy', 'weak drive to explore new relations', 'lack of a proactive strategy', 'self-serving' and 'wait-and-see attitude'. The only positive/neutral images in this context include: 'generous development assistance', 'positive role in climate change' and 'trade negotiator'.

More generally, the EU is commonly viewed as a global economic power with an often normative impact and a great regulatory potential, in spite of exhibiting an inconsistent role in diplomatic affairs and exercising virtually no clout over military issues (see Table 10.2). According to most respondents, the EU's overall strengths as an international power pertain to its sheer size and weight in the world economy, with specific focus on areas such as aid and trade. While the virtuosity of Scandinavian countries finds common agreement among the respondents, the whole EU is also included among the most progressive donors, owing to its generosity in providing aid. The EU is also praised for its success in preserving and promoting diversity and in showing how different traditions, experiences and styles can coexist and lead to overall progress. Additionally, the EU is perceived as a sincere promoter of the fight against poverty, open to the world and dedicated to promoting core values, such as the respect of human rights, aspiration to a better life and cultural diversity in partner countries. Finally, several respondents appear to perceive a lower level of selfishness in EU development strategy compared to the USA, especially in the linking of economic and security goals.

Moving to the main weaknesses, the respondents often perceive the EU as divided and inconsistent. Some of the respondents point to the fact that it is not a

*Table 10.2*  Defining the EU's power (% of respondents)

| *Which type of international power?* | |
| --- | --- |
| Purely economic | 44.44 |
| Economic and normative | 22.22 |
| Economic and diplomatic | 16.67 |
| Economic, diplomatic and normative | 16.67 |
| Military | 0 |

Note
Sample: $n = 18$, top political and technical World Bank management staff.

member of the Bank, and that the EU executive directors are at times only 'weakly coordinated in the Board'. On a more general level, some respondents remark that the EU is absent from the directing rooms of some key global governance institutions ('it is not a member of the United Nations Security Council') and perceive it as not being 'interested in shaping its role and influence in multilateral institutions'. Finally, some officials note that the EU is not ready to make use of its potential to the fullest, or to advance political values in economic and development programmes, at times appearing unclear in its setting of strategic objectives.

Some exceptions to what appears to be rather negative assessment of the EU's political ambitions in global security affairs come from respondents working in the Middle East and North Africa (MENA) Washington-based regional unit as well as in the Africa unit. The respondents foresee an important role for the EU in supporting negotiations and peacekeeping operations in these two regions, albeit contingent upon the member states' ability to overcome existing differences and divergent national policy goals.

## Issues and policies: aid, trade and poverty reduction

According to the World Bank, the EU's role in fields such as aid effectiveness, donor coordination, trade, agricultural policies and climate change appear to be critical issues for the overall Bank's policy making . However, as frequent reference was made by several respondents to the high regional variability in policy outcomes, this part of the chapter offers an additional insight into specific views from different regional units and opinions on the policy impacts in these geographical areas.[6]

A consensus emerged on the need for both the Bank and the EU to improve coordination in client countries and harmonize strategies with other donors. As expected, efforts from the EU to sustain the Paris Agenda (along with other global initiatives on aid effectiveness) is a most welcome development in the eyes of high level World Bank staff, as it touches upon key aspects of the Bank's development mission.[7] In addition to softening conditionality, the effort to coordinate policies governing 'how to distribute the aid that we each give' is seen by the Bank as a constructive strategy to 'find a middle ground' with the EU and better coordinate their actions and policies towards the reduction of world poverty. In this context, the Paris Agenda, and the Limelette Process within it, are perceived by most top officials as unprecedented steps towards an increased synergy in the cooperation between the EU and the World Bank.[8]

Nevertheless, the debate on aid effectiveness also highlights differences and contentious issues between the EU and the Bank in terms of strategy, policy design, operations, disbursement and implementation (World Bank 2007b). Some officers contrast the smooth nature of high level contacts between Washington and Brussels with on-the-ground problematic and often unsatisfactory compromises reached with the EU. They describe the Union as 'overly bureaucratic' and 'slow', and link these policy processes back to their general weaknesses 'the EU is very bureaucratic and foreign aid is no exception'.

With respect to international trade, the relationship is described as 'critical', 'contentious' and displaying 'frictions'. Technical references to agricultural issues, trade diversion and negative impacts on regional integration processes are mentioned, particularly in light of the debate concerning the Economic Partnership Agreements (EPAs). Firm criticism of the Common Agricultural Policy and its distorting effect on trade is quite common across all the interviewees, who also criticize the seemingly passive (and at times regressive) stance of the EU with regard to the multiple mechanisms through which trade policies impact on poverty and aid policies.

On the contrary, respondents from the Europe and Central Asia unit point to an 'excellent and cooperative dialogue' with the EU, supported by regular contacts with different directorate-generals, with European bilateral donors and with development banks such as the European Investment Bank and the European Bank for Reconstruction and Development. The existence of a common development agenda is viewed as the main reason behind this positive perception, which confirms that the synergy achieved during the enlargement process has generated positive results in terms of cooperation between the EU and the Bank. Some criticisms of inconsistency were raised in relation to the disparity of approaches adopted by the EU towards the Balkans and Eastern Europe, which on the one hand received specific attention from the EU, and the countries of the Commonwealth of Independent States (CIS) and Central Asian partners, which in contrast appeared to be left out of the EU's development agenda.[9] Effectiveness outside the former Soviet Union in the non-CIS area was highly praised in the case of the Balkans, where the approach of the EU was described as 'innovative' and 'fast' in reacting to the multiple changes that had happened in the 1990s.

Based both on the interviews and documentary evidence, views from the MENA regional unit acknowledge the high potential for current and future joint action against the backdrop of existing differences in the two institutions' goals and interests (World Bank 2003). In this regard, political instability and diverging operational objectives are seen as factors affecting the EU's role in the region. Poor preparation for the Association Agreements in the EuroMed process, launched in 1995, and a strategy of shallow integration (most prominent culprit, the exclusion of services and sensitive products) were criticized in the past (Nabli 2001; Müller-Jentsch 2004). Currently, the EU's policies in the region are perceived as being 'generally effective', although there is significant room for improvement according to a number of respondents. For instance, inconsistencies in the enforcement of good governance criteria is viewed as a sensitive topic. In this regard, the EU could greatly improve the impact of its economic policies in the region by being more 'objective in assessing the progress made in economic and political governance', as well as more transparent in communicating it consistently to its partner countries.

Views from several units on EU–World Bank relations in sub-Saharan Africa hinged around the issues of trade, donor coordination and support for development in conflict-torn states. They convey a mixed picture about the quality and effectiveness of EU–WB interaction, both at the high strategic level, through the Paris Process, and in partner countries. Views on the effectiveness of EU development policies in the region are mixed. On the one side there is a positive assessment of the role played by the EU in the initiatives on development coordination and aid harmonization. On the other side, negative remarks refer to the cumbersome, slow approach of the EU to development finance, with both political and bureaucratic factors quoted as obstacles that delay the attainment of development objectives 'even if the commitment is there'. All in all, however, the present situation is described as greatly improved, and current EU efforts are appreciated over past ones.

The EU is viewed as a remarkable example of how diversity can coexist and lead to peaceful progress, especially among officers working in the South Asia and East Asia-Pacific regions. The 'EU as a conscience of the world' is sometimes seen as a model in South Asia, and is favoured ideologically in this specific respect (i.e. as a model for cooperation and integration in the case of the South Asian Association for Regional Cooperation, over the USA, which is nonetheless perceived as a key player in the region and as an ally by India).

Aside from coordination issues, voices from different units, executive directorates, regions and functional units remark on how the EU does not always appear capable of taking full advantage of its economic weight to advance its preferred political values in its development policies. This gap casts a somewhat sombre shadow on the implications of the current EU attempts to gain visibility in international affairs, as some put it. Many of the top political and technical officials indeed appreciate that the Union is making a special effort to define its role and image in world politics in order to make its influence on world affairs more effective and purposive. However, increased visibility with lower effectiveness in key areas such as development aid and trade may not give the Union the effect on its reputation that it wants to achieve. Finally, EU protectionism in trade and agriculture appeared with almost no exception in all interviews, and were also the target of numerous criticisms in the Bank's newsletters and policy research working papers.

## Understanding the World Bank's views of the EU

The evidence presented above has provided several insightful elements into the sources of the World Bank's images of the EU. Contingent variables appear to explain a large portion of the variation in the views from the World Bank. Such positional factors as the organizational role and culture of the interviewees (the Bank and the EU's respective missions, the respondents' role in the Bank), as well as relational elements, such as current or recent policy interactions, clearly emerge in the findings. However, longer-term factors (i.e. framework variables) also appear to be at work, as traits bearing on the respondents' political identity, history and conception of world order are clearly identifiable in a good portion of the answers. With respect to the former, the organizational role and culture, as well as policy interactions, appear of paramount importance. Elements pertaining to the two organizations' respective missions and goal attainment functions are more frequent in the words of top technical staff, while views on relative overlaps (or the absence thereof) between the EU's foreign policy and constituency-specific priorities more often appear to influence the perceptions of top political staff. In the latter case, emphasis is put more frequently on strategic and planning levels within the Bank at the headquarters in Washington, Brussels and other EU capitals, or in top-level world meetings, while in the former it is the policy inter-actions in client and partner countries that appear to orient views on the EU.

Organizational roles and functions appear to be a key variable in explaining the variance in the perceptions on the EU's approach to development issues in different parts of the world. Showing a trait common to most complex organiza-tions with a high degree of internal diversification, several respondents indeed qualified that a large portion of their answers pertained specifically to issues and regions in which they were involved at the time of the interview, or in which they had been involved previously. The lamented poor level of policy coherence indeed emerged from respondents who had been exposed to interactions with the EU in several regions and on different issues in time. The EU's neglect of key development issues in the Pacific, or in the countries of the CIS, as well as dispar-ities in enforcing governance criteria among different countries in the group of the Euro-Mediterranean Partners, as seen above, is perceived very distinctly by officials who operate in these areas. Critical, detailed opinions on trade discrimi-nation are doubtless ascribable to the respondents' in-depth knowledge of these issues in either regions where there is a great deal of trade with the EU (notably MENA and Africa) or in technical units that deal specifically with trade policies. Equally, praise for the EU's action in speeding development in the new member countries of Eastern Europe, or for its constructive role in conflict mediation in MENA and Africa can be explained based on role and function-specific elements. A general orientation to technical problem solving and goal attainment functions, on the other side, may help to explain several Bank-wide aspects that emerged in the answers relative to the EU's perceived high degree of bureaucratization and poor coordination mechanisms, both in the design and implementation phases.

Perceptions vary between technical and political roles. Relative to the issue of internal EU cohesion, to quote a prominent example, opinions from the Board lament the low assertiveness with which EU member states on the Board are able to coordinate and support common EU positions consistently throughout a range of decision processes, often resulting in fragmented action. The absence of an all-EU constituency on the Board (EU member states are currently spread over eight different constituencies) is clearly perceived as a symptom of disu-nity, further reinforcing the view that 'The EU is not a member of the World Bank.' However, the EU, through the Commission and its member states, cur-rently provides the main financial contribution to the Bank's overall budget: the net effect is often interpreted as one of 'under-representation'.[10] Technical know-ledge, on the other side (organizational culture and background), and interaction elements are most likely at the root of perceptions of the EU's inconsistencies in trade and agricultural policies.

Framework variables also play a key role in the Bank as sources of the views on the EU. Almost uniformly across the interviews a preference emerged for a pluralistic world order (possibly the result of both framework elements, such as political identity and the very conception of world order, and contingent elements, such as a policy and organizational culture based on a philosophy of multilateral management of both local and global issues), pointing to a view of the EU as an inclusive, mediating, cooperative and soft-power type of actor, as opposed to a more coercive, selfish and hard-power actor type (identified either with the USA or, less often, with China). Specific political identities can also be quoted, for example, to explain the emphasis on perceptions of the EU's action in the field of social cohesion, with respondents of Northern European origin appearing to be most critical of the EU's differential approach to the issue, on the domestic and external fronts respectively. However, instances of geo-political and cultural identity variables as a source of critical opinions of the EU along the North–South divide appear practically non-existent, as criticism on the Union's discriminatory approach points more to its current sectoral and geographical interests, and is shared across the Bank, when it is not unit-specific, as noted above. History and past occurrences also appear to be at work in the process of image formation, as particular praise for the specific European model of conflict resolution through development tools emanates from respondents from countries/regions with a history of conflict between different ethnic/religious groups.

## Conclusions and recommendations: coordination or competition?

> I've often said development is a team sport, there are a lot of players on the field but we have to cover all the positions. We can't all be strikers; is that the term you use in Europe; we can't all be goalies, every position needs to be covered, that means we need to work together, work as a team and I very much appreciate the teamwork that I find between the World Bank at the country level and at the Headquarters level and the European Commission.
> (Paul Wolfowitz, former World Bank President, Brussels, November 2006)[11]

While there is still the need ultimately to filter perceptions through both institutional and policy transmission mechanisms, based on image feedback from key actors in the Bank, several policy recommendations are put forward here on possible policy courses to improve the EU's action in the fields of its external aid, trade and development policies.[12] Standard-bearer of the promotion of 'good' socio-economic values (poverty reduction, non-discrimination, social inclusion, environmental awareness), as well as guarantor of key individual rights, the EU appears to bear the responsibility for a less than development-friendly stance in its agricultural policies, and, increasingly, in its trade policies. Considered a unique model for social, political and economic development, the EU is, however, criticized for its current discriminatory approach in some development policy and geographical areas.

Undoubtedly a heavyweight in trade negotiations, and a generous partner in providing aid, the EU is still retained a weak actor in security matters at the world level. However, its complex mission, perceived as 'both political and economic' by Bank officials, entails a great potential for the redefinition of a more balanced, yet still synergic, role as a 'security promoter through development'.

What are the implications of these perceptions for the credibility of the EU in the network of development policy makers? The EU's restrictive and ambiguous stance on several technical issues in the EPA negotiations and its emphasis on maintaining agricultural subsidies risk 'destroying part of the role' that it has built over the years as a honest and committed supporter of the twin causes of development and poverty reduction. Twenty years ago, against the background of a nascent multilateral development community, this would have had negative, but manageable implications. Today, with an increased voice and role for all partners in the global political economy, the negative repercussions on the future of the EU's external role risk being much more severe. The weak support given by the EU to pro-poor policies in countries undergoing EPA-led trade reforms casts serious doubts on the Union's ability to formulate poverty-focused trade policies with developing countries. To the direct transmission effects quoted in the Bank interviews and documents (market disruption, incentives to adverse restructuring and consequent market losses, trade diversion), one should add the longer-term implications stemming from the existing dynamics of aid policies in client countries. The opportunity cost of displeasing African partners, 'a beautiful bride' (*The Economist*, 6 December 2007), is much higher now, as new aid providers have, rightfully, entered the market with their own goals, styles and practices. While the Bank has greatly supported and warmly welcomes the 'graduation' of China to donor status and its increased contribution to International Development Agency resources, if looked at from the EU standpoint, new entries accompanied by its own loss in reputation may have negative implications on the future of the Union in the overall process of development support.

Second, while criticism of the EU's low level of effectiveness and high level of bureaucratization surface more seriously in the implementation phases, critical views from top level Bank officials indicate that both the Union's policy making and role definition may be at stake. It therefore appears important for the Union to reflect carefully on these aspects and possibly sharpen its current effort. While scaling-up is already underway, a reconsideration of methods and approaches may improve the effort to coordinate with the Bank.

Third, and closely connected with the point quoted above, the lamented lack of internal and geographical consistency entails consequences that have impaired the EU's action and credibility, both at project and regional levels.

Bearing in mind the necessary caveats, we may take several cues from the previous analysis to improve the Union's reputational capital in development policy making. Additionally, a few, general suggestions can be made for the improvement of the EU's own action in its development policies, and for the betterment of its synergic cooperation with the Bank in the fight against poverty. Less weight on immediate 'general visibility' targets, and a renewed emphasis on redefining goals and methods could perhaps be fruitful. Complex political and economic priorities could be better harmonized in the EU's own strategies to ensure consistency, both in the eyes of partner countries and at the Bank. If aid is linked to the attainment of governance standards, the EU should be clearer in its definition of these benchmarks, as well as more consistent in evaluating the countries' achievements and the allocation of funds. *Ex ante* disbursements do not appear to go in this direction, while objectiveness in *ex post* assessments can do a lot on both the policy effectiveness and reputational fronts. Also, the EU could better capitalize on the trusting relationship that it enjoys with the Bank. A widened dialogue could be pursued by all the directorate-generals involved in development policies, and DG Development (EuropeAid) could positively entertain more regular exchanges of information with relevant counterparts at the Bank. The EU could also place more trust in the Bank's approach characterized by a generally neutral pursuit of development goals. Closeness to the EU approach, especially on social issues such as cohesion and gender, as well as on environmental themes, proves that a substantial overlap exists between the two institutions in these policy areas too, in addition to the shared commitment to foster development and reduce poverty. Additionally, in order to develop synergies by building on existing comparative advantages, the EU could positively rely on the extensive knowledge that the Bank has not just of technical issues in aid management but also of institutions in partner countries, which are key actors in the making, and the success, of development policies.

Finally, the Union could give a clearer definition of its goals according to its mission and role, focusing on its comparative advantages and relying on the Bank to complement its efforts. This would provide a means to tackle the perceived lack of expertise, and the ensuing reputational effect, while allowing some time for the EU to improve its expertise where it deems necessary. Alternatively, the EU could focus on prioritizing its strategic goals and coordinating them with those of the Bank in areas of mutual interest, and pursue them in the respect of the other's institutional and policy specificities. The political nature of the Union, its ideological drive and the 'emulation capital' that it enjoys in the eyes of the Bank and of partner countries provide an exceptional basis for developing more ambitious foreign policy goals.

Strong commonality of objectives and close cooperation normally entail more opportunities for dissent, potentially opening the way to tensions. Wherever there is close contact, there emerge opportunities to cooperate, as well as chances to conflict. It is therefore down to these two players, the EU and the World Bank, which largely share similar objectives in the area of development, to reinforce cooperation where this already exists, and to turn differences into challenges in order to build cooperation where collaboration is still in the initial stages.

## Notes

1 This chapter draws from my research undertaken in the context of the *Survey on the External Image of the EU* presented in the introduction to this volume. I am grateful

to Chiara Franchini for her excellent research support, and to Lisa Tormena, who has kindly assisted me in a number of different tasks. Lastly, I owe my heartfelt gratitude to all the World Bank officials, top political and technical management staff, in both Washington, DC, and Brussels, who kindly agreed to lend me their time and insight into World Bank–EU relations.

2  Research in the area of foreign policy has long explored the role of national leaders' own beliefs in their decision making, while political and IR research on how perceptions form and evolve at the aggregate (national, multilateral) level has to date produced a consistent body of literature (Adler 1987; Goldstein and Keohane 1993; Wendt 1999; Legro 1995, 2005). The debate on the role of the EU in international affairs has recently benefited from these insights, with studies that explore the role of collective ideas on the EU from national and multilateral sources (Lucarelli 2007; Elgström and Smith 2006).

3  While the documentary survey spans a greater period of time, it reports positions that were either publicly available on World Bank external websites between December and February 2008, or in a number of the Bank's paper publications mostly released between 1999 and 2008. While enjoying the benefit of ample time coverage, the documentary overview presented here does not claim the historical exhaustiveness of a detailed archive search. World Bank official documents comprise the *World Development Report*, *Global Monitoring Report*, policy briefs and regional reports, as well as official statements by the Bank's representatives, as reported by both the Bank and external sources (e.g. the *Financial Times*, *China Daily*, *Strait Times*, *Wall Street Journal* and others). Non-official documents are mostly limited to World Bank papers by research staff.

4  The interviews, conducted between January and February 2008, are based on semi-structured questionnaires given to a non-statistically representative sample (18 staff interviewed in an organization with around 10,000 employees overall, of whom two-thirds are based at the Washington headquarters). In this chapter, the adjective 'technical' refers both to top and senior management staff levels (vice-presidents, sector managers, sector directors, senior advisers, special representatives, senior economists and senior consultants), while the adjective 'political' applies either to executive directors or alternate executive directors. Answers on and from the World Bank's regional units pertain exclusively to Washington-based officials. *Non certa che ci sia bisogno di specificarlo, visto che ho indicato sopra la location delle interviste, ma, in caso vogliate dare ai lettori una indicazione chiara sin da subito riguardo ai riferimenti alle unità regionali.*

5  Additional details on the methodology and scope of the survey can be found in Baroncelli (2008b).

6  The evidence from the documentary portion of the survey, to which reference is also made in the following text, largely supports the views expressed in the interviews.

7  On the Paris Agenda see World Bank (2006), on harmonization and donor coordination see World Bank (2007a).

8  See EU Commission–DG Development and the World Bank (2007) and World Bank Brussels Office (2007a).

9  The CIS was formed in 1991 and comprises 12 former Soviet republics. Non-CIS countries include the three Baltic republics and the other Central and Eastern European countries that are part of the Europe and Central Asia regional unit.

10 On the debate over the reform of World Bank internal governance see Eurodad (2006).

11 World Bank external website (2008).

12 Studies in comparative political economy have also shown how and when ideational elements matter in the making of EU foreign policies (see Baroncelli 2008a).

# References

Adler, E. (1987) *The Power of Ideology: the quest for technological autonomy in Argentina and Brazil*, Berkeley, CA: University of California Press.

Baroncelli, E. (2008a) 'Preferenze, istituzioni e idee: il "policy making" economico esterno dell'Unione europea', in M. Ferrera and M. Giuliani (eds) *Governance e politiche nell'Unione Europea*, Bologna: Il Mulino.

Baroncelli, E. (2008b) 'The External Image of the EU in Multilateral Settings: a view from the World Bank', in Forum per i Problemi della Pace e della Guerra-GARNET, Jointly Executed Research Project 5.2.1, S. Lucarelli and L. Fioramonti (coordinators) *The External Image of the European Union (Phase Two)*.

Commission of the EU (2008) *The EU: a global partner for development. Speeding up progress towards the Millennium Development Goals*, Brussels, 9 April 2008, COM(2008) 177 final.

Elgström, O. (2006) 'Leader or Foot-Dragger? Perceptions of the European Union in multilateral international negotiations', *SIEPS Report 1*.

Elgström, O. and Smith, M. (2006) 'Introduction', in O. Elgström and M. Smith (eds) *The European Union's Roles in International Politics*, London, Routledge, pp. 1–10.

EU Commission–DG Development and The World Bank (2007) 'European Commission–World Bank Meeting with Civil Society on EC–World Bank Collaboration on Africa', note, Brussels, 17 September.

Eurodad (2006) 'European Coordination at the World Bank and International Monetary Fund: a question of harmony?' *European Network on Debt and Development*, Brussels, January 2006.

Goldstein, J. and Keohane, R. (1993) *Ideas and Foreign Policy: beliefs, institutions, and political change*, Ithaca, NY: Cornell University Press.

Legro, J. (1995) *Cooperation under Fire*, Ithaca, NY and London: Cornell University Press.

Legro, J. (2005) *Rethinking the World, Great Power Strategies and International Order*, Ithaca, NY and London: Cornell University Press.

Lucarelli, S. (2007) 'The European Union in the Eyes of Others: towards filling a gap in the literature', *European Foreign Affairs Review*, 12 (3): 249–70.

Müller-Jentsch, D. (2004) 'Deeper Integration and Trade in Services in the Euro-Mediterranean Region: southern dimensions of a 'wider Europe', 32530, World Bank/ European Commission Programme on Private Participation in Mediterranean Infrastructure, work-in-progress for public discussion.

Nabli, M.K. (2001) 'The EU–Med Partnership: stocktaking and long-term challenges ahead', Chief Economist, Middle East and North Africa Region, The World Bank, presented at International Development Research Center Trade Workshop: *Trade Negotiations and Trade Policies in Developing Countries: what role for capacity building and research?* Ottawa, Canada, 28 March.

Wendt, A. (1999) *Social Theory of International Politics*, Cambridge: Cambridge University Press.

World Bank (2003) 'Engaging with the World: trade, investment and development in MENA', MENA development report, Washington DC: The World Bank.

World Bank (2006) 'Paris Declaration at a Glance', prepared by the World Bank OPCS. Online, available at: http://info.worldbank.org/etools/docs/library/238766/H&A%20 Menu%20rev%202%20English.pdf (accessed 31 January 2009).

World Bank (2007a) 'Aid Architecture: an overview of the main trends in official development assistance flows', background report, Washington DC.

World Bank (2007b) 'Country-Based Scaling Up: assessment of progress and agenda for action', background report for the 21 October Development Committee Meeting.

World Bank (2008) Paul Wolfowitz, press call Brussels, 15 November 2006, Online, available at: http://web.worldbank.org/WBSITE/EXTERNAL/NEWS/0,,contentMDK: 21131393~menuPK:64255981~pagePK:34370~piPK:34424~theSitePK:4607,00.html (accessed 31 January 2009).

World Bank Brussels Office (2007a) European Commission–World Bank Group 'Lime-lette' Partnership, background note for meeting with Civil Society Organization, Brussels, 26 April.

World Bank Brussels Office (2007b) 'The World Bank in Brussels', prepared by the World Bank Office in Brussels, June. Online, available at: www.worldbank.org/eu (accessed 31 January 2009).

# 11 The EU through the eyes of the United Nations

## The quest for unity

*Franziska Brantner*

## Introduction[1]

The 2003 European Security Strategy expresses a strong commitment to the United Nations (UN), highlighting that 'strengthening the United Nations, equipping it to fulfil its responsibilities and to act effectively, is a European priority' (European Council 2003). Diplomats from the 27 member states of the European Union (EU) meet about a 1,000 times a year in New York alone, and the EU presidencies issue approximately 200 statements on the Union's behalf during their six-month tenure. In addition, the EU Commission is now an important financial partner of the UN operational system on the ground.

Although EU unity has not yet been fully achieved at the UN Security Council – suffice it to think of the divisions over the war in Iraq in 2003 – the EU increasingly speaks with one voice inside the UN assembly across a wide range of issue areas (Luif 2003; Smith 2006a; Laatikainen and Smith 2006; Young and Rees 2005; Wouters *et al.* 2006). For instance, the EU has rarely split on votes at the Human Rights Council since its creation in 2006 (Brantner and Gowan 2008). This chapter studies whether such unity is reflected in perceptions of the EU at the UN. It focuses specifically on whether the EU is perceived as a unitary actor, with a selection of documents and interviews conducted in the UN hallways, UN Secretariat members and representatives of non-EU countries in New York.

First of all, it should be recognized that the EU has a 'split personality' at the UN as 'both an actor in its own right and an arena for the expression of member-state interests' (Jørgensen and Laatikainen 2006: 10). In this respect, the Security Council, with the two permanent members France and the United Kingdom, represents a regular test of the EU's 'actorness' (Hill 1996). On the whole, the collective 'presence' of the EU in the international arena has been achieved 'through cumbersome consultative procedures and partially effective diplomatic, economic and military instruments' (Hill and Wallace 1996: 13). Third countries are hence still left 'to cope with relations with the European Community (through the Commission) alongside bilateral relations with the Member States' (Hill and Wallace 1996: 13). The UN is also a forum and an actor at the same time. This creates a complicated net of interactions, which is likely to affect the way in which UN Secretariat staff and other UN state representatives perceive the EU and its member states. Two main questions will guide this analysis: (a) do UN officials and other UN members' delegates perceive the EU institutions – the Presidency and the Commission – or rather EU member states individually, as the key interlocutors? (b) what kind of actor do they think the EU is?

The structure of this chapter includes a preliminary part describing the cooperation framework between the EU and the UN system and the methodological approach. The central parts present the results of the study and are followed by an analysis of the potential factors influencing the perceptions of the EU at the UN.

## The context: EU–UN cooperation

While the European Community (EC) is an observer at the UN General Assembly (not at the Security Council) represented by the European Commission, the EU has no official status as it lacks legal personality. In areas such as trade and fisheries, the Commission represents EU member states, but in all other areas without full EC competency, the EU Presidency therefore speaks 'on behalf' of the EU.

Operationally, EU member states together are the largest financial contributor to the UN system, paying 38 per cent of the UN's regular budget, more than two-fifths of UN peacekeeping operations and around half of all contributions to voluntarily funded UN funds and programmes. A total of more than €1 billion was approved by the European Commission to be channelled to the UN system in 2007 for the implementation of projects and programmes.[2]

In 2003, the Commission agreed with the UN on an updated Financial and Administrative Framework Agreement, with the goal of facilitating programmatic cooperation. The Commission has furthermore signed formal strategic partnerships or initiated correspondence with over ten agencies.

In the peace and security field, Chapter VIII of the UN Charter provides for cooperation with regional organizations. Under this provision, the EU has cooperated with the UN regarding various conflicts, such as Chad and the Central African Republic among others. Furthermore, the EU is involved in a wide array of groups, such as the Middle East Quartet or the Millennium Development Goals Africa Steering Group, which the Secretary-General established to bring together the African Union, the EU and other multilateral organizations. The EU also financially supports other regional organizations, such as the African Union, to carry out UN Security Council mandates.

In order to clarify the context of this analysis, it might also be worth taking a brief look at the EU member states' behaviour at the UN. Despite the inherent limitations of voting analyses at the UN – as only a minor part of decisions are actually brought to a vote – voting patterns are one indicator of EU cohesiveness (Kissack 2007). Even in the most divisive period of the 2003 Iraq crisis, EU member states voted together on more than 60 per cent of the votes at the General Assembly; and at the best times the share of united voting is above 85 per cent (Brantner and Gowan 2008). Such cohesion should increase the likelihood of others perceiving the EU as a united actor.

## Methodology

The general difficulty of assessing perceptions (as discussed in the introduction to this volume) is further complicated by the complex net of dynamics involving both the UN and the EU. First, UN staff come from many different cultural, ethnic and social backgrounds. Some work in New York and Geneva, while others are operatives in conflict zones, administrators or senior managers. Some are regularly in contact with EU institutions while others are never in touch with them at all. This study focuses only on UN officials based in New York and Brussels who work closely with EU institutions and are supposedly knowledgeable about European policies.

Moreover, diplomats tend to have a general perception of the EU (say its domestic and external policies) and a specific evaluation of the EU's role within the UN. Even though these two types of perception are difficult to discern, this research focuses on how UN delegates perceive the EU's role *within* the UN core institutions (therefore excluding specific programmes, offices and parallel agencies operating within the extended UN family) rather than the actual EU per se.

This work draws on a variety of sources in order to increase the validity and reliability of the results. First of all, I analysed all UN Secretariat press releases from January 2007 to March 2008 containing the words 'European Union' or 'EU' in the body of the text, which resulted in 420 hits. Of these releases, 90 per cent report statements given by the EU Presidency with no commentary by the Secretariat. An additional 5 per cent explain the composition of the Middle East Quartet, listing the EU as one of the four actors composing it. Only the remaining 5 per cent really deal with the EU, providing in-depth information on how the EU is officially represented by the UN Secretariat.

An additional source of information was provided by the UN reports on financial cooperation with the European Commission in 2005, 2006 and 2007 and by the major annual publications prepared by the Division for Economic and Social Affairs within the UN Secretariat, the *World Economic Situation and Prospects* and the *World Economic and Social Survey* for the years 2005 to 2008. The latter group of publications covers facts and figures about economic and social development worldwide, including Europe.

Regarding perceptions of the EU among the wider UN membership community in New York, this chapter draws on the few session summaries of government statements at the General Assembly, which exceptionally relate some direct comments about the EU. Moreover, standardized interviews were conducted with UN member state diplomats in New York during two fieldwork sessions. The first set comprised 40 interviews carried out in 2006 and 2007 with high-level diplomats and officials, while the second set was undertaken in March 2008 resulting in 12 face-to-face interviews with non-European delegates to the General Assembly.[3]

The remainder of the chapter presents the perceptions of the EU at the UN, starting with perceptions transpiring from UN documents, then relating non-EU member state representatives' perceptions. It is understood that, given the complexity of the topic, data and results cannot be exhaustive.

## Perceptions of the EU in UN documents

### *Press releases and reports*

When analysing Secretariat discourse via its press releases and reports about UN–EU Commission financial cooperation, the Deputy Secretary-General rather than the Secretary-General emerges as the main interlocutor. These documents also present the EU and the UN as sharing the same *universal* values, as being partners and the UN as providing the legitimacy and the EU the resources. The following gives some citations to exemplify this pattern.

The UN report 'Improving Lives: results from the partnership of the United Nations and the European Commission in 2006' begins by highlighting that the UN and EU 'are united by common values and principles – by a shared commitment to the essential rights and freedoms outlined in the Charter of the United Nations' (United Nations 2007: 1).[4] According to the UN Deputy Secretary-General Asha-Rose Migiro, not only do the 'European Union and the United Nations have so much in common', but they are also 'founded on the same universal values', as the 'Union represents an unprecedented project towards the peaceful unification of a continent'.[5] The EU is also presented as a 'natural partner' because 'the EU is one of the great supporters of multilateralism' or because it is a regional organization, like the African Union, and regional organizations are partners of the UN under Chapter VIII.[6] At times a distinction is made between 'natural allies' and 'essential partners': the EU is a natural ally supposedly due to sharing the same values but also an 'essential partner' in terms of actually carrying out the common commitment and agenda.[7] In short: 'The United Nations and the European Union are engaged in a vital, tremendously complementary partnership.'[8]

Complementarities are identified as legitimacy on one side and material resources and innovation on the other. Whereas the EU's resources are crucial and welcomed, the 'comparative advantage' of the UN is its universal membership and therewith the legitimacy it can bring to EU activities.

The structure and substance of the report by the UN team in Brussels on the partnership between the UN and the EU Commission is a good example of this. The report attempts to categorize the cases in which the EC works in partnership with the UN; for example, when the EU prefers to spend its money via the UN rather than bilaterally or via another third agent. The report identifies the cases as the following: (i) on sensitive issues that require the legitimacy and impartiality of the UN, (ii) in fragile country situations where consistent field presence and combined UN mandates facilitate transition out of crises, (iii) where donor coordination is at a premium and (iv) in thematic areas where the UN has particular expertise.

The perception of UN officials is hence that the UN's legitimacy and expertise is an important element for EU decision makers, tilting their preference towards acting multilaterally via the UN instead of bilaterally or via other third actors. Implicitly this assumes that the EU lacks these elements; despite shared values, EU actions lack legitimacy.

We can find this logic in several other statements. For example, during a speech at the European Parliament, the Deputy Secretary-General repeated that:

> The United Nations brings to this relationship its unique global legitimacy and impartiality; its longstanding presence, especially in fragile countries; and its deep expertise in economic and social development.... You [the EU] bring resources, creativity, innovation and the inspiring example of a continent that has proved to the world that peace, stability and human security can be achieved through cross-border cooperation.[9]

The only time that the legitimacy–resources pattern is switched around is a press release by Carla Del Ponte, at the time Prosecutor of the International Criminal Tribunal for the Former Yugoslavia, calling upon 'European Union Member States and the European Commission [to] maintain their principled position by insisting on Serbia's full cooperation as a condition in the European Union pre-accession and accession process' in order to guarantee the legitimacy and functioning of the tribunal.[10] Carla Del Ponte establishes a link between the potential effectiveness of the UN mechanism and EU policies, where the effectiveness and credibility of the UN hinges upon the EU.

Besides this overall pattern, the EU is mentioned positively due to its leadership role in combating climate change and its peacekeeping efforts, but is called upon to engage more seriously in peacekeeping efforts in Africa.[11] Its support for the Millennium Development Goals is lauded, but the praise sounds more like a plea to the EU not to renounce on its commitment.

To summarize, the documents analysed share a positive tone in highlighting common values, which support the EU's normative discourse while drawing a line between the EU and the UN so as to avoid competition.[12] This feeds back into the funding dimension of the EU–UN partnership, the EU being the payer and the UN the global player. This perception might be influenced by the asymmetric power relationship due to funding dependencies as well as interaction variables in terms of concrete interface at the operational level.

### *UN publications in the economic and social field*

Given the EU's level of integration in the economic field, one might expect the major annual UN publications in this sector to report consistently on the EU as an entity and not only its member states individually. But the World Economic Situation and Prospects (WESP) and the World Economic and Social Survey

(WESS)[13] from 2005–2008 very inconsistently use either the EU or the member states as the relevant unit of analysis, though all heavily rely on European Commission statistics as a source of data – where both levels are always provided. The WESP 2007 statistical tables, for example, sometimes cover both EU member states and the aggregate EU level, some have only EU member states listed (such as for growth expectancies) and the table about foreign direct investments and textile imports mentions only the EU as an entity alongside the USA. The WESS 2007 addressed migration and ageing patterns within the EU while a similar 2001 UN study focused on specific countries including France, Germany, Italy and the United Kingdom (UK). There is hence recognition of the EU as the relevant level of analysis, but not consistently, and there is never an explanation as to why either the EU aggregate or the individual member state level is chosen.

Substantively, the reports mention in a positive light the economic impact of enlargement on the joining countries (WESS 2006). The WESP 2007 report is similarly upfront about benefits from the relocation of production to the ten new member states of the enlarged EU. It traces how firms have shifted production from the 15 old to the new EU member states with a clarity that EU internal reports often lack. But at the same time the reports warn against signs of increased EU protectionism and other distortions to world trade, for example limits on imports of certain Chinese textiles and the use of non-tariff barriers (WESP 2007). The WESS 2005 analyses, among other things, the impact of regional economic integration on global free trade. It distinguishes between earlier and more recent integration processes, identifying more recent cases as being open towards the outside, in contrast to the earlier EU project. Furthermore, the WESS 2006 report examines at length the long-term effects on economic development of 'European colonialism' (WESS 2006: 10, 127–30). It is highly critical of former European colonial powers and often hints at parallelisms between colonial policies and current EU trade policies.

Overall, while the facts presented are often based on EU statistics or policy interactions, their reading is tainted by broader framework variables, such as the North–South cleavage lens invoking memories of colonialism.

## Perceptions from non-EU delegates

If memories of colonialism were evoked by the Secretariat, what can be expected of the states delegates' perceptions of the EU? The following tries to identify a few trends that crossed regional differences. Furthermore, since 2003 and the beginning of the Iraq war, the UN has been haunted by the resurgence of a North–South divide (Benner 2006; Traub 2006). It is in this polarized political context that interviews have been conducted.

The interviews were conducted per issue area; diplomats at the UN in New York are responsible for specific issue areas, and the smaller the delegation, the more issue areas one diplomat must cover.[14] The first part of the standardized questionnaire required interviewees to identify the most relevant actors in their

*Table 11.1* Perception of the EU in different issue areas: 'do you agree that...'

| | Economic and social field | Human rights | Management | Peacebuilding | Security council | Total |
|---|---|---|---|---|---|---|
| ...the EU is a key actor? | 8 | 10 | 11 | 4 | – | 26 |
| ...the EU member states behave differently from the EU as a whole? | – | 2 | 2 | 11 | 10 | 25 |

Source: author's interviews.

Note
Cells show number of interviewees who agreed with the statement.

respective issue area. Next, they were asked about the role of the EU presidencies. The interviewees were then asked to characterize the role of the EU, in comparison with the United States of America (USA) and in relation to the challenges at stake in the area in question.

Regarding the first question, the results are clear: the EU is considered an important actor across issue areas, but with limitations that increase with the salience of the area to the five permanent members of the Security Council, as Table 11.1 shows.

When prompted about differences among presidencies, more than half of the interviewees answered in the same vein as one diplomat who said bluntly: 'It does not really matter who the presidency is: you anyway know who you have to speak to inside the EU.' However, they noted a difference in the style of the presidencies and individual diplomats' tones, which could either exacerbate or mollify existing tensions. Contingent interaction variables do hence complement broader power-related variables. The following will delve into each issue area to fine-tune the analysis.

### *The economic and social area*

All nine diplomats from the economic and social area identified the EU as a key actor together with the Group of 77 and the USA. This reflects the cohesive representation of the EU in this area. Overall, the EU is seen as playing a more positive role than the USA. For instance, they all believed that the EU, in contrast to the USA, would not want to reopen the Monterrey Consensus on 'Financing for Development'.[13] According to one interviewee: 'It is good that the Nordics guarantee that the other EU countries cannot bring the entire EU to renounce completely on its development commitments.'

Yet, the EU is not spared accusations of double standards. During the 2007 General Assembly debate, the Minister of Foreign Affairs of Guyana stated that: 'In a show of bad faith, the EU denounced the Sugar Protocol, which protected sugar-exporting countries in Africa, the Caribbean and the Pacific, contradicting its own sermons on partnership and good governance.'[16] Similarly, answers by diplomats on the role of the EU in the economic and social field at the UN were largely dominated by their perception of EU policies at the World Trade Organization (WTO). All developing country diplomats constantly referred to the EU's self-interested stance in the current WTO Doha Development Round and to what extent these negotiations would paralyse much of the UN economic and social processes. It is hence not so much direct interaction at the UN that influences perceptions, as policy interaction in another international forum.

### *Human rights*

It is worth mentioning that more emphasis is given to EU member states when analysing policies concerning human rights, especially the UK, Germany and France. The EU as a whole is viewed as the leader of the International Criminal Court although it was criticized for its lack of interest in economic and social rights. Some went so far as to argue that the EU is only perceived as a strong defender of human rights because the USA 'is so bad'.

The following statement by the delegate of Zimbabwe at the General Assembly is certainly an extreme accusation, but it contains two elements that were raised throughout the interviews with the human rights-focused diplomats. Despite speaking with one voice, the EU is perceived as being dominated by some of its member states, especially the UK and France. Second, and related to this, current European initiatives are filtered through Europe's colonial past:

> Instead of using human rights issues to settle political scores and carrying on arms races, the European Union and its allies should provide more resources to the fulfilment of those rights. The statement by the Union on human rights in Zimbabwe was inspired by the United Kingdom Government's objective of 'regime change' in the country, after it lost the war to perpetuate its subjugation.[17]

In a similar vein, during the debate about a moratorium on the death penalty, the representative of Singapore lamented that the EU 'wanted everyone to think as they did. When their values "shift", our values must also "shift"'.[18] This accusation of the EU's desire to impose its own values coupled with the reproach of 'neo-colonialism' was raised by all non-Western interviewees (nine out of 11). In this perspective, the perception of the EU is again based on concrete interaction but imbued in a world vision structured by colonial memories.

The EU was furthermore accused by all non-Western interviewees of double standards. The EU would only single out those countries for condemnation where the price of attack was not too high compared to potential gains. The interviewees did not criticize the EU per se for following such a utilitarian approach, but rather the EU blaming others for doing the same. As one delegate bluntly put it: 'The EU blames us for not defending human rights. They think we refuse to accuse certain countries because doing so would be too costly for us. But the EU does not want to acknowledge that it is doing just the same.' Another delegate from Africa further noted that the EU had the same tendency as the African Union to gang up to defend a member of its group under attack. This is echoed for example in the statement by the representative of Iran who maintained that since the EU 'turned a blind eye to its own problems with human rights', he wished 'to be informed of the existence of illegal detention centres within the European Union territory'.[19] In addition, the delegate from Indonesia criticized the incoherence between the EU's action at the UN and in other forums or in bilateral relations,[20] a recurrent topic throughout the interviews. These perceptions of double standards and incoherence are partially based on policies by the EU and its member states outside the UN context, but also on concrete EU choices at the UN in terms of selecting the countries to be targeted.

At another level, one interviewee argued that South Africa for example 'was second to none on human rights and democracy and that the behaviour of some EU ambassadors was just so humiliating'. In this example, it is the behaviour of individual EU member states' ambassadors that influences the perceptions of the EU, rather than an overall policy.

### *Management of the Secretariat*

In the management area concerned with the work, functioning and accountability of the UN Secretariat, all of the 11 expert diplomats mentioned the EU as a key actor, in addition to the USA, the G77 and Japan; two interviewees cited as key actors both the EU and France and the UK. During the ensuing conversation, interviewees recognized that they often summed up donors as the EU. The diplomats continued to describe a specific EU (and not Western) attitude as that of Europeans behaving as 'having on the right the crazy and unsophisticated USA, on the left the stupid developing countries, and both need our help'. Yet they themselves did not perceive the EU as being in the middle, but as a lighter version of the USA. For the majority of the diplomats interviewed, EU decisions to side with the American government on budgetary and management questions, such as the budget spending cap introduced in 2005 by the USA and the vote in 2006 on management reform, represented litmus tests for EU distinctiveness. Such moments 'defined where the EU is', for example, vis-à-vis the USA. This rendered it difficult or impossible for the EU to be the bridge-builder towards the South. Diplomats from developing and middle-income countries commented on 'Western triumphalism after the end of the Cold War', and a 'We won' ideology, translating into a Western attitude of 'We know how things should be done without any interest in what others think.' These perceptions are based both on broader geopolitical frameworks and visions of world order. On the other side of the spectrum we find comments from John Bolton, former US ambassador in New York, who grew infuriated with the EU's 'prodigious diplomatic "bridging"' and concluded that the USA should bargain with the G77, 'cut the deal we want, and marginalize the EU, thus also frustrating their global governance agenda' (Bolton 2007: 446).

Overall, the EU's attempts at being a 'bridge-builder' are hence recognized, but rendered impossible by its perceived closeness to the USA on one side and the Americans' rejection of such a role on the other.


## *Peace and security*

In the broader peacebuilding area, four out of the 11 diplomats mentioned the EU as a central actor and all underlined the EU's crucial role in bringing peace-building issues to the UN agenda. France and the UK were included by all as key actors. In the narrower Security Council area, the EU was not mentioned by any of the interviewees. When prompted to assess the EU's actorness in UN peacekeeping and peacebuilding, five of the 11 interviewees told in an amused way the story of EU representation at the new Peacebuilding Commission. The Commission, the Council Secretariat and the Presidency all wanted to play a role there, and this without the EU having a legal status at the UN. Only in December 2007 (two years after the establishment of the Peacebuilding Commission) did the Organizational Committee agree to allow the representatives of the Presidency of the Council of the EU and the European Commission to have two seats behind a single 'European Community' nameplate during future country-specific meetings.

While the importance of the European integration project in bringing peace to the European continent was underscored by two-thirds of the interviewees, the EU is rather seen as an alliance of interests when it comes to peacebuilding, which can be positive for the UN when these interests coincide with the wider UN membership. Seven of the 11 pointed out the difference in EU commitment to the Balkans and Africa or Asia, highlighting the Darfur crisis. France was identified as the leader of the EU's commitment and missions to Africa by all interviewees, independently of their origin. This was mostly seen as a 'Europeanization of French colonial policies', 'an attempt by France to give a multilateral flavour to bilateral relations' – but also as a welcomed coincidence of views between French, and partially British, interests on the African continent and humanitarian concerns. A lack of illusions as to EU motivations can easily change into suspicions as to their inspiration.

Regarding the deployment of EU troops, two patterns emerged: the EU seen as a rival to the United Nations and the EU troops as important partners for the UN. Those fearing EU competition critically claimed that common EU troops would diminish the likelihood of EU member states putting their soldiers at the disposal of the UN command. They also feared that short-term EU interventions would undermine the credibility of the UN forces in the longer term: 'The EU comes and goes with all capabilities and the UN's lack thereof is even clearer once the EU has left the field.' But the majority of interviewees welcomed the EU's capacities and identified a shift towards more openness with regard to regional groups in general following the parallel engagement of other regional units such as the Economic Community of West African States and the African Union on behalf of the UN. Nonetheless, the interviewees from developing countries all insisted that 'the UN had to remain the primary body'. Instead of direct EU troop intervention, all African, Asian and Latin American interviewees preferred the EU approach of capacity building and giving financial support to African peacebuilding efforts, such as the African Peace Facility. Nonetheless, the Africans raised a question mark as to the 'ownership' issue, and emphasized that its understanding still needed to be enhanced.

When prompted as to whether there was a distinction between the EU and the military forces of the North Atlantic Treaty Organization (NATO), all clearly pinpointed one, with NATO being 'purely linked to geopolitical interests' and the EU having the moral 'duty to export security after having exported insecurity around the globe for centuries'. But African diplomats were well aware that NATO helps in the deployment of EU troops to the African continent and that it was difficult to keep the two distinct on the ground.

To summarize, what emerges is a picture of the EU where its leadership role is recognized in the human rights area, and to a lesser extent in peacebuilding, but where its overall impact is limited by EU or EU member state policies outside UN hallways. This could be at the WTO or its bilateral human rights policy vis-à-vis Indonesia, as well as the EU's concrete policies at the UN, such as its stance on budgetary and management matters in defending donors' interests or human rights policy choices. Any EU policy is susceptible to reading through the 'neo-colonialism' lens, which seems to be an overarching framework of analysis for developing country diplomats. The latter can be related to the strong and again increasing group identity of the developing country coalitions, central to which is the North–South cleavage.

## Conclusions and recommendations

This chapter presents a first glimpse of how the EU is perceived at the UN. The EU is undeniably perceived as an actor. However, the parallel ongoing activism of its member states and the lack of coherence in its external action allow other actors to project everything and nothing on to the EU banner. Being divided into the intergovernmental arena of the Common Foreign and Security Policy (CFSP) and the supranational initiatives directed by the Commission, the EU is faced by a twofold challenge. The first challenge concerns lack of unity among EU member states, as the EU is automatically held responsible for everything its member states choose to do (or not to do) individually, without being in a position really to have an impact on their international strategies. The second challenge concerns the fact that when common positions are agreed among member states, they usually follow a lowest common denominator approach, which often tends to be too mild and ineffective in the international arena. Paradoxically, though, this 'soft unity' often triggers equally united opposite blocs at the UN, especially among less developed nations.

In all the documents studied and the interviews, non-EU actors tend to subsume EU member states, their history and policies, under the EU banner – or at least they do not clearly distinguish between proper 'EU' policies in terms of

CFSP or Commission policies, and those of its member states. External developments like EU politics at the WTO have an equal impact on perceptions of the EU as historical readings of colonialism and contingent interaction at the UN with the member states. The history, policies and behaviour of member state diplomats are hence projected on to and ascribed to the EU. Other actors try to identify and read EU policies via the lens with which they read the policies of its member states. For them, EU member states cannot escape their own past and current policies by hiding behind the EU 'normative power' shield. They do not tend to believe that EU member states change by merely acting together: for them, the Nordics are more inclined towards multilateralism and international solidarity; the former colonial powers want to maintain their sphere of influence; and the sum – that is, the EU – tends to reflect the latter, even if the former permit the EU to be perceived as 'less bad' than the USA. Even the Secretariat press releases, the most inclined to subscribe to a normative EU discourse, argue that the EU lacks the legitimacy to act on its own in third countries. Reading between the lines it transpires why: because of the history and current policies of its member states in those very third countries.

Furthermore, EU member states acting and speaking together impact the overall dynamics at the UN, especially at the General Assembly. UN member states' coalition patterns are influenced: EU member states with their individual interests do not necessarily align with those inside the UN that share their views, but first negotiate within the EU. African or Latin American states increasingly tend to do the same. The compromise within each group tends to be characterized by the least willing to promote universal human rights and multilateral action in order to achieve the goals of the UN as set out in its Charter. As a consequence, groups negotiate lowest denominator compromises instead of like-minded groups coming to agreements. This study cannot say how different the outcome of a compromise of compromises may be to an agreement negotiated between like-minded countries – with on one side those most interested in advancing multilateral action and the promotion of human rights and on the other those opposing such an agenda. However, the risk of polarization and bloc confrontation is real and EU member states should be aware of this consequence of unity, which might hamper the effective promotion of their interests.

This analysis makes it doubly difficult to make any easy recommendation. While the first dimension of the EU unity trap would suggest increasing unity even further, e.g. limiting the actions of individual EU member states and increasing cross-issue and cross-arena coherence, the second dimension could recommend loosening coordination and calls for more cross-regional outreach and alliances. Remedying the negative consequences of multiple actors perceived as 'the EU' might however increase the negative consequences of EU unity on UN negotiation dynamics. The EU is hence trapped.

Given this analysis, one exit strategy could be a shift from unanimity to majority voting when it comes to determining EU positions within UN forums. Unless this becomes a reality, when interests diverge within the EU, member states should seek to reach out to other actors across the system according to interest similarity, facilitated by looser EU cooperation mechanisms, instead of spending endless hours in order to reach a compromise, which does not inspire any other actor in the system. Also, it would be advisable to be aware of group dynamics and the blocking force of a North–South divide, and to avoid policies and behaviour that sustain and increase appearances of 'neo-colonialism'. More precisely, it would be wise to abandon a normative discourse that might give a sense of superiority in favour of discourse that is self-reflective and focuses on new alliances in order to define common agendas and policies for promoting universal human rights and sustainable development.

## Notes

1　I am grateful to Karen Smith, Knud Erik Jørgensen and the editors of this volume for their detailed comments, and to all those who accepted to be interviewed for this study and shared their insights with me.
2　For further information see the website of the European Commission at the United Nations, online, available at: www.europa-eu-un.org (accessed 31 January 2009).
3　Argentina, Brazil, Canada, Chile, Costa Rica, Cuba, Egypt, India, Jamaica, Japan, Kenya, Malaysia, Mexico, New Zealand, Nigeria, Pakistan, Panama, Peru, Russia, Rwanda, South Africa, Switzerland, Thailand, United States and Yemen. For some countries, I conducted interviews with several diplomats, one for each issue area.
4　The 2007 report about cooperation equally states: 'This year marks the 60th anniversary of the Universal Declaration of Human Rights, which lies at the heart of the cooperation between the UN and the Commission' (United Nations 2008: 11).
5　'Universal values make United Nations, European Union natural partners, says Deputy Secretary-General at concert marking body's 50th Anniversary', UN press release, 29 March 2007.
6　'United Nations, European Union share many objectives, Deputy Secretary-General says at launch of report in Brussels', UN press release, 15 March 2007; '"Life and Death" matter for millions, at European Union-Africa Summit, Deputy Secretary-General Asha-Rose Migiro to the European Union-Africa Summit in Lisbon, Portugal, on 8 December', UN press release, 10 December 2007.
7　'Reforms will make UN more responsive, accountable, Deputy-Secretary General says in Bonn meeting with European Union Development Ministers', UN press release, 13 March 2007.
8　'United Nations, European Union engaged in vital, complementary partnership, says Deputy Secretary-General in Strasbourg speech', UN press release, 14 March 2007.
9　'United Nations, European Union engaged in vital, complementary partnership, says Deputy Secretary-General in Strasbourg speech', UN press release, 14 March 2007. This citation raises another perception: the EU as a model for peace based on regional integration.
10　'Enduring freedom of suspects indicted on genocide charges "a stain" on former Yugoslavia tribunal's work, prosecutor tells Security Council', UN press release, 10 December 2007.
11　'Secretary-General welcomes European Union decision to establish targets for energy efficiency, use of renewable energy sources', UN press release, 9 March 2007; 'Security Council says drug trafficking undermines Guinea-Bissau peace consolidation, calls for urgent steps to confront threat', UN press release, 19 October 2007. See also 'Deputy Secretary-General says Africa's quest for development, human rights, peace, security is "Life and Death" matter for millions, at European Union–Africa Summit, Deputy Secretary-General Asha-Rose Migiro to the European Union–Africa Summit in Lisbon, Portugal, on 8 December', UN press release, 10 December 2007.

12 A normative power approach (Manners 2002) suggests that the EU is a spearhead of human rights and international law. As Thomas Diez underlines: 'One difference between the EU and the US, however, is that the US has sought to project, and often impose, its own norms while (unlike the EU) refusing to bind itself to international treaties' (2005: 622). Karen Smith echoes similar views when maintaining that: '[The] EU's foreign policy reflects the view that the imperatives of cooperation, and of compliance with international law and norms, limit the freedom of states to do whatever they wish domestically and externally' (2003: 199).

13 Data is online, available at: www.un.org/esa/policy/wess/wesp.html (WESP) and www.un.org/esa/policy/wess/index.html (WESS) (accessed 31 January 2009).

14 A total of nine interviews were conducted on the economic and social field, 11 on human rights, management and peacebuilding and ten on security.

15 The Monterrey Consensus was the outcome of the 2002 Monterrey Conference, the United Nations' International Conference on Financing for Development. New development aid commitments for the United States and the European Union and other countries were made at the conference.

16 'National security strategies, non-proliferation, "credible deterrence", conflicts in Horn of Africa among topics as General Assembly debate nears conclusion', UN press release, 2 October 2007.

17 'Capital punishment not prohibited under international law, Third Committee told', UN press release, 30 October 2007.

18 'Ten amendments to draft proposing moratorium on use of death penalty, rejected by recorded votes in Third Committee. Assembly called upon to ensure realization of Millennium Development Goals for persons with disabilities', UN press release, 14 November 2007.

19 'Third Committee calls on international community to focus on upcoming review of Madrid Plan of Action on Ageing', UN press release, 25 October 2007.

20 'Capital punishment not prohibited under international law, Third Committee told', UN press release, 30 October 2007.

## References

Benner, T. (2006) Editorial, *International Herald Tribune*, 4 October.

Bolton, J. (2007) *Surrender Is Not an Option: defending America at the United Nations and abroad*, New York: Threshold Editions/Simon & Schuster.

Brantner, F. and Gowan, R. (2008) *A Global Force for Human Rights? An audit of European power at the UN*, London: European Council on Foreign Relations.

Diez, T. (2005) 'Constructing the Self and Changing Others: reconsidering "normative power Europe"', *Millennium: Journal of International Studies*, 33 (3): 613–36.

European Council (2003) *A Secure Europe in a Better World: European security strategy*, Brussels: European Council, 12 December.

Hill, C. (ed.) (1996) *The Actors in Europe's Foreign Policy*, London: Routledge.

Hill, C. and Wallace, W. (1996) 'Introduction, Actors and Actions', in C. Hill (ed.) *The Actors in Europe's Foreign Policy*, London: Routledge.

Jørgensen, K.E. and Laatikainen, K.V. (2006) 'The EU @ the UN: multilateralism in a new key?' paper presented at the ISA Annual Convention, San Diego, CA, USA, 22–25 March.

Kissack, R. (2007) 'European Union Member States Coordination in the United Nations System: towards a methodology for analysis', *Working Paper 20071/1*, European Foreign Policy Unit.

Laatikainen, K.V. and Smith, K.E. (eds) (2006) *The European Union at the United Nations: intersecting multilateralisms*, Basingstoke: Palgrave Macmillan.

Luif, P. (2003) 'EU Cohesion in the UN General Assembly', *EU-ISS Occasional Paper 49*.

Manners, I. (2002) 'Normative Power Europe: a contradiction in terms?' *Journal of Common Market Studies*, 37 (3): 235–58.

Smith, K.E. (2003) *European Union Foreign Policy in a Changing World*, Cambridge: Polity Press.

Smith, K.E. (2006) 'Speaking with One Voice? European Union coordination on human rights issues at the United Nations', *Journal of Common Market Studies*, 44 (1): 113–37.

Traub, J. (2006) *The Best Intentions: Kofi Annan and the UN in the era of American world power*, New York: Farrar, Strauss, Giroux.

Wouters, J., Hoffmeister, F. and Ruys, T. (eds) (2006) *The United Nations and the European Union: an ever stronger partnership*, The Hague: TMC Asser Press.

United Nations (2007) 'Improving Lives: results from the partnership of the United Nations and the European Commission in 2006', United Nations System in Brussels. Online, available at: http://ec.europa.eu/development/icenter/repository/2nd-annual-report-on-EC-UN-relations-2006_en.pdf (accessed 31 January 2009).

United Nations (2008) 'Improving Lives: results from the partnership of the United Nations and the European Commission in 2007', United Nations System in Brussels. Online, available at: www.europa-eu-un.org/documents/en/UN-EC-partnership-report.pdf (accessed 31 January 2009).

Young, H. and Rees, N. (2005) 'EU Voting in the UN General Assembly, 1990–2002: the EU's Europeanising tendencies', *Irish Studies in International Affairs*, 19: 193–207.

# 12 Regional partners?

## Perceptions and criticisms at the African Union

*Daniela Sicurelli*

## Introduction

Since the early 2000s the relationship between European and African countries has witnessed key changes both in the type of actors involved and in the contents of the bi- and multilateral policies. The Cotonou Agreement in 2000, which reframed the overall development and trade relations between the EU and the countries from the African, Caribbean and Pacific group, the creation of the African Union (AU) in 2002 as an amalgamation of the outdated Organization of African Unity and the African Economic Community, and the series of European Security and Defence Policy (ESDP) missions in Africa from 2003 onwards have marked a turning point in Europe–Africa relations. These events have pushed in the direction of more institutionalized interregional relations, the liberalization of trade relations and the securitization of EU policies towards Africa.

Importantly, the creation of the AU as the institutional interlocutor for the EU provides a common platform for African governments to share their views, appreciation and criticisms of EU foreign policy. As a matter of fact, representatives of AU institutions often make explicit reference to the EU in their declarations, which further confirms that the AU can be seen as an important locus for collecting African views of the EU. The EU has gained such relevance in the African debate due to at least two factors. The first factor concerns the recent changes in EU trade and foreign policy towards Africa, which have intensified the relationship between the EU and African states. The second factor concerns the role of the EU as a reference point and successful model for the newly established AU. Despite these changes, though, the way AU leaders view the EU reveals a certain degree of continuity with traditional patterns of interaction between Africa and Europe. The colonial history binding the two continents still affects the image AU leaders have of the EU. The memory of the colonial past contributes to building expectations of compensation and disappointment when EU actions do not fulfil this need. Moreover, macro-structural factors, such as the asymmetric North–South distribution of power that has outlived colonization, tend to influence the way AU leaders view the EU.

This chapter aims to capture the different dimensions of the EU's image emerging from AU official documents, speeches and interviews with AU leaders.

It analyses the positions of representatives of subregional organizations (such as the Regional Economic Communities) and includes data on the AU member states' governments in order to provide a deeper look at the different voices emerging within the AU itself. As the main sectors in which EU–Africa relations play themselves out, the chapter will focus on trade policies and peace-keeping operations. The first part of the chapter analyses the key changes in the EU–Africa trade relationship and the reactions of AU leaders to these changes. The second part focuses on EU peacekeeping missions and analyses the perceptions of the EU in this sector. Finally, the chapter discusses the sectors that have contributed to shaping the various images and draws some recommendations for the EU with a view to building on the positive aspects of its relationship with the AU.

## Images of the EU at the AU

### Trade controversies

Reacting to pressures from the World Trade Organization (WTO) and to the common perception that the Lomé Conventions (1975–2000) had failed to respond to the development needs of African, Caribbean and Pacific (ACP) countries, the new Cotonou Agreement signed in 2000 marked the beginning of a liberalization philosophy with respect to trade relations between Europe and the ACP. The two parties committed to building the foundations for free trade areas within the ACP region and with EU counterparts. Between 2000 and 2007, the EU promoted the creation of subregional organizations within the ACP group in order to conclude separate Economic Partnership Agreements (EPAs) with each regional grouping. In the case of African countries, the subregional group-ings only partially overlap with pre-existing regional economic communities and customs unions.

Despite directly involving only sub-Saharan countries, EPAs became a con-tended issue between the EU and the whole of Africa during the course of 2007. This eventually led to the impossibility to reach an agreement with all African partners by the end of the year as had been requested by the WTO waiver granted to the EU and ACP.

EU positions in the EPA negotiations have raised critical remarks from African negotiators. A first key criticism concerns the volume of liberalization the EU expects from ACP countries. According to article 24 of the General Agreement on Tariffs and Trade (GATT), liberalization in a free trade area should cover 'substantially all trade'. The GATT does not specify, however, what percentage of trade should fall under this term. The EU proposed to define 'substantially all trade' as 90 per cent of trade between the EU and ACP. The AU rejected this proposal, lamenting the 'EC's rather restrictive interpretation of Article 24 of GATT 1994 as it relates to the definitions of substantially all trade' (AU 2008). According to a representative of the ACP secretariat: 'Some African countries argue that 70% (or even 60%) of the ACP products should be subject to liberalization, not 80% as the EU says. 70% can be accepted by the WTO.'[1]

A second criticism concerns the relationship between trade and development. According to AU leaders, EU pressures for the liberalization of African economies do not appear equally supported by development assistance projects. In this respect, in 2006 the AU trade ministers expressed their 'profound disappointment at the stance taken by negotiators of the European Commission in so far as it does not adequately address the development concerns that must be the basis of relations with Africa' (AU 2006). A year later the AU trade ministers noted the 'delay by the European Commission to respond to certain issues submitted by the African negotiators related, *inter alia*, to the development dimension' (AU 2007a). This concern recalls the complaint raised by ACP negotiators involved in the EPAs (see Chapter 9 in this volume). More generally, the problem raised by the AU seems to mirror a perception, shared by ACP representatives, of a loss of importance of African development for the EU. A representative at the Brussels headquarters of the ACP Secretariat pointed out that the attention of EU trade commissioners to development aid has decreased in recent times, with the transition from the socialist Pascal Lamy (Commissioner from 1999 to 2004), who was more prone to take African development concerns into account, to the British Labour minister Peter Mandelson (Commissioner from 2004 to 2009).[2]

AU leaders argue that not only does the EU overlook the development demands of its African counterparts, but it also limits EU market access for African products, thereby contributing to keeping African economies in a disadvantaged position. Notwithstanding its pressures for liberalization agreements, the EU has not yet dismantled protectionist measures against foreign products. In the words of representatives of the AU Commission's Department of Trade and Industry:

> Africa has … pointed out the extensive protectionism and subsidisation done in developed countries including in Europe. The protectionism limits trade opportunities for African producers. The subsidisation of European producers gives them an unfair advantage over African producers, again limiting trade opportunities.
>
> (AU 2007b)

The problem is evident especially in the case of sugar. Erastus Mwencha, the Secretary-General of the Common Markets for Eastern and Southern Africa, said that the EU should take special care of nations that depend on sugar exports. EPA negotiations have not solved this problem, as most agricultural products are included in the liberalization process. According to the trade ministers of the AU member states, the lack of market access for African products is still a key problem for AU–EU relations (AU 2007a). A survey by the African Trade Policy Center (2007), based on a questionnaire to representatives of African subregions involved in the EPA negotiations, specifies that duty-free access to the

European market, especially when it comes to agricultural goods, is the major concession the delegates of African regions participating in the EPAs expect from the EU.

The way in which the European Commission has operated to secure the various EPAs has also affected the way in which the EU promotes regional integration in Africa. In this regard, the perceptions of AU leaders are mixed. Some African leaders consider EU pressures for intra-African integration as a positive step towards further economic and political integration in Africa. For example, the Ghanaian Chairperson of the Economic Community of West African States, Mohamed I. Chambas, recognizes the contribution of EU trade policy to fostering unity among African negotiators (Ndiaye 2007). Similarly, the AU Commission's Department of Trade and Industry states that 'the emphasis given to regional integration [by the EU] is welcome, as the economic integration of Africa is the overarching development strategy adopted by Africa' (AU 2007b).

At the same time, though, the EU strategy aimed at dividing Africa into subregional groupings for the EPA negotiations is viewed by the AU as being at odds with its parallel promotion of pan-African integration and, perhaps, as revealing the traditional 'divide-and-rule' approach adopted by European countries during the colonial era. A representative of the AU Permanent Mission in Brussels argued that this inconsistency undermined the efforts of the AU Commission to coordinate the African subregions involved in the EPA negotiations. 'The EU breaks these efforts because it provides each region with different offers, which end up putting them one against the other.'[3] In this respect, the AU seems to voice the same concern that was expressed by ACP negotiators (as shown in Chapter 9). In the eyes of several AU representatives, more specifically, EU positions in the EPA negotiations clash with the results of previous attempts by African countries to bring about economic integration in Africa. Representatives of the AU Department of Trade and Industry argued that:

> Africa has been firm in insisting that EPAs must not undermine the process of economic integration in Africa. Projections are that, with reciprocal trade under EPAs, intra-Africa trade will be reduced by up to 16%; and that European imports will displace intra-regional exports. Such reduction of intra-Africa trade does not promote and strengthen economic integration in Africa; rather, it enhances the lopsided colonial oriented trade structures.
>
> (AU 2007b)

Given this inconsistency between EU economic strategies and its political support to pan-African integration, AU trade ministers concluded by declaring their expectation that 'the African regions will be allowed to pursue their regional integration processes at a pace that is commensurate with their political, economical and social capacities' (AU 2007a). Moreover, African leaders involved in the EPA negotiations lamented their difficult position in the talks, given their lack of expertise and technical knowledge, which increased the asymmetric power relations between the parties in the negotiations (African Trade

Policy Center 2007). AU trade ministers also underlined the lack of support from the EU to cover this 'knowledge gap' and lamented the 'lack of completion of country-specific impact assessment studies' by the time negotiations began (AU 2007a).

When it was clear that the deadline for the EPA negotiations needed to be extended, the negative reactions of AU leaders to the EU positions in the negotiations appeared even more explicit. In the ninth AU summit that took place in Accra (Ghana) in 2007, AU member states remarked on their dissatisfaction with the EU positions towards the EPAs and urged 'the EU to consider putting in place transitional measures that will safeguard the continued entry of African exports to the EU market beyond December 2007' (AU 2007e). The EU addressed this request by proposing interim agreements aimed at reducing the effects of the stalemate on the negotiations. Nevertheless, as of December 2007, only 18 out of 47 of the sub-Saharan African countries had accepted to endorse interim deals with the EU.

Even the concluded interim deals were not able to reduce the main problems perceived by AU leaders. After the December 2007 deadline had expired, the AU Commissioner for Trade and Industry remarked that the AU regions involved in the EPA negotiations had requested the EU:

> to give binding commitments on the provision of adequate, predictable and additional resources, over and above European Development Fund (EDF), to deal with supply-side constraints, to build production and trade capacities, and to meet the adjustment costs of opening African markets to EU products

but these requests were 'not [...] addressed by the EU' (AU 2008). According to the Commissioner, the interim agreements 'have also resulted in the breaking of solidarity and unity of our Member States and the weakening rather than the strengthening of Africa's regional integration initiatives'.

Finally, even the Everything But Arms (EBA) scheme, which grants free access to the least developed countries (LDC), raised criticism among African leaders, specifically in those countries excluded by the EBA. African trade ministers criticized the fact that the EBA undermines the principle of 'equal treatment for all', which is the basis of the WTO (Epawatch 2005). In a declaration by AU trade ministers, it was asked to maintain 'duty free and quota free treatment for least developed countries' and extend 'the same treatment to African non-least developed countries' (AU 2006). A representative of the ACP Secretariat explained the problem raised by the EBAs, arguing that 'since it establishes different relations with the LDCs and the other ACP countries, it disrupts regionalization. It makes harmonization of policies difficult.'[4] Table 12.1 presents a summary of the main view of the EU as a trade actor in Africa.

*Table 12.1* AU views of EU trade policy

| EU actions | AU views |
| --- | --- |
| EU promotion of liberalization | The AU shares the EU position in favour of liberalizing the African economy, but it provides a more flexible interpretation of WTO requirements. |
| EU development cooperation measures | The AU laments that the EU does not provide substantial development measures in support of the liberalization of African trade and does not provide African products with sufficient access to the EU market. |
| EU promotion of regionalization | The AU supports EU attempts to promote regional integration, but it considers these efforts as inconsistent and, ultimately, ineffective. |

## *Partnership for peace?*

The EU started to be involved in peace operations and democracy support in Africa in the 1980s. Yet its involvement has radically increased over time, especially since 2000. This activism has raised positive reactions from AU leaders, but also cautious remarks. On the one hand, they positively acknowledge the European contribution to peace and stability in Africa and the model of peace-through-integration the EU promotes with its example. On the other hand, they have expressed their concern over the actual limits of the EU as a security actor and its attempt to impose its own norms on AU member states.

Back in the 1960s, the then European Economic Community (EEC) began to devise programmes to support human rights and democratization (mainly through the EDF). During the 1980s, the EEC started imposing sanctions for human rights violations in Africa and, in the following decade, the first European election observation missions took place. Since 2000, the number of election monitoring missions implemented by the EU in Africa has increased, as well as the number of economic and diplomatic sanctions against African regimes accused of violating human rights and democratic norms. Since 2002, the EU has imposed diplomatic sanctions against the Zimbabwean President Mugabe and his government, accused of human rights violations and election rigging. More recently, the EU has threatened to impose sanctions against the Sudanese government if those responsible for the genocide and human rights abuse are not reported before the International Criminal Court.

Moreover, since the establishment of the ESDP in 2003 the EU has carried out more than 20 missions aimed at contributing to conflict prevention and management in sub-Saharan Africa, from the Democratic Republic of Congo to Chad. Since 2004, the EU has also begun to finance AU-led conflict management and prevention initiatives, through the so-called African Peace Facility, which has been used so far to co-fund peacebuilding activities in Sudan and Somalia. Finally, in the past ten years the EU has introduced conditionality measures to promote human rights in Africa, ranging from the human rights clause of the Cotonou Agreement to the conditions attached to the so-called 'Generalized System of Preferences (GSP) Plus', which requires beneficiary countries to ratify a number of international conventions concerning core human and labour rights, good governance and environmental issues.

Overall, AU perceptions of the EU in peacekeeping and democracy promotion are more positive than those triggered by EU trade policy (see Table 12.2 for a summary). The preference of the EU for civilian operations and long-term peacebuilding strategies based on conflict prevention has raised broad consensus within the AU. 'The Africa–EU Strategic Partnership' adopted in the Lisbon Summit (8–9 December 2007) elaborates on this shared view of peacebuilding. According to this document:

> Due to their history and experience, Africa and Europe understand the importance of peace and security as preconditions for political, economic and social development. On this basis, the two continents have laid the foundation for successful cooperation based on the need to promote holistic approaches to security, encompassing conflict prevention and long-term peace-building, conflict resolution and post-conflict reconstruction, linked to governance and sustainable development, with a view to addressing the root causes of conflicts.

Furthermore, AU leaders tend to depict the EU as a model of achieving and maintaining peace. Back in 2002, Ambassador Said Djinnit (at that time Assist-

*Table 12.2* AU views of EU peacekeeping policies

| EU actions | AU views |
| --- | --- |
| EU promotion of the European model of peace through integration | The AU recognizes the EU peace and security model, but AU member states express resistance to delegating sovereignty to the supra-national level. |
| EU support of AU-led peacekeeping missions | The EU decision to co-fund AU peacekeeping missions through the African Peace Facility is considered positively. Nevertheless, AU representatives criticize the decision of the EU to finance the facility with funds destined to the ACP, rather than to open a new chapter of development funds for the AU. |
| ESDP operations | The AU welcomes ESDP operations as long as they are based on an AU–EU agreement. Criticisms against the implementation of these operations, though, concern the modest mandate and internal division of the EU. |
| EU promotion of democracy and human rights | EU attempts to promote democracy and human rights in the African continent are considered positively by the AU as long as they do not take place through hard measures (such as sanctions and other types of conditionality). |

ant Secretary-General of the Organization for African Unity, in charge of political affairs) considered the EU as a model of integration. In a document entitled *Building an Effective African Union* he argued:

> I strongly believe that an effective African Union should be built on a solid ground and on a set of shared values in the areas of security, stability, development and cooperation. The EU construction has been possible only when the European countries agreed on common values to sustain their common endeavour.

(Djinnit 2002)

More recently, referring to the challenges Africa has to face in the fields of peace and security, governance and economic globalization, Maxwell M. Mkwezalamba, Commissioner for Economic Affairs at the AU Commission, clearly stated that the EU should be a model for Africa: 'In view of the significant progress made by the European Union in similar endeavours, the AU stands to draw valuable lessons from the European experience' (Mkwezalamba 2007).

That said, the willingness of AU leaders to learn from the EU model has its limits. In fact, AU leaders do not share with the Europeans the need to pool sovereignty. Members of the AU Commission argue that the establishment of the AU has affected the distribution of sovereignty in the African continent, but only to a limited extent. According to the Commission, while the Organization of African Unity was based on a purely intergovernmental approach, the creation of the AU has made the 'community and inter-governmental approach possible'. Beside the 'respect for national authority', the AU has also introduced the 'right to intervene' in member states' domestic politics. At the same time, though, the Commission stresses that the AU has this right to intervene only 'in grave circumstances' (AU 2004a: 23–4).

In a way, it is fair to argue that AU member states do not hold similar views when it comes to the possibility of sharing sovereignty. Publicly, many will probably agree with the Algerian Foreign Affairs Minister who argued that the AU needs to go beyond negative integration and that 'a resolute effort would have to be made to harmonise institutions and economic policies at continental level' (AU 2007c). At the same time, though, there is enough evidence that African leaders are not willing to give up any significant component of their national sovereignty. As maintained by a Mauritian diplomat in Brussels, the African leaders and public do not share the Europeans' willingness for a political union.[5]

EU peacekeeping operations in Africa have also received positive and negative feedback. Not surprisingly, positive reactions have been expressed on the establishment of the African Peace Facility, which followed a request by the AU to combine 'strong African ownership of programme design and implementation with provisions for strategic and political EU-level involvement' (European Union and African Union 2007). Said Djinnit, AU Commissioner for Peace and Security, argued that the facility was crucial in order to make AU peacekeeping missions possible and that '[t]his is particularly true with the current efforts at peacekeeping in the Darfur region which enabled the AU to extend the mandate of the mission in Sudan by three months as a result of the contribution of 30 million Euro by the EU' (Djinnit, quoted in Reuters 2006). The way the facility was implemented, though, raised criticism from the AU leadership. A key problem is that, in order to finance this peace instrument, the EU uses the EDF budget, which is formally meant for development cooperation. AU Commissioner Djinnit pointed at the negative consequences of this choice, arguing that: 'the commitment of European funding initially earmarked for development to finance peacekeeping operations raised ethical and moral problems' (Djinnit 2007). Another problem highlighted by a representative of the AU mission in Brussels was that 'European funds for the facility are allocated to the ACP group first, and to the AU only at a later stage. This contributes to increasing bureaucracy and delays.'[6]

Also the results of the ESDP missions and EU support to African governments in conflict areas (from Darfur to the Democratic Republic of Congo and Somalia) have been criticized for their inconsistency and limited effectiveness. With respect to the EU mission to Darfur, the Chairperson of the AU Commission, Konare, hailed the cooperation between the AU, the United Nations (UN), the United States of America, Canada and the EU that led to the signing of the Darfur Peace Agreement, as a report in the AU Commission official newsletter notes. Nevertheless, the newsletter continues, this international effort involving the EU was not completely effective in furthering peace in Darfur, since 'two rebel groups are still holding out' (AU Commission 2006). In order to assess the EU contribution to peacebuilding in Darfur, the Deputy Secretary-General of the UN, Mallock-Brown, also pointed at the need of the EU to strengthen its internal cohesion:

> The EU is important because I suspect that [the government in Sudan] sees differences of emphasis even within Europe. If Barroso can narrow those differences and give a sense of demonstrating a common Europe anxiety and urgency, then that is the key.
>
> (Beatty 2006)

The first military mission of the EU in the Democratic Republic of Congo (Artemis), which took place in 2003, is emblematic of the different reactions of AU leaders with respect to European programmes aimed at improving security and humanitarian conditions. The South African contribution of troops to Artemis confirms that the role of the EU in this field is positively appreciated, particularly if one considers the key role of South Africa in the AU security policy. Nevertheless, the head of the UN mission in Bunia, Alpha Sow, raised criticisms about Artemis, pointing at its limited scope, and therefore effectiveness, because of its short mandate and the small region it targeted (Sow 2004).

Another key case that shows the perception of the limits in the EU peacebuilding strategy is the contribution of the EU to solving the Somali crisis. On the one hand, AU leaders consider EU involvement in the Horn of Africa crucial for the stabilization of the area. In 2004 the AU Peace and Security Council described the financial support provided by the EU to the peace process in Somalia as 'badly needed' (AU 2004b). A representative of the AU mission in Brussels commented that EU support for the Traditional Federal Government in Somalia was welcome, as it was the outcome of an agreement with the AU.[7] On the other hand, the assessment of the contribution of the EU to bringing peace to Somalia appears more cautious. Abdullahi Mohamed Dualeh, the Foreign Minister of the self-declared state of Somaliland, commented that attempts by the EU to build peace were bound to fail because of the EU support of Somalia's Transitional Federal Government, which appears unwilling to reconcile the country's many ethnic groups, as EU officials came to admit later on (Beatty 2007).

Besides peacekeeping activities, EU initiatives of democracy promotion and human rights have also proved successful in gathering a certain degree of consensus among African leaders, although even in this case the EU was not spared criticism. Back in 1994, the Council of the Organization of African Unity stated that the EU was a major partner of democracy promotion in South Africa and commented on 'the positive contribution of the UN, the Commonwealth and the European Union Observer Missions in South Africa' after the end of apartheid (OAU 1994). Similarly, the AU Political Affairs Directorate recently noted that:

> The establishment of the Resource Center for Governance, Democracy and Human Rights of the AU testifies to the partnership between the African Union, the European Union and the Office of the United Nations High Commissioner for Human Rights to promote Governance, Democracy, Human Rights and Gender Equality as the cornerstones of Africa's renaissance.
>
> (Shawul 2005)

Nevertheless, the use of conditionality measures in the fields of *human rights*, such as those included in the GSP Plus provisions, raised harsh criticism among AU leaders. A representative of the AU pointed at the neo-colonial features of these conditionalities.[8] This concern also emerged from declarations of representatives of African civil society. In this respect, the Chair of the Cluster session of the African Civil Society Organizations' Consultation, Bayo Olukoshi, remarked that Africa should be a co-definer of conditionality measures as 'there is no basis for Africa to accept conditions that are pre-determined by others as pre-conditions for partnerships' (AU 2007d).

Finally, EU promotion of human rights through sanctions raises different comments within the AU, as shown by the case of Zimbabwe. The decision of Mugabe to participate in the AU–EU Lisbon Summit in 2007 triggered a harsh debate within the EU. A group of EU member states, led by the United Kingdom, was against his participation, in accordance with the sanctions imposed by the EU, whereas other member states were less rigid in opposing his presence. Finally, the EU accepted his presence in Lisbon. This debate within the EU raised mixed reactions from AU leaders. On the one hand, AU member states supported the EU in expressing its concern about crucial cases of bad governance and human rights violations in Zimbabwe (Kotsopoulos and Sidiropoulos 2007). On the other hand, the President of the AU Commission, Alpha Ouman Konare, said:

> What we would like is the summit between the EU and Africa, a very important and historic summit, to concentrate on the documents which are to be approved and not on President Robert Mugabe. [...] There are problems of governance, but Africans themselves have to sort these out, to tackle them head on. Otherwise we won't be able to get beyond our difficulties.
>
> (Doyle 2007)

These statements confirm that the AU officially shares EU concern for human rights violations in Zimbabwe, but suggest that even AU leaders did not consider this problem a priority for key AU–EU summits such as that of Lisbon.

## Understanding EU images

The analysis of public declarations, official documents and face-to-face interviews with leaders and officials of the AU reveal that this young regional organization has been vocal in expressing both positive and negative assessments of the EU, especially with respect to trade and peacekeeping policies. AU representatives depict the EU as a model for integration and a key partner for economic development and democratization. At the same time, though, they point out the lack of coherence between EU trade and development policies and criticize the way in which the EU imposes its model of integration and its conditions for development aid. At times, they also question the effectiveness of the EU as a partner for conflict management and peacebuilding in certain areas.

It appears that changes in EU–Africa relations since the turn of the millennium have contributed to shaping a multifaceted image of the EU in the eyes of the AU. While representatives of AU institutions continue to consider the EU a supporter of the integration of African markets into the global economy and a crucial partner in the construction of peace in Africa, they nevertheless detect meaningful limits in the way the EU promotes liberalization and security. Indeed, AU leaders assess the success and limits of EU trade and foreign policies on the basis of their economic and security interests. It is worth noting that other variables also contribute to explaining how AU leaders interpret EU actions, that is to say, identity and historical and structural variables. First, the way AU leaders view the EU can be understood in the context of the AU's own process of identity building. The AU is constructing its own identity as a regional organization in comparison to the EU, both taking inspiration from that model and highlighting the differences from it. AU declarations depict the EU as a successful experiment of conflict prevention and economic cooperation that can be exported to Africa and, thus, contributes to the AU's self-representation as a trade and security organization. Nevertheless, the AU warns against 'how' this influence is exerted, which might easily turn into a forceful imposition of conditions, pace and direction on to Africa rather than an incentive for this continent to find its own way towards integration.

Second, the importance of the 'colonial factor' emerges from the speeches and interviews. For instance, criticisms of the EU's hard tactics, such as economic protectionism and conditionality measures, explicitly recall the asymmetric relationship of the colonial era. Moreover, the tone adopted by AU leaders when criticizing the limitations of the EU development policy is undoubtedly influenced by an expectation of 'compensation' filtering their discourse about Europe and the EU. In a sense, it also appears that the rhetoric of EU leaders on the development power of Europe further contributes to increasing the expectations/response gap in the eyes of AU representatives.

Third, the disadvantaged position of African countries in the global distribution of economic and technological resources, which is only partially associated with the colonial past, clearly affects the way AU leaders view the EU. AU representatives tend to remark on their relative lack of expertise in the international negotiations as an indicator of this asymmetric relation with the global North, of which the EU is a key component. From these declarations, the EU appears as a powerful bloc and an unequal counterpart, which contributes towards keeping Africa countries in a subordinated position.

## Conclusions and recommendations

AU reactions to EU policies provide key challenges for EU policies towards Africa. These challenges increase further if one takes into account that other international players are interested in establishing political relations with the AU. China, India and Russia, among others, are becoming more and more attractive for the AU as partners in development and peace (Wissenbach 2007; McCormick 2008). While these partners do not have the same colonial baggage as the EU, they seem to be more lax when it comes to conditionality measures. If the EU is genuinely interested in strengthening its partnership with African countries 'as equals', as the Portuguese Presidency stated in the Lisbon Summit, then it will need to take into account the emergence of these competing powers and their potential impact on EU–Africa relations.

In this regard, it is paramount that the EU provides answers to the reiterated requests of the AU and its member states. First, the call for coherence between EU development and trade policy. The EU has tried to address this demand by reforming the Lomé agreements in Cotonou, but the failure of the EPA negotiations proves that no relevant progress has been made in this direction. Other attempts to reform EU development cooperation policy are visible in the decision to untie its aid allocation to Africa, following a recommendation from the Organization for Economic Cooperation and Development. Parallel to this process, the time has come for the EU to adopt serious measures to allow access to the European market for African goods, especially those that are sensitive for the economy of African countries. As repeatedly underlined by African leaders and opinion makers, the EU will also need to simplify its complex system of non-tariff barriers, such as rules of origins and production standards for imported goods. Moreover, a decision to extend the EBA agreement to all African countries that do not belong to the LDC group, proposed by the AU but also by the Swedish, Danish and UK governments in 2002 (Elgström and Pilegaard 2008), would help provide AU countries as a whole with greater opportunities to become fully integrated in the global market.

Second, EU negotiators should try to address the demand by African representatives for a better knowledge of their political and economic contexts in order to build local expertise. This demand has been expressed with respect to both trade policy and peacekeeping operations. As far as trade policy is concerned, EU institutions should coordinate with local negotiators in order to gather data on the country-specific economic context and be able to adjust their positions to those contexts. Moreover, the EU should provide AU subregions with expertise and technical assistance in order to strengthen their capacity to take advantage of trade with Europe. More specifically, capacity-building programmes aimed at supporting the harmonization of customs policies within the AU would contribute to intra-African trade liberalization. The EU should also try to find an agreement with AU negotiators on the timing of the removal of the preferential trade relationship with ACP countries compatibly with the schedule required by the process of trade liberalization within sub-Saharan regions. With respect to peacekeeping, EU institutions are called upon to gather systematic information on local conflicts and their implications for civilian populations. To this end, the EU should improve the coordination of European delegates in Africa (the special representatives and the external delegations of the European Commission). Furthermore, it should further increase its diplomatic presence in the continent, for example, by appointing a Special Representative to Somalia, following a proposal of the Italian and Swedish governments.

Finally, to address the criticism against its attempt to impose models of integration, the EU needs to take into account the steps African countries have already taken in the direction of integration and *leave it up to the AU and the subregional groupings to define their pace of integration*. At the same time, though, the EU should provide these organizations with the incentives to build on these steps. More specifically, in order to foster intra-Africa integration, it should encourage infrastructure development within these subregions, which would contribute to improving internal communication and trade.

These proposed changes in European policies towards Africa would probably bring about relative economic costs for the EU in the short term. Nevertheless, they are functional to redefining the way AU leaders perceive the EU. Only by improving its image as an equal partner and positive model can the EU overcome its historical label of colonial power, and compete with emerging powers that are appearing more and more attractive for Africa.

## Notes

1 Interview in Brussels, 16 September 2008.
2 Interview in Brussels, 8 February 2007.
3 Interview in Brussels, 15 September 2008.
4 Interview in Brussels, 8 February 2007.
5 Interview in Brussels, 13 February 2007.
6 Interview in Brussels, 16 September 2008.
7 Interview in Brussels, 16 September 2008.
8 Interview in Brussels, 13 February 2007.

## References

African Trade Policy Centre (2007) 'EPA Negotiations: African countries continental review', 19 February. Online, available at: www.africa-union.org (accessed 31 January 2009).

AU (2004a) 'Mission and Vision of the African Union, Strategic Plan of the African Union Commission', 1, Addis Ababa, May. Online, available at: www.africa-union.org (accessed 31 January 2009).

AU (2004b) 'Communiqué of the Solemn Launching of the Tenth Meeting of the Peace and Security Council', PSC/AHG/Comm. (X), Addis Ababa, 24 May. Online, available at: www.africa-union.org (accessed 31 January 2009).

AU (2006) 'AU Conference of Ministers of Trade', Fourth Ordinary Session, 12–14 April. Online, available at: www.africa-union.org (accessed 31 January 2009).

AU (2007a) 'Conference of Ministers of Trade of the African Union', Third Extra-ordinary Session, Addis Ababa, 15–16 January. Online, available at: www.africa-union.org (accessed 31 January 2009).

AU (2007b) 'Brief on Negotiations for Economic Partnership Agreements', African Union Commission Department of Trade and Industry, 26 May. Online, available at: www.africa-union.org (accessed 31 January 2009).

AU (2007c) 'Second Conference of African Ministers in Charge of Integration' (COMAI II), Ministerial Conference, Kigali, 26–27 July. Online, available at: www.africa-union. org (accessed 31 January 2009).

AU (2007d) 'Report of the African Civil Society Organizations' Consultation on AU/EU Joint Strategy for Africa's Development', Accra, 26–28 March. Online, available at: www.africa-union.org (accessed 31 January 2009).

AU (2007e) 'Decision on the Status of Negotiations of Economic Partnership Agreements with the European Union', Doc EX.CL/358 (XI), Ninth AU Summit, Accra, 25 June to 6 July. Online, available at: www.africa-union.org (accessed 31 January 2009).

AU (2008) 'Statement by Mrs Elisabeth Tankeu, AU Commissioner for Trade and Industry', Opening Session of the Conference of Ministers of Trade and Finance, Addis Ababa, 3 April. Online, available at: www.africa-union.org (accessed 31 January 2009).

AU Commission (2006) 'Chairperson Visits Darfur to Assess the Situation', *AU Commission News*, 10 June. Online, available at: www.africa-union.org (accessed 31 January 2009).

Beatty, A. (2006) 'Mallock Brown's Last Push for Darfur', *European Voice*, 12 (36). Online, available at: http://europeanvoice.com (accessed 31 January 2009).

Beatty, A. (2007) 'Presidency Ponders Special Envoy to War-torn Somalia', *European Voice*, 13 (17). Online, available at: http://europeanvoice.com (accessed 31 January 2009).

Djinnit, S. (2002) 'Building an Effective African Union', speech, Addis Ababa, 7 March. Online, available at: http://uneca.org (accessed 31 January 2009).

Djinnit, S. (2007) 'Speech at the UN Security Council 5649th Meeting', S/PV.5649: 7, New York, 28 March. Online, available at: http://undemocracy.com (accessed 31 January 2009).

Doyle, M. (2007) 'Tough Issues Dog Ambitious Summit', *BBC News*, Lisbon, 9 December. Online, available at: http://news.bbc.co.uk (accessed 31 January 2009).

Elgström, O. and Pilegaard, J. (2008) 'Imposed Coherence: negotiating economic partnership agreements', *Journal of European Integration*, 30 (3): 363–380.

Epawatch (2005) 'The Financial Times Highlights Differences between Mandelson and African Trade Ministers on the Singapore Issues'. Online, available at: http://epawatch. net (accessed 31 January 2009).

European Union and African Union (2007) 'The Africa–EU Strategic Partnership: a joint Africa–EU strategy', Lisbon, 9 December, article 33.

Kotsopoulos, J. and Sidiropoulos, E. (2007) 'Continental Shift? Redefining EU–Africa relations', European Policy Paper, Brussels. Online, available at: http://epc.eu (accessed 31 January 2009).

McCormick, D. (2008) 'China and India as Africa's New Donors: the impact of aid on development', *Review of African Political Economy*, 35 (1): 73–92.

Mkwezalamba, M.M. (2007) 'Speech at the Opening of the Joint Ministerial Preparatory Conference for the Second Africa–Europe Summit', Sharm El Sheikh, 5 December. Online, available at: www.africa-union.org (accessed 31 January 2009).

Ndiaye, M. (2007) 'Time Factor may Wreck EU–ACP Negotiations', *Agence de Press Africaine*, 12 March. Online, available at: http://apanews.net (accessed 31 January 2009).

OAU (1994) 'Resolution on the Report of the Standing Committee on the Review of the Scale of Assessment of the Organization of African Unity', Fifth Ordinary Session of the Council of Ministers of the OAU, CM/Res.1479–1513 (LIX), Addis Ababa, 31 January to 4 February. Online, available at: www.africa-union.org (accessed 31 January 2009).

Reuters (2006) 'EU Loan Saved Darfur Peacekeeping Mission', 29 September. Online, available at: www.sudantribune.com (accessed 31 January 2009).

Shawul, T. (2005) 'Resource Center for Governance, Democracy and Human Rights: a source of inspiration', *AU Commission News*, 2 October. Online, available at: www. africa-union.org (accessed 31 January 2009).

Sow, A. (2004) 'Achievements of the Interim Emergency Multinational Force and Future Scenarios', in M. Malan and J.G. Porto (eds) *Challenges of Peace Implementation: the UN mission in the Democratic Republic of the Congo*, Pretoria: Institute for Security Studies.

Wissenbach, U. (2007) 'Africa's Attractions', *World Today*, 63 (4): 7–9.

# 13  Non-Western media and the EU

## Perspectives from Al Jazeera

*Donatella Della Ratta*[1]

## Introduction

In the past years, after 9/11 and the following wars in Afghanistan and Iraq, the rise of 'global terror' and the consequent strict laws on travelling and visas have dramatically contributed to turning cultural relations into media-*mediated* relations,[2] particularly influenced by television. Nowadays cultural relations are filtered more than ever through media images, as a result making the television screen a key 'cultural mediator'.

With Al Jazeera providing exclusive pictures of the most important breaking news events in recent years, the entire world has had to wake up to the idea that a mature Arab media system exists and communicates on a global scale. Al Jazeera, representing one segment of a complex Arab media system made up of more than 400 TV channels, has proved to be a very powerful tool in shaping Arab public opinion and feeding it with images of the outside world. By introducing the *opinion and counter opinion* editorial principle[3] and by substituting the former information system based on consensus with inflammatory and controversial debates, Al Jazeera has strongly contributed to turning passive Arab viewers into an active Arab public opinion. Many taboos and issues that had never been represented on Arab television were to find a place in public discussion through the mediation of Al Jazeera TV screens.

While the station plays such a central role in shaping internal relations inside the Arab world, at the same time it is also very important at the external level, since it is a strong tool for articulating and distributing meaningful images of the non-Arab world to the Arab audience. In this respect, 9/11 dramatically influenced cultural relations between the Western and the Arab worlds by introducing the idea of the alleged 'clash of civilizations'. Meanwhile, on a global scale the majority of media outlets began to polarize around the rhetoric of 'You' against 'Us', which has also dramatically affected TV news by moving its principal value from objectivity to empathy and shared emotional participation with the audience.[4] While the core of Al Jazeera narratives lies mainly inside the Arab world, it is indeed true that the Arab TV station has started to pay more attention to 'Western issues' by following this global media trend of emotional participation, mostly after 2003 and the US-led attack on Iraq (see also El Nawawy and Iskandar 2002).

In this new global framework, where the media has turned into a central actor in world public diplomacy (to the extent that the latter has become mostly *media diplomacy*), it is of key importance to analyse what kind of images of the outside world are conveyed to the Arab audiences through these powerful media outlets. With that, the main aim of this chapter is to understand how the European Union (EU) is depicted in Al Jazeera programming, and if the EU is represented independently or, on the contrary, under the generic label of the 'West'. After analysing the news in Al Jazeera TV listings plus programme schedules, and studying the values assigned to EU issues, the chapter tries to add some final considerations on how the EU could work to improve its image through media diplomacy.

## Al Jazeera, more than ten years of Arab TV news

Al Jazeera was founded in November 1996, with an initial six hours programming slot before moving to 24 hours non-stop (see also Della Ratta 2005; El Nawawy and Iskandar 2002; Lynch 2006; Miles 2005; Zayani 2005).

The channel, headquartered in Doha, Qatar, was the first all-news channel in the Arab world, and it soon started to be considered a reliable news source in the Arab region, particularly after its extensive coverage of the Palestinian Intifada of 2000. This event marked the coming of a new era in terms of TV news: it was the very first time that audiences all across the Arab world were able to watch an uprising of the Palestinian people, the most important and most followed pan-Arab issue, live on their TV screens. During the 2000 Intifada, the BBC started to quote Al Jazeera as a reliable news source in the region (Sullivan 2001), but it was only in 2001 that Al Jazeera made its international debut and became a real global player in the news-making arena. The broadcasting of Bin Laden's videos helped Al Jazeera capture international attention and raised many polemics, particularly from the American administration, due to the channel's decision to distribute a message that could have led to more terror and violence after the 9/11 turmoil.

After the US-led attack on Afghanistan in 2001 and, later in 2003, on Iraq, Al Jazeera gained an international reputation as a global news provider[5] although it has always been very much linked to polemics and critiques against its alleged violent anti-American (and, more generally, anti-Western) attitude.

Al Jazeera was not new to this criticism: since the outset the station has always been labelled by many Arab states as controversial and, sometimes, as a real threat to national security. The reason lies in the very editorial principle behind the station's programmes: 'the opinion and the counter opinion'. By following this principle, Al Jazeera has given the floor to the opposition movements of many Arab regimes. It was the first time that an Arab broadcaster had broken the unwritten but largely followed rule of 'protocol news', which has always meant that TV news was the safest place for the ruling government to exercise its power and authority.

This taboo-breaking behaviour – which has always been claimed by the station to be the source of its added professional value and audience success –

has led many Arab countries to protest formally or break diplomatic ties with Qatar. This tiny Gulf state, ruled since 1995 by the enlightened Emir Sheikh Hamad Bin Khalifa Al-Thani, has always supported Al Jazeera financially, although it was formally launched as a private station driven by a commercial goal. Despite its international success, the channel has never been able to collect as much advertising revenue as its global reputation deserves, due to a 'de facto embargo' laid by Saudi Arabia. There are many reasons[6] for Saudi Arabia's opposition to Al Jazeera and its editorial policy: the result of which has been to block or dramatically reduce the channel's capability to break even financially. Although the relations between the Kingdom and the channel (and the state that is behind it) have improved over the last few years, the channel is still believed to depend on personal cheques from the Emir of Qatar (Hammond 2007; Worth 2008).

Over more than ten years of broadcasting, Al Jazeera has grown from a single all-news channel to a network of themed offers (a sports channel, an English channel, a live channel and a children channel) and has expanded its influence into many different activities (for example, the training field, after launching one of the most highly reputable training centres for journalists in the Arab region).

Its average audience is reputed to count around 50 million Arabic-speaking people from all over the world (Gibson 2005).[7]

## Methodological note

The aim of this research is to underline the main perspectives conveyed to the Arabic-speaking audiences concerning the EU. As a result, the English channel, which was launched in November 2006, does not fall under this analysis, as it is an autonomous station with its own programming tailored towards English-speaking targets.

As we have seen, given the gap in the literature regarding this topic, this chapter is the result of field research undertaken in Doha in December 2007. The fieldwork consisted both of collecting and analysing programmes, as well as carrying out interviews. The analysis was conducted on the results of a search in the Al Jazeera archives that used selected keywords[8] referring to EU topics and related events over the past ten years (1998–2008). Given the fact that search criteria differ according to the different types of programmes and the methodology used to archive them, it was not possible to select one particular time span, for this would have limited the search and may have brought with it few results. Moreover, the goal was also to analyse Al Jazeera as a dynamic and evolving institution that has changed over the years in line with media transformations and geopolitical events. Interestingly enough, the search showed how the bulk of items dealing with the EU (or related issues) have been broadcast only since 2003, a phenomenon that I will try to explain better below.

Among the talk shows, the analysis included many flagship programmes such as *Al ittijah al moakis* (Opposite Direction), *Shariaa wal hayat* (Religion and Life), *Akthar min ray* (More than One Opinion), *Hiwar maftuah* (Open Dialogue) and *Bila hudud* (No Frontiers).[9]

Special attention was devoted to *Min Uroba* (From Europe), a 26-minute weekly programme created by Ahmed Kamel, the former head of the Al Jazeera bureau in Brussels. Broadcast from 2003 until 2005, the programme was dedicated entirely to Europe, and dealt with institutional, political, cultural and social aspects of the European Union.

In order to be analysed properly, the Al Jazeera TV schedule was divided in two main areas: news bulletins and talk shows – the latter being the most important genre among the channel's programmes. It might be useful to say a few words on the different production routines employed in the news-making process on the one hand, and in programme production on the other, as this helps to explain the research findings. The news-making routine falls under the responsibility of the news department: the production process is strictly monitored by a selected group of people and supervised by an editorial committee that is responsible for maintaining the quality of the news items. Talk shows are part of the programme department but they are usually managed by small production units where the producer works closely with the show's author. The latter is usually the host of the show, too, and enjoys great freedom in choosing the topics and the guests for the programme. Therefore, while news making is more a collective and cross-checked process, talk shows are usually the result of more individual choices made in editorial autonomy and mostly based on personal tastes, according to the author/host's style. These two different organizational routines result in different perspectives on the topic of our interest as I will underline and explain below.

The analysis of news items and programmes has been integrated by qualitative in-depth interviews with the channel management and staff from both the news and the programme departments,[10] including Ahmed Kamel (who left Al Jazeera just after *Min Uroba* was cancelled). The aim of these qualitative interviews was to investigate and evaluate different aspects of Al Jazeera's coverage of the EU. A first series of questions was devoted to the *newsworthiness* of the EU, in order to understand the degree of informative value that Al Jazeera assigns to EU-related issues and the kind of relevance that these issues assume compared to others. A second series aimed to evaluate the *quantity* and *quality* of the station's coverage of EU issues, both in the news programmes and talk shows, according to the interviewees' perspectives. The third set analysed the *definition of Europe* to discover if the latter was regarded as a self-standing political and cultural unit or classified under the generic label of the 'West' together with the USA. The fourth set aimed to ask the interviewees their personal opinions and evaluations about the EU's 'communication strategy' towards the Arab world, and its strong and weak points as a 'brand' to be 'advertised' through Arab TV screens.

## The EU according to Al Jazeera: an analysis of the main findings

As underlined above, the US attack on Iraq in 2003 could be interpreted as the leading factor in shifting Al Jazeera's attention and coverage towards pan-Arab issues. Containing a strong emotional value, these topics may have contributed to consolidating the 'empathy' between the station and its viewers. Since pan-Arab issues like the war in Iraq, the Israeli–Palestinian conflict and the Lebanon crisis are very closely related to European and American policies and attitudes towards the Arab region, this has resulted in a growing coverage of the EU and the USA since 2003. I have investigated *how* and *in which way* Al Jazeera's renewed pan-Arab focus has contributed to its discourse on Europe, that is, in terms of the *quality* of the coverage and its *exactness*.

After analysing Al Jazeera coverage in the news and talk shows, it is fair to state that, generally speaking, there are 'two Al Jazeeras', which speak about the EU in very different ways.

Since news bulletins are usually neutral in their reporting and mainly stick to the news item itself, it is in the talk shows that one can find the most sharp and culturally significant perceptions of the EU. Whereas the analysed news items are balanced, informative and very precise in defining the EU as a self-standing political entity inside which many differences in political cultural and economic orientations can be found, the talk shows introduce opinions and views that melt together different arguments and even different political players (like the EU and the USA, usually labelled as a generic 'West'). An Arab viewer who only watches the news on Al Jazeera could have a dissonant and totally opposite vision of the EU compared to a talk-show viewer.

This could be interpreted as a direct consequence of the different organiza-tional routines employed in making the news programmes and talk shows as underlined above; but it is also strictly related to the very nature of the two TV genres. The difference between news bulletins and talk shows is equivalent, for a broadcaster, to the difference between news and column articles in the printed press. While accuracy in reporting the news is an added value for a communica-tion medium – be it for the printed press or a broadcast – it is the opinions expressed in the columns and the TV programmes that ultimately make the dif-ference between one type of media and another, that is, builds its particular flavour and style. Moreover, due to the appeal enjoyed by 'emotional' elements in TV programmes, talk shows are regaining attention as the ideal place to express empathy with the viewers by dealing with opinions/emotions over facts/rationality.

Overall, the analysis shows that in terms of *newsworthiness* (in the news as well as in talk shows), the EU becomes a more valuable topic when it is directly related to the Arab world. This is of course more evident in talk shows, where the EU is not relevant at all if not strictly linked to the Arab world.[11] As the author of the top-rated show, *Al ittijah al moakis*, points out:

> Generally I don't deal with the EU because of its lack of TV appeal and the lack of a unified policy among its members. Sometimes I do debate Euro-pean topics when it comes to the Euromediterranean partnership; the EU as a model of unity and political economic cooperation for Arabs; when Israel and Palestinian issues are involved; when there is a clash or a divergent

opinion between America and Europe; when it comes to the Arab presence in Europe; when there are laws affecting European Muslim communities, like the French one against the veil; when it comes to new member states joining the EU, particularly Turkey, because it is regarded as a Muslim country. I remember I made a show on the Turkey issue where the core of the debate was: is Turkey a part of the Muslim world or is it a part of Europe?[12]

In news bulletins things are slightly different, as the EU is covered when it becomes relevant as an international player, and not only if directly related to the Arab world. Nevertheless, even inside news bulletins the news value accorded to individual EU member states is far higher than the value attributed to the EU as an independent institution. In terms of news priority, European nation states are still more important than the EU as a whole. The Deputy Chief Editor admitted:

> We might pay more attention to a decision issued by the UK or France as single countries rather than EU collective decisions. We look at Europe, we are interested in it and our audiences are interested in it, but we still consider it as a conglomerate of different nation states rather than a coherent block.[13]

When it comes to the *quality* of the EU coverage – both as resulting from the programme analysis and from the perceptions of the interviewees themselves – the difference between news broadcasts and talk shows becomes clearer and more marked, particularly in terms of accuracy in reporting the story and using the correct terminology. In the news bulletins the EU is always described in a correct and fair way, even in linguistic terms. There is no approximation, and every divergent position within the EU is reported correctly and in a neutral, professional style. According to one of the senior editors:

> Al Jazeera always differentiates between the USA and the EU. Even within the EU itself we differentiate if there is a disagreement among the members. In the news department we are very acutely aware that the EU doesn't speak in one single voice when it comes to foreign policy and sometimes when it comes to internal policy too. We always report on newcomers to the EU and we explain that these newcomers are not at the same economic level as the core countries of the Union but they have the same rights inside it. We never use the term 'West' and we would never say something like 'Western attitude to Iraq' which is very imprecise and inaccurate as there is not such a thing as a unified attitude to Iraq. And not even in the Danish cartoon case would we use terms like 'Western freedom of expression'. We could use this expression only when we quote people talking about freedom of expression in the West, which is an opinion coming from people, not our point of view.[14]

When it comes to talk shows the quality decreases, as the personal opinions of the host and guests take over the informative value, thus undermining the accuracy in terminology, too. As openly admitted by the author and host of *Al ittijah al moakis*:

> We hardly distinguish between Europe and the USA, we tend to put them in the same basket [...] The media after 9/11 – and the Western media in particular – started talking about Europe and the USA as one thing, portraying everything as a civilization clash. In TV language it is much better to have one only enemy to fight against.[15]

It can happen that the EU and US are presented as separate entities: but this is always done to serve the logic of TV spectacle rather than to create a better understanding.[16] Generally speaking, the talk shows maintain a linguistic ambiguity and approximation in referring to Europe as an 'undistinguished West'.

As for the *quantity*, EU-related news is quite limited and, according to the majority of the interviewees, not yet sufficient. Also in relative terms, EU coverage results lower if compared to US coverage. If we think that Al Jazeera has seven bureaux located all across Europe, with a total of 14 correspondents out of 75 all around the world (quite a good percentage if we consider that the strongest concentration is naturally in the Arab region), this also shows that the core problem with the scarce quantity of the EU coverage does not lie in a lack of staff or weak territorial presence.

Many reasons could explain the limited coverage, among them the headquarters' difficulty in understanding how the EU political process works as underlined by the chief of the Brussels bureau. He explains this clearly:

> From the Doha perspective it is very hard to understand how Europe works. For example, it is difficult to judge the importance that something like a project discussed within the EU could have, even if it has not become a decision yet. But when I propose a feature on a EU project I always find it very hard to explain its importance. It is easier to understand the behaviour of nation states rather than this collective EU bureaucratic machine.[17]

Another reason has to do with what is considered to be the greater appeal enjoyed by the USA as opposed to the EU, which is widely viewed as 'not sexy enough' for TV screens.[18]

Though there has been a decrease in the attention placed on the EU by Al Jazeera schedules in the past years (also due to the cancellation of *Min Uroba*), on the contrary since 2003 there has been a slight increase in the number of talk shows discussing issues somehow related to Europe.[19] As already underlined, the aftermath of the US attack on Iraq and the increasing turmoil in the Arab region have contributed to polarizing the world media around a 'West against the Arab world' attitude. This has resulted in Al Jazeera increasing its focus on pan-Arab issues with an emotional and mobilizing approach at the expense of more 'rational', educational and informative topics. This renewed pan-Arab focus has also increased the attention paid by opinion-led programmes to the EU where the latter usually stands as the 'enemy' under the generic label of the 'West'.

As regards the EU's 'communication strategy' towards the Arab world, one thing that has to be mentioned here – found both in the programme analysis and in the qualitative interviews – is the strong value attributed to the EU in terms of *soft power*. Both in the news and in talk shows, the EU is always portrayed as a model of unity to be followed by Arabs. In the episode from 27 June 2003, *Akthar min ray* stressed the concept of uniting 25 states under the same flag, quoting it as General De Gaulle's accomplished dream. The episode of *Al Ittijah al moakis* from 28 January 2003 reminded the audience that a union of so many states clearly had a strong military and economic power, which thereby resulted in a stronger global strategic position. As remarked by the show's host:

> I wanted to tell the Arabs: look at the Europeans … they have gone to war more than once in history, they killed each other and look at them now! Even though they speak different languages they are melting together and uniting! In this case I use the EU as an example to follow and encourage Arabs to do the same.[20]

In news coverage, the idea of the EU as a model of unity for the Arabs is implicit in many items, such as the coverage of the single currency (the euro) as an example of an accomplished and successful economic model. 'The EU model (first a monetary union, followed later by a political one) represents a strong example for Arabs', affirms Ahmad Beshto, host of the programme *Iktisad wa nass*.[21] The idea of the EU as an integrated system offering opportunity and access even to weaker economic subjects is also present in news regarding the debate over the admission of Turkey to the EU.

It is therefore clear that, both in news bulletins and talk shows, the EU is portrayed as a positive and successful model of unity for the Arab world that would result in an increase of its *soft power* appeal.

### *A case study: Min Uroba*

*Min Uroba* deserves some specific considerations, as it was designed to be an informative weekly space for in-depth analysis of the EU. According to its creator and host, the programme was meant 'to present Europe […] in every aspect of its daily life and culture, even if not directly related to the Arab world'. It was 'aimed to show to Arabs – who often have lots of stereotypes on Europe – how Europeans live and think'.[22]

The first episode was broadcast by Al Jazeera on 3 February 2003. It lasted until 2005, in all producing 87 episodes. To give an idea, the 2003 edition produced a total amount of 260 features and 313 news items, from 70 cities in 33 countries. In fact *Min Uroba* featured a concept of an 'enlarged' Union, covering not only the official EU member states, but also countries like Serbia, Russia and Turkey, to embrace a wider idea of Europe.

The programme structure was divided into a first part dealing with EU institutions (the Parliament, Commission, European Council), while the second half was devoted to culture and society. Each episode was completed by a 'news flash', a sort of quick news bulletin on EU decisions and European societies.

The analysis of the 2003–2005 editions of *Min Uroba* shows that the programme was rich in contents, and very informative and accurate in terms of describing and defining the EU. Generally speaking, the characteristics found in the news coverage – accuracy in terminology, balance, richness in information, etc. – could also be referred to this show, which was the only space entirely devoted to the EU not only in Al Jazeera's programming but all across the Arab media.

The core topic of *Min Uroba* was the EU and Europe at large, and it never focused only on the relations between the EU and the Arab world. Many issues were tackled, even if not related to the Arab region. On the contrary, the aim seemed to be to 'educate' the Arab audiences to the democratic process of the EU institutions, giving precise knowledge of the procedures and processes governing the admission of new member states and the relations between the newcomers and the founders of the Union. The programme was therefore a truly educational programme on the EU and Europe, whose aim was to inform Arab audiences and perhaps – even if not directly – provide them with a model of unity.

The reasons why *Min Uroba* was prevented from broadcasting after 2005 are still unclear. Most probably a major shift occurred in Al Jazeera editorial policy after a management turnover in mid 2003.[23] The new management urged a change in the schedule as it wanted to turn Al Jazeera into a pure information channel that concentrated on news rather than programmes. Reportage programmes like *Murasilu Al Jazeera* (Al Jazeera correspondents) and other current affairs programmes were shelved. The number of talk shows, on the contrary, stayed the same, even if they were shortened in length. The result was to strengthen breaking news slots and increase the amount of news bulletins. But the topics that were privileged during the aftermath of the US attack on Iraq and the worsening of the general situation in the Arab region were pan-Arab in nature, at the expense of educational and informative items not directly connected to the Arab world. This is most probably the reason why a programme like *Min Uroba* might have been shelved, for it dealt with the EU institutions and European cultural and social life as something not directly related to the dramatic developments in the Arab region. As one of the senior editors pointed out:

> After the Iraqi occupation of 2003 the entire region changed: there was a need to report extensively what had been happening there and also to try to explain the reasons for this situation. […] The increased pan-Arab coverage would come at the expense of other programmes: those in charge of programming would find it hard to position a programme about the EU, or South America, or Asia while Iraq, Palestine and Lebanon were burning. I

think that in normal circumstances it would be important to have such programmes but at this particular time everything becomes different.[24]

## EU media strategy in the Arab world: remarks and recommendations

As showed by the analysis above, there are many weak points in the TV portrayal of the EU on Al Jazeera screens, sometimes resulting in evident misrepresentation.

The first weak point that makes it so hard to represent the EU properly in front of Arab TV audiences is the difficulty in *understanding* its complex political nature and bureaucratic way of functioning. Arab viewers are used to dealing with strong individual political powers. They are not accustomed to 'softer entities', where the decision-making process has to go through multiple rounds of negotiations and complex systems of collegial decisions.

TV representation is also a critical point, whereas the EU lacks an image that can get across its values through the media. This is the result of the lack of a united foreign policy that could convey a stronger image of a united political entity. Furthermore, it would drive the Arab media to focus its attention on the Union's policy rather than the behaviour and decisions of single member states.

The lack of EU representatives that are willing to talk to Arab audiences through the media is another issue that needs to be tackled in the future if the EU wishes to improve its image in the Arab world.

Many decades have passed since the colonial times when European states operated in the Arab world through their own media outlets targeting local audiences. These media services – like the first pan-Arab radio stations targeted at the Middle East and operated by Radio Bari, BBC Arabic, Voice of America and Monte Carlo Moyen Orient – were broadcasting in the total absence of any local audiovisual media. Therefore, they were filling a big communication gap in providing information and entertainment to the Arab region. Nowadays the situation has changed dramatically: powerful media outlets – like Al Jazeera and many others among the 400 TV channels that make up the contemporary Arab media landscape – operate in the Arab region. They speak Arabic and they are produced by the Arabs themselves, for the first time providing an 'Arab point of view' on world events. For this reason, the Arab media system, which has reached a high standard of maturity over the past few years, has to be acknowledged and not ignored by Europe if it still wants to play an important role in the Arab region. This role would be strategic to head towards cooperation and mutual understanding rather than in the direction of targeting the Arab viewers with political propaganda or a post-colonial 'educational' attitude.

*Media diplomacy* provides the EU with an enormous opportunity: it lies in its *soft power*, in its being interpreted as a model of unity by an Arab region that aspires to move in a similar direction. The EU needs to regard this privileged position as a starting point for building – even through the media – cooperation and mutual understanding with the Arab world at a time when they are needed more urgently than ever.

## Notes

1 The author wishes to thank the Al Jazeera International Media Relations Department, the Al Jazeera Library and the Al Jazeera Newsroom and Programme Department for their support and kind help. Due to the lack of pre-existing sources on the topic under discussion, this chapter is mainly the result of fieldwork and a programme analysis conducted from December 2007 until May 2008.
2 I am grateful to Jihad N. Fakhreddine for this concept.

> The fear is that with less personal interaction with Westerners, Arabs will interact more with images of the West. In such an environment the media is likely to become the sole channel for the conveyance of these images, and the media, as we know, are not usually neutral.
>
> (Fakhreddine 2004)

3 This is the Al Jazeera motto.
4 This process – known as 'commercialization of the news' – had already started at the beginning of the 1990s. See Hallin 1996 as an example.
5 In 2004, according to Brandchannel.com, Al Jazeera was ranked fifth among the most powerful brands in the world.
6 The channel was the first to give wide TV visibility to all the opposition movements to the ruling Saudi regime, hosting many of them in inflammatory talk shows. But there is also a geopolitical reason, very much linked to the loss of regional importance Saudi Arabia had to face particularly in 2003, when the US decided to move its biggest regional military base from the Kingdom to Qatar.
7 This is a pure estimate since there is not an agreed audience measurement system in the Arab region yet.
8 A number of alternative keywords not directly linked to the European Union but concerning relevant facts occurring in Europe or involving Europe directly (for example, the Danish caricatures of the Prophet Muhammad) were also used to find additional audiovisual material on the EU.
9 The English titles of the programmes are given as they appear in the Al Jazeera archives, therefore according to the Al Jazeera translation.
10 The people interviewed at the Doha headquarters were: Faysal Al Kasim, author and host of the talk show *Al ittiijah al moakis*, Muetaz Al Khatib, author and producer of the talk show *Sharia wal hayat*, Ahmed Beshto, author and presenter of the programme *Iktisad wa nass*, Ayman Gaballah, Deputy Chief Editor, Aref Hijjawi, Head of Programming, Samir Khader, Senior Programme Editor, and Hassan Shawki, Senior Programme Editor. Two other key interviews were added: Labib Fahmi, Al Jazeera correspondent and current chief of the bureau in Brussels, and Ahmed Kamel, former author of the programme *Min Uroba* and former chief of the Brussels bureau.
11 The only significant exception to this trend is *Akthar min ray*. The London-based talk show is more open to dealing with EU themes as independent topics, maybe also as a result of its geographic location.
12 Faysal Al Kasim, author interview, December 2007.
13 Ayman Gaballah, author interview, December 2007.
14 Hassan Shawki, author interview, December 2007.
15 Faysal Al Kasim, author interview, December 2007.
16 Like in the *Al Ittijah al moakis* episode from 28 January 2003. Al Kasim's introduction to this episode – which is built around his powerful rhetoric of presenting the

good aspects of one point of view and, immediately after, the good aspects of its counter opinion – addresses the Arabs by asking the following question:

> Why are Arabs the chicken, the caviar and the petrol in the American salad? Why don't they choose to be ingredients of another salad, the European one? Isn't it true that Europe and America are diverging about how to deal with the Iraqi affair? Isn't it true that European countries are opposing the war in Iraq in a stronger and more determined way than the Arab countries themselves? Isn't Europe closer to us than America? Isn't the Mediterranean a shared affair that interests us the Arabs in the same way as them the Europeans?

17  Labib Fahmi, author interview, May 2008.
18  Labib Fahmi, author interview, May 2008. The majority of the interviewees agree with this vision, with the significant exception of Ahmed Kamel, the Brussels-based author of *Min Uroba.*
19  Hassan Shawki, author interview, December 2007.
20  Faysal Al Kasim, personal interview, December 2007.
21  Ahmad Beshto, author interview, December 2007.
22  Ahmed Kamel, personal interview, May 2008.
23  Mohamed Jasim Al Ali, the former general manager of Al Jazeera, was substituted by Adnan Sharif and, later, by Wadah Khanfar, who still holds this position in the channel.
24  Hassan Shawki, personal interview, December 2007.

# References

Della Ratta, D. (2005) *Al Jazeera. Media e società arabe nel nuovo millennio*, Milan: Bruno Mondadori.

El Nawawy, M. and Iskandar, A. (2002) *Al Jazeera: how the free Arab news network scooped the world and changed the Middle East*, Cambridge, MA: Westview Press.

Fakhreddine, J.N. (2004) *Trojan Horse? On the Arab media as a portal for Western goods and values*, Transnational Broadcasting Studies, 12 (spring/summer).

Gibson, O. (2005) 'BBC Goes Head-to-head with Al Jazeera', *Guardian*, 26 October.

Hallin, D. (1996) 'Commercialism and Professionalism in the American News Media', in J. Curran and M. Gurevitch (eds) *Mass Media and Society*, London: Arnold.

Hammond, A. (2007) 'Concerns over Al Jazeera's Saudi coverage', *Arabian Business*, 13 December.

Lynch, M. (2006) *Voices of the New Arab Public: Iraq, Al Jazeera and Middle East politics today*, New York: Columbia University Press.

Miles, H. (2005) *Al Jazeera: how Arab TV news challenged the world*, London: Abacus.

Sullivan, S. (2001) *The Courting of Al Jazeera*, Transnational Broadcasting Studies online, 7, fall/winter.

Worth, R.F. (2008) 'Al Jazeera No Longer Nips at Saudis', *New York Times*, 4 January.

Zayani, M. (ed.) (2005) *The Al Jazeera Phenomenon: critical perspectives on new Arab media*, London: Pluto Press.

# 14 Close enough?

## The EU's global role described by non-European diplomats in Brussels

*Caterina Carta*

### Introduction: a closer insight into the 'nature of the beast'

This chapter focuses on the views and opinions of non-European diplomats based in Brussels. The privileged position of diplomats to the European Union (EU) constitutes a complementary perspective to the analysis set out in this book. Diplomats are agents of the state, who act on specific instructions and contribute to foreign policy making by virtue of their professional authoritativeness. On the one hand, they constitute an 'exclusive fraternity' of potentially likeminded individuals thanks to 'a universal diplomatic culture' (Cohen 1991: 3). On the other hand, they are constantly confronted with a double-edged responsibility, which is likely to shape their conceptions and beliefs. Due to the complexity of the EU's institutional machinery, it is expected that the views of diplomats posted in Brussels will be based on more hands-on knowledge of the Union's 'engine room', thus revealing a more nuanced portrait of its external image.

The international identity and role of the EU is indeed a complex issue. It is characterized by a triangular system of external relations (comprising the foreign policy systems of the Commission, the Council and the member states). As described in the Introduction to this volume, most analysts regard the EU as a 'different' global actor due to its foundations grounded in international peace, its multilateral vocation and its structural foreign policy (Lucarelli and Manners 2006; Lucarelli 2007).

However, this acclaimed distinctiveness also entails precise limits to the EU's international capability to act, due to the plurality of national identities and interests that converge in the Union. These intrinsic inconsistencies, coupled with the complexity of the system, contribute to explaining the citizens' and elite's struggle to understand what kind of 'animal' the EU is. In this regard, the views of Brussels-based diplomats might help us overcome this knowledge gap.

In order to identify their views of the EU as a global actor, non-European diplomats were interviewed on two main topics: how they defined the EU and how they viewed its global role, including its strengths and weaknesses.[1]

The chapter analyses the data collected by drawing upon the well-known distinction between presence and actorness.[2] The chapter ends by recapping the main conclusions and puts forward some policy recommendations for the EU.

## The EU's presence in the world: what is the EU?

The diplomats tend to conceive the EU as an atypical international actor, with some state-like characteristics though marred by critical limits, invariably dependent on its fragmented policy-making power in foreign affairs (Figure 14.1). Nonetheless, the unitary factor, that is, the attempt to represent different member states, is seen as a powerful credential for the EU on the international scene. According to a Japanese diplomat, 'numbers are a strength, because the EU represents the will of its 27 member states' (JA3). The 'power of numbers' is also conceived as an important element in deepening the EU's relations with the rest of the world, as the various member states have different capacities to reach out to other countries, particularly due to historical links and versatile expertise (AU2, IR2). In the eyes of a Chinese diplomat, this is the key factor that makes the EU such an important economic power vis-à-vis nation states (CH1).

Nevertheless, most respondents agreed that the EU's main weakness lies in the difficulty of creating unity out of this diversity. Particularly, in the field of hard-core traditional foreign policy, this plurality represents two sides of the same coin: while diversity is a strength in terms of reaching out to the world, lack of unity can be a serious impediment when it comes to adopting important foreign policy measures (US2). Hence, the widely heralded 'power of numbers'

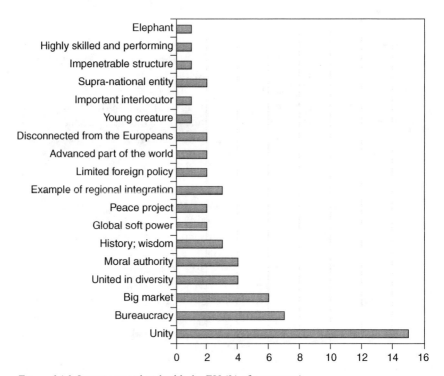

*Figure 14.1* Images associated with the EU (% of responses).

can also be 'a challenge and trial for the future' (JA3), especially with respect to the EU's international actorness.

In general, though, the image of 'a union of states' is by far the most recurrent among the positive images associated by the respondents with the EU. This is further reinforced by a number of positive images describing the EU's international presence, which include peace, wisdom, honest brokering, mediator, non-imperial power, balanced interlocutor and a unique project of regional integration. In the eyes of most of the diplomats, the EU stands out as an agent of peace, both in relation to its internal role of supranational power within the European continent as well as its international strategy to resolve controversies through diplomatic means. This characteristic gives the EU a 'moral authority' given that 'it is a supranational organization like no other, [...] based on the idea of agreement, union, dialogue and human rights' (IS1). According to some Japanese and American diplomats, this is often an asset, particularly in international forums, owing both to the moral authority that the EU carries and to its added value to reach common positions (JA2, JA3, US3).

At the same time, the integration process within the EU has given rise to an immense amount of bureaucracy 'that nourishes itself' (RU1). Bureaucracy ranks, indeed, among the most quoted images defining the EU's presence. When moving on to the internal complexity of the EU, most of the diplomats recognize the pitfalls of its intricate institutional apparatus, which inevitably affect its foreign policy aspirations. The institutional intricacy of the EU makes it quite complicated for external diplomats to identify responsibilities, interlocutors and channels of communication. On a more general level, the EU's over-bureaucratization affects its legitimacy vis-à-vis other governments insofar as it widens the gap between the institutional representatives and the citizens of Europe (US3, IR2). European citizens, it is claimed, do not understand the complexity of the EU and the underlying principles of the integration process (IR2): this also undermines the international credibility of the EU as a promoter of democracy and human rights.

Thus, the EU is conceived as having a peculiar international presence in the light of its complex and multinational composition. At the same time, the diplomats are fully aware of the crucial limitations concerning the EU's governance of external affairs and also tend to intertwine their perceptions of what the EU is at the international level with the complexity of its internal decision-making structure.

## The EU's international actorness: what does the EU do?

Similarly to its international presence, respondents appear to describe the EU's international actorness as influenced by its atypical character as a multinational, non-state actor. While this distinctiveness was viewed as a constitutive trait of its international presence, it is now described as the key limit to a satisfactory performance at the global level. The interplay between the two dimensions (international presence and global actorness) is easily unveiled: the EU's atypical entity as a new type of international player (which is seen as a strong element of its presence) invariably raises expectations as to what it should do; yet, its ambiguity limits its role performance fuelling harsh criticisms with regard to its actual global actorness. Paradoxically, what was seen as a key strength in defining the EU's international presence is also regarded as its main weakness in terms of actorness. In this regard, some of the diplomats highlight how the distinction between high and low policies in EU external relations (Hoffmann 1966) contributes to delineating the EU role (JA2, SA1, ME3).

Whereas some important competencies – such as international trade – are handled at the Community level, others – such as foreign policy, security and justice and home affairs – are conceived as standing firmly at the national level. The EU is generally described as an effective actor in those areas where there are clear delegated competencies at the Community level. In those areas, as we will see, the EU is seen to have a strong, undisputed role on the international scene (Figure 14.2).

This is the case for international trade and technological development (IN2), but also for regulation, a sector in which the EU is said to play a powerful role, probably more so than the US (JA2, IS1, US3). However, this strong relevance is often criticized as way of maintaining a privileged economic position on the international scene. As put by a South African diplomat, the developing world tends to see the EU as protectionist bloc, which uses technical barriers in order to protect its market while promoting an official policy of tariff removals (SA1). According to an Indian diplomat, the powerful role that the EU plays in international trade affords it a disproportionate representation in the World Trade Organization (WTO), which brings into question the actual multilateral vocation of the EU itself (IN2). The EU is also blamed for not being particularly transparent in its regulatory processes (IS1, US3). Furthermore, over-regulation is not only seen as a tacit instrument of power, but also as a burden on other countries, which inevitably slows down international cooperation (AU1).

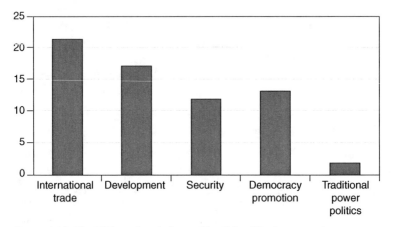

*Figure 14.2* The EU's main role in world politics (% of responses).

When it comes to traditional foreign policy matters, the EU is accused of not being able to express reliable and common positions. For some, foreign policy is a trade-off between the oft-diverging interests of the various member states (SA1). Although they are all well aware of the nuances of the EU policy-making processes governing foreign policy, most respondents admit that such complexity only serves the purpose of hiding a simple truth, that is, the absence of a real European foreign policy.

Of course, there are slight differences depending on the type of foreign policy issue. In some areas, the EU is perceived as more coherent and prompt. As cases in point, respondents mention the European Security and Defence Policy (ESDP) mission in the Pacific, particularly in Aceh (AU1, AU2, AU3), or the various missions in Africa (SA1, CH1). However, these best practices do not alter the overall perception of the EU as a global actor with poor credibility and serious deficiencies, especially when divergent interests are at stake. In cases in which the EU is seen as more effective, its intervention tends to be regarded as limited in scope, as it mainly deals with humanitarian aid and conflict prevention (CH1). An American diplomat points out that the EU's inability to act in foreign and security policy matters also depends on the lack of investment by member states, above all in the military sector (US1).

Generally speaking, though, divisions among member states are regarded as the main reason undermining the pursuit of a coherent EU foreign policy. On many issues the result of member states' bargaining over foreign policy decisions is a compromise position, which may even be seen as 'a camouflage for the lack of a common position' (IS1). In certain situations, the EU's incapability to act is said to represent an important aspect of its presence: the EU is not able to produce sound responses to sensitive and complicated situations (IS1, RU2, US1). Although respondents are aware that decisions based on the lowest common denominator might sometimes constitute the only way to reach initial positions upon which further consensus can be built, the non-European diplomats point out that this makes it difficult for the EU's counterparts to develop a response (IS1).

Rather negative perceptions also regard other sectors of intergovernmental cooperation, such as justice and home affairs and security-related matters. In security matters, the EU is mainly seen as having a 'back-seat approach', which clouds the EU's visibility and makes international coordination difficult (AU3). In general, the EU is not portrayed as a player on 'big issues'. In the words of an Australian diplomat, the EU's strength 'does not obviously rely on its foreign policy and, after September 11, not even on security-related issues' where member states still play the leading role in the game (AU1). Yet, the role of the EU in security-related matters is not delineated in wholly negative terms, with some respondents looking with interest at the developments in the ESDP (RU2, US1, LE1).

Furthermore, the term 'security' is subject to various interpretations, due to the multifaceted nature of the concept (CH1, JA1, RU1, ME3, SA1). For one Russian diplomat, the EU pursues security action only insofar as internal security is concerned (RU1). In this view, the EU's security capabilities are highly dependent on how security is defined: whereas in human security the EU can play an important role, in military terms this role is still questionable (SA1). Analogously, the EU has been able to establish 'concrete strategies and goals' to combat climate change and in this field build upon 'experience and technologies to play a leading role' (CH1). This vision is echoed by a Japanese diplomat who concedes that the EU has played a large role in security matters, based on the fact that, with its presence and by acting as a negotiator (JA1) and advocating multilateralism (IN1), it guarantees a different international climate without any recent incident of violent conflicts. Iranian diplomats also share this view, but denounce the EU's vassalage to the USA, making it clear that a better-equipped Europe in critical foreign policy matters would be particularly welcome as a credible counterforce to the hegemonic position of the USA (IR1, IR2).

Across the board, it is widely recognized that the EU 'invests lots of money in development' (AU1). This guarantees the EU an almost undisputed role in this area (US, ME, LE, IN1, CH, JA, IR1). Through development aid, the EU is also said to pursue an important role at the global level, with an important impact on human security (ME2). The idea that the EU pursues an overall approach, which mixes trade and development strategies, is shared by the diplomats, although the effectiveness of its action is not always ascertained (IN2, SA2). An Indian diplomat argues that the EU's policies to fight poverty are not proportionally distributed across the globe and points out an alarming lack of investment in South Asia, where the majority of the world's poor live (IN2). According to his South African colleague, the EU promotes an 'unequal partnership', similarly to other rich countries, which is deeply rooted in a 'superiority complex' and a 'top-down' approach towards less developed countries (SA2). In their view, this threatens the EU's credibility and ability to build trust among its partners.

In general, it is a common view that the EU does not perform traditional power politics, either due to its incapacity to do so or to its manifest rejection of this approach. However, this opinion does not necessarily include all member states, in particular France and Britain, which, through their special relationship with former colonies, are seen as maintaining their areas of influence, while pursuing a power policy on their own. In the economic sphere, though, some elements of power politics can be found. Besides its control over the WTO, the EU enjoys a fairly high stake of representation and control within the International Monetary Fund and the World Bank, not to mention the seats that three of its member states have within the United Nations (UN) Security Council (IN2). In this regard, the position of the EU regarding the reform of the UN Security Council inevitably contradicts its multilateral vocation. To an extent, this does not surprise many of the diplomats, as diplomacy and foreign policy 'are all about [national] interests' (SA, IN1, CH1). Nevertheless, it tends to contrast with the EU's publicized tendency to promote a 'megaphone diplomacy' – that is to say, the Union's intransigency and tendency to issue grand declarations based on principles regardless of their feasibility (IS2) – and to 'act as a teacher telling pupils how to behave' (SA2). Moreover, the EU tends to neglect some aspects of communication related to power politics: it lacks the ability to control the media on a global scale and to 'produce' effective, credible opinion makers, for instance through non-governmental organizations (NGOs), the media, academic institutions and think tanks. In their view, the US is still monopolizing the production of knowledge and cultural symbols, which is further strengthened by its capacity to attract the best human resources, particularly from emerging giants such as India and China. In this regard, the EU is seen as short-sighted, especially with respect to its immigration policies and its incapacity to attract new talents that could then be used to propagate European values and forge the opinions of many countries' future ruling classes (IN2).

Interestingly, the respondents' opinions regarding the EU's democracy promotion policies are contrasting. As an Australian diplomat puts it, 'the EU stands for human rights, not for democracy promotion, while the US is the opposite way round' (AU1). By contrast, the EU is seen as a 'credible living example' and an 'obliged term of reference' for democracy promotion according to his Mexican counterparts (ME1, ME2). The credibility of the EU in this field derives from values that 'originate from the EU', like democracy and human rights (CH1). The strength of the EU in this area descends directly from 'the philosophy of the EU: governance, democracy, the fight against poverty, rules, norms, conciliation of interests' (ME2) and also 'because it is setting an example to other countries and, in doing so, it impacts on people' (US3). Yet, very critical remarks are not spared.

According to a Russian diplomat, the EU does not possess the credentials to export democracy, as it neglects its internal democratic deficit, while 'imposing standards outside' (RU1). Furthermore, the EU – the Russian diplomats add – does not pay enough attention to violations of human rights in its own territory, as is the case of Russian minorities in some Baltic countries (RU1, RU2). Other respondents also point out the EU's lack of attention towards other cultures' values while propagating its norms and rules. In this regard, the main weakness of the EU is 'arrogance' rather than the inability to act as a top rank international actor in foreign policy (RU1). For other respondents, the EU might not be imposing cultural standards, but it is definitely 'dictating policies' (SA2) or imposing commercial and regulatory norms (US2, US3). Finally, most of the diplomats warn against the risk of imposing standards and conditions through trade and development, the policy areas in which the EU is more powerful and where the temptation to adopt the instrument of power politics is always present. At the same time, some acknowledge that most EU values are in fact universal principles (ME1). In this regard, the critical element is not which kinds of values are promoted, but how they are transmitted to other countries.

## Conclusions and recommendations

The diplomats hold a complex and well-established vision of where the Union stands in world politics. Their privileged position helps them frame judgements and beliefs from direct knowledge of how the EU works in practice. In this sense, the exposure to European institutions helps them substantiate their views with an analysis of institutional constraints. Thus, in spite of being representatives of countries with different interests vis-à-vis the EU, the diplomats hold similar views regarding the strengths and weaknesses of the EU, mainly based on their knowledge of its institutional machinery and their day-to-day experience.

Even though the diplomats perceive the EU in generally positive terms, they believe the EU's global role is inevitably curtailed by some serious pitfalls. The EU is criticized for its over-bureaucratization and slow-paced decision making, as well as its democratic deficit and low approval rate in the hearts and minds of the European citizens. The diplomats believe that the EU should open up a debate on its achievements and limitations, with a view to encouraging a more direct relationship with national constituencies, which will in turn promote a stronger feeling of European citizenship. All these initiatives could benefit its international appeal and reputation tremendously, especially in the eyes of other democratic powers.

Indeed, from a foreign policy perspective, the democratic deficit equates to a legitimacy deficit and has negative effects on the reputation of the EU as an 'exporter' of democracy and human rights. Moreover, it also influences the credibility of the EU as an international partner, especially when member states cleverly use its poor political legitimacy to discredit EU decisions in the eyes of external observers in order to promote national interests. As a recommendation, the non-European diplomats believe that the EU should improve its strategy of internal communication, while also strengthening its capacity to communicate directly with the political elite and civil society in their countries.

This criticism is often coupled with the impression that the EU does not make enough effort to publicize itself outside 'fortress Europe'. The diplomats point out the absence of an overall EU strategy to reach the common citizens and inform them about the EU's missions and activities in the world with a language that is accessible to everyone, within Europe and beyond its borders.

As regards external communication, in spite of existing efforts, the European Commission delegations might be used more effectively in order to illustrate better the EU to local communities. A possible instrument to improve external communication might be for local radios to broadcast common news in local languages. This might be a good idea to ensure some coverage of the EU in industrialized and developing countries, building, for instance, on the experience of Euronews.

The diplomats responding to our survey also point out that the EU should be more careful when dealing with non-Western cultures. The risk of cultural misunderstanding is always present and it might lead to undesirable consequences, even when the interaction is motivated by good intentions. Intercultural sensitivity and mutual understanding might be pursued by way of a twin-track approach: first, by improving cultural exchanges and reciprocal comprehension and, second, by developing serious common migration policies. Those measures would prove to be useful both for pursuing cultural understanding and for improving the overall competitiveness of the EU.

In terms of cultural understanding, the EU promotes cultural exchange programmes with nearly all the countries involved. Yet, most of the diplomats interviewed for this research do not think the existing initiatives are sufficient actually to achieve reciprocal understanding. Programmes such as Socrates, Leonardo, Youth, the Town Twinning Programme and MEDIA 2007 might be broadened to create better cultural and academic exchanges among European and non-European citizens. Through these programmes, the EU might well trigger virtuous processes capable of generating cross-cultural learning at the grassroots level.

As regards migration, a different policy approach may also contribute to improving cultural interchange and understanding. In the eyes of an Indian diplomat, the EU's current approach still reveals a tendency to depict migration as a menace, rather than as a resource. Only recently, the EU common immigration policy started including measures for attracting highly skilled nationals from third countries. The 2005/71/EC Directive sets out procedures for the admission of third country nationals for scientific research. In the same direction, the Policy Plan on Legal Migration defines a road map for the remaining period of The Hague Programme (2006–2009), which includes a proposal for highly skilled immigration from non-European countries. At the same time, though, attracting highly skilled nationals from other countries, especially less industrialized nations, is quite problematic since the brain drain towards Europe is having a negative impact on many poor countries. It would also be useful to guarantee that adequate compensation is given to countries losing skilled labour, while promoting incentive schemes that also encourage skilled Europeans to work in poorer countries.

With regard to the direct role of the EU in world affairs, a clear distinction is made between its 'presence' and 'actorness', which reveals the direct correlation between growing expectations and institutional constraints. In terms of 'presence', the EU is described as an important player thanks to its internal diversity, which leads to a multifaceted capacity to dialogue with different counterparts and a natural propensity to adopt multilateral initiatives. The various images employed to describe the EU point to its 'consensual' nature, its ability to spread peace in the European continent and to stand for 'universal values', such as democracy, human rights and the rule of law. When it comes to its 'actorness', the argument is reversed. In this case, the plurality of identities and interests as well as the multifaceted approach are seen as the main factors causing its lack of global actorness. The fact that the EU often adopts the lowest common denominator line gives rise to two apparently contradictory arguments: on the one hand, this practice allows the EU to assume a balanced position that tends towards dialogue and cooperation; on the other, the EU is unlikely to be a reliable partner, above all in dealing with situations of crisis, as its position might easily change at any minimal contrast among the 27 member states.

The diplomats tend to refer to the institutional engineering of the EU to explain the limited international role in hard-core matters pertaining to foreign policy, such as security, the fight against terrorism and other intergovernmental sectors of cooperation. This process makes the EU's moves difficult to predict and assess. This overall criticism also touches upon the material difficulties experienced by the diplomats in their daily work in singling out their interlocutors at the EU level.

The hypothesis of a double-hatted High Representative for Foreign Affairs and Security Policy and Vice-President of the Commission and the subsequent better coordination of the Commission's and Council's services is, in general, a welcome step towards the achievement of a more understandable and accessible system of external relations. Even if the diplomats do not propose any detailed recipe for improving the EU's external effectiveness, simplification and better coordination of the different services dealing with external relations seem to be the most viable guidelines in order to proceed towards a reform. Unifying the services, within the margins of the division of competencies, would address the notorious issue of giving the EU a telephone number, in order to create a better connection with external partners. In general, the diplomats included in this research believe that a reform of the EU's system of external relations is critical for the credibility of the EU in the world, even independently of the ratification of the Lisbon Treaty.

When talking about the EU's international role in more general terms, the diplomats identify some major contradictions in its conduct. While the EU is keen on adopting 'megaphone' diplomacy on issues where its power is limited, it does refrain from resorting to restrictive and unilateral initiatives on matters where its leverage is particularly significant.

A far more positive role performance is recognized in relation to other areas of international cooperation, especially those in which there are clear competencies bestowed upon Community institutions. Hence, in the areas of trade, development and human rights, the EU is recognized as a rather significant international actor. Yet, important inconsistencies are identified by the non-European diplomats, particularly with regard to sensitive issues, such as energy, trade barriers and over regulation. Indeed, many respondents warn that the fame of the EU as an 'honest broker' and a 'moral authority' is being questioned all over the world. In actual fact, the EU is portrayed more and more as imposing its own rules in financial, commercial and development matters. Furthermore, it is accused of double standards due to modifying its approach from case to case and, chiefly, to not upholding those very same values at home. In this sense, the diplomats tend to agree that the EU should have a less aggressive policy in those areas in which its power is stronger in order to avoid the ever-present temptation of imposing standards and values on other countries and cultures.

Within this limited framework, the non-European diplomats recognize the willingness of the EU to champion global efforts such as the fight against global warming and the promotion of sustainable development. In these areas, the EU is still seen as a forerunner, especially due to the conservative attitude of the current US administration.

# Notes

1 Semi-structured interviews were conducted with 26 non-European diplomats dealing with European affairs in Brussels. Interviews were conducted between January and May 2008, with diplomats of the following embassies/missions to the EU: Australia, China, Japan, India, Iran, Israel, Lebanon, Mexico, South Africa, Russia and the United States of America. The countries were selected with the aim of covering a large part of the nations included in the rest of the volume. For the sake of discretion, names and diplomatic ranks are not reported here. Interviewees are identified using the following country codes: AU (Australia), CH (China), JA (Japan), IN (India), IR (Iran), IS (Israel), LE (Lebanon), ME (Mexico), SA (South Africa), RU (Russia) and US (United States). The numbers next to the country codes indicate the sequence of the interviews: 1 (first interviewee), 2 (second interviewee) and 3 (third interviewee). My deepest gratitude goes to all the diplomats who spared some time to answer my questions.
2 Bretherton and Vogler suggest that 'presence' is a sort of 'latent actorness' (1999: 257). The concept of presence was elaborated in order to capture tangible and intangible patterns that characterize the 'complex and institutionalized expression of "Western Europe"' (Allen and Smith 1990). The concept of actorness was elaborated in order to set up a series of criteria for defining an actor's capability to act, without aligning the EU to other existing categories of international actors (such as states) (Manners and Whitman 1998: 233).

# References

Allen, D. and Smith, M. (1990) 'Western Europe's Presence in the Contemporary International Arena', *Review of International Studies*, 16 (1): 19–37.

Bretherton, C. and Vogler, J. (1999) *The European Union as a Global Actor*, London: Routledge.

Cohen, R. (1991) *Negotiating across Cultures*, Washington, DC: United States Institute of Peace Press.

Hoffmann, S. (1966) 'Obstinate or Obsolete? The fate of the nation-state and the case of Western Europe', *Daedalus*, 3 (95): 862–915.

Lucarelli, S. (2007) 'The European Union in the Eyes of Others: towards filling a gap in the literature', *European Foreign Affairs Review*, 12 (3): 249–70.

Lucarelli, S. and Manners, I. (2006) *Values and Principles in European Foreign Policy*, London: Routledge.

Manners, I.J. and Whitman, R.G. (1998) 'Towards Identifying the International Identity of the European Union: a framework for analysis of the EU's network of relationships', *Journal of European Integration*, 21 (3): 231–49.

# 15 Conclusion

## Self-representations and external perceptions – can the EU bridge the gap?

*Lorenzo Fioramonti and Sonia Lucarelli*

This book is the first attempt to provide a global analysis of the external perceptions of the European Union (EU). As discussed in the introduction to this volume, the 'external image of the EU' is a rather new topic of research for academics as well as political analysts and journalists, despite the fact that external perceptions and images are crucial factors in foreign policy. Perhaps this lack of focus on the global perceptions of the EU is due to the relative novelty of the EU as an international player. Internally fragmented, due to opposing foreign policy interests among the 27 member states, and institutionally redundant, due to overlapping mandates between its supranational and intergovernmental institutions, the EU is the global actor in the making par excellence. In a world still dominated by nation states and power politics, where global governance is far from being consolidated, the EU has been struggling to carve out a relevant space. Nevertheless, in the past decade, it has definitely become a player to reckon with.

The chapters in this book confirm this general description. The EU's political and social image is still fragmented, while the European project remains vastly unknown to the citizens of non-European countries.

In emerging powers such as India and Brazil, most citizens are unaware of the existence or purpose of the EU, while in South Africa it is viewed as a rather ineffective actor by the few who have an opinion about it.

Knowledge and approval of the EU is highly correlated to levels of education, that is, better-educated people are much more familiar with the EU and tend to evaluate it more positively. Although education plays an important role in shaping perceptions of the EU, the analyses of national elites provide mixed results. Across the globe, political elites hold serious doubts about the effectiveness and credibility of the EU as a 'new type' of global actor. For instance, American political elites do not see the EU as a significant actor in international affairs. According to James Sperling (Chapter 2), many US politicians and bureaucrats 'discount the importance of the EU as an autonomous actor, preferring to see it as a cipher for the national interests of the individual member states or as an impenetrable bureaucratic maze'. Similarly Sharon Pardo's analysis of Israeli perceptions (Chapter 5) aptly confirms that, although Israelis feel close to Europe culturally and politically (so close that they entertain the thought of becoming full members of the EU in the near future), they are nevertheless persuaded that the Union is a 'non-factor' in the Middle East peace process. Interestingly, the analysis of Palestinian views (Chapter 6) confirms the perception of the EU as a marginal factor in the Israeli–Palestinian conflict. According to the two authors, Simona Santoro and Rami Nasrallah, not only do Palestinian elites view the EU's internal policy making as hampering the effectiveness of its foreign policy, but they also believe that in the past few years the Union has endorsed a 'subordinate position' vis-à-vis the United States of America (USA) as far as the Middle East peace process is concerned. Along the same lines, Santini, Mauriello and Trombetta (Chapter 4) argue that Iran and Lebanon do not perceive the EU as a fully fledged actor in world affairs 'due to its lack of internal unity and its Eurocentric attitude'. In Iran, political elites and civil society see the EU as 'as passively receiving and accepting negative biases on Iran from other foreign policy actors', especially the USA. Perhaps more importantly, European powers are accused of 'failing to recognize the important role Iran plays and wants to play in the Middle East and still tend to treat it from a position of asymmetrical power'. In Lebanon, although the EU is appreciated for having been directly involved in the post-2006 stabilization process, local constituencies are nevertheless wary of the EU's alleged interest in democracy promotion mainly due to the Union's double standards and uncertainties in this field. In this regard, the EU is harshly criticized for failing to recognize Hizbullah as a crucial national political force and is described as 'oscillating' and 'unable to react to the flagrant violations of international law and the destabilization of the region perpetuated by Israel'.

While both China and Russia may view the EU as a more collaborative and cooperative partner than the USA, they nevertheless perceive it to be rather weak in international politics and often hostage to US-made strategies (Chapter 3). Obviously, there are differences in the perceptive patterns of Russia and China. As underlined by Mara Morini, Arlo Poletti and Roberto Peruzzi:

> while Chinese perceptions take shape in a context where 'hard' security and economic conflicts with the EU are not likely to be on the agenda, Russian views evolve within a much more dynamic, complex and potentially problematic framework of mutual relations.

According to the authors, the main negative factors influencing Chinese perceptions of the EU have to do with economic disputes (from the arms embargo to protectionist policies), while in the case of Russia there are a number of 'potentially troubling issues', ranging from the definition of EU borders, the relationship with the post-2004 member states and ongoing territorial disputes in Central Asia.

According to some recent surveys, most citizens and opinion makers around the world do not consider that the EU will play a leading political role in future decades. The USA, China and some regional players (such as India and Brazil) are believed to be those 'calling the shots' in the future global governance.

Similar conclusions are drawn by Franziska Brantner, who has analysed the views of the EU at the United Nations (UN). According to her interviewees (see Chapter 11), the EU's image at the UN is undermined by the lack of unity among European member states in international politics, while the lowest-common-denominator approach adopted by the EU in foreign policy is widely perceived as producing ineffective and unreliable decisions in the international arena. For the most well-known Arab media network, Al Jazeera, the EU is a difficult topic 'to sell'. As explained by Donatella Della Ratta (Chapter 13), 'Arab viewers are used to dealing with strong individual political powers. They are not accustomed to "softer entities", where the decision-making process has to go through multiple rounds of negotiations and complex systems of collegial decisions.' According to Al Jazeera's editors, the EU is too complicated and bureaucratic to become an interesting topic for Arab TV stations.

In spite of its limited 'political' image, the EU has gradually acquired a significant weight in global economic matters. Of all the economic images of the EU, the one depicting a trade and economic 'giant' is possibly the most frequent and powerful. Throughout the book, the EU is often described as the largest market in the world and an example of economic development and stability. Trade with the EU is often considered crucial in order to promote social and economic development in other regions of the world, from Latin America to Africa and Asia. As remarked by Alejandro Chanona in Chapter 8, the EU is viewed as a crucial partner by Mexico and the upgrading of their bilateral trade partnership is an important element of debate in this country. Similarly, business elites and the press in India, Brazil and South Africa emphasize the importance of the EU as an economic actor in today's world, particularly with regard to the developmental ambitions of many countries in less industrialized regions. As additional evidence of the primacy of the EU's economic image, it may be useful to recall that across all countries surveyed for our research, the EU is far more covered by newspapers and magazines concerned with economic and financial policies than it is by the political and social press.

Nonetheless, the reputation of the EU as a trade and economic 'partner' has been significantly damaged in the past couple of years, especially vis-à-vis less developed countries. In the words of Gerrit Olivier and Lorenzo Fioramonti, who have studied the EU image in the IBSA countries (Chapter 7), '[a]gricultural subsidies, non-tariff barriers and other protectionist measures against emerging economies of the "global south" contribute to reinforcing the perception of the EU as a neo-colonial power'. Even at the World Bank, perceptions of the EU as a protectionist actor are not uncommon. As remarked by Eugenia Baroncelli (Chapter 10), in spite of being seen as a 'standard-bearer' of socioeconomic values and a guarantor of key individual rights, 'the EU appears to bear the responsibility for a less than development-friendly stance in its agricultural policies, and, increasingly, in its trade policies'. Similarly, the analysis of EU perceptions at the African Union (AU) underlines the gap between African developmental expectations and the Union's economic policies. As explained by Daniela Sicurelli (Chapter 12), although 'AU representatives depict the EU as a model for integration and a key partner for economic development', they firmly criticize 'the lack of coherence between EU trade and development policies' and 'the way in which the EU imposes its model of integration and its conditions for development aid'. Since 2007, such a critical view of the EU has been exacerbated by the European insistence on establishing Economic Partnership Agreements (EPAs) with the African, Caribbean and Pacific countries (ACP). Initially designed to replace long-standing trade and development policies between Europe and its former colonies with new arrangements inspired by the liberalization philosophy of the World Trade Organization, the EPAs soon became a catalyst of tensions and contrast in an era characterized by financial uncertainty and widespread opposition to the free-trade mantra of the 1990s. Ole Elgström (Chapter 9) gives a suggestive description of the negative impact of the EPA negotiations on the EU's reputation as a development partner to the ACP countries. In his face-to-face interviews with an ACP delegate, 'Commission negotiators are characterized as patronizing and showing little understanding and sympathy towards ACP needs.' Moreover, the EU's 'use of warnings (by many ACP representatives seen as threats) and deadlines to put pressure on its opponent' was viewed as being 'in sharp contrast to what should be expected from a "partner"'. In this regard, it appears as if the enthusiasm declared by the EU for the recent adoption of strategic partnerships with a number of emerging powers (from India to Brazil and the whole African continent) has not really affected the latter's negative assessment of certain core EU policies. By and large, the adoption of strategic partnerships with the EU has not produced any meaningful public debate in these countries.

Besides its economic might, the EU is also perceived as a 'model of regional integration' and a 'promoter of democracy'. The Union is widely recognized as the most successful example of regional integration in the contemporary world. Its mechanisms and policies to help poorer member states acquire higher levels of economic well-being are also praised by civil society organizations around the world. In the view of many of the respondents involved in this research, this founding element of equitable development and cross-national subsidization is also derived from deeply entrenched European values, which also distinguish the way in which the EU operates globally vis-à-vis, for instance, the USA. In this regard, the EU approach to democracy promotion, characterized by a mix of soft power, incentives and political dialogue, is often contrasted with the aggressive way of 'exporting democracy' adopted by the USA.

At the same time, though, the EU is also criticized for inconsistencies and double standards. African decision makers lament that EU financial and trade policies hamper indigenous integration in Africa. The EPAs are explicitly mentioned as a case in point since they are aimed at dividing Africa into subregional groupings, which are 'at odds with its parallel promotion of pan-African integration' and reveal 'the traditional "divide-and-rule" approach adopted by European countries during the colonial era' (Chapter 12). Moreover, political conditionality attached to development aid and trade arrangements is increasingly seen as imposing and inconsistent. Conditions on democratic reforms and good governance are criticized for being inspired by Eurocentric values. At the same time, the EU is accused of being eager to punish weaker countries in sub-Saharan Africa, where its economic leverage is higher, while glossing over abuse in powerful countries such as China or in the Middle East. In addition to that, the EU is also stigmatized for its internal democratic deficit. As observed by Caterina Carta (Chapter 14) in her analysis of non-European diplomats located in Brussels, the democratic deficit within the EU 'has negative effects on the reputation of the EU as an "exporter" of democracy and human rights' and 'influences the credibility of the EU as an international partner'.

On a positive note, civil society organizations and political elites recognize that the EU has been at the forefront of important global campaigns, from the fight against climate change to the adoption of international agreements based on the rule of law. In a word, the EU is perceived as a beacon of multilateralism in global affairs. Nevertheless, this multilateral character is interpreted quite differently in the various countries. In China, for instance, the public discourse of political elites suggests a very different understanding of what multilateralism means, which is undoubtedly at odds with the EU's declared preference for a system of international policy making able to move beyond national sovereignty. On the contrary, Chinese elites use multilateralism to define what would be better described as a multipolar world: a system of international governance based on the leadership of a few leading powers (e.g. the five permanent members of the United Nations Security Council or an extended G8) and firmly anchored on the prerogatives of national sovereignty. Quite similar are the views of governmental elites in India and Russia, who emphasize the importance of national sovereignty in global governance to demonstrate the legitimacy of their security concerns and justify their policies towards neighbouring countries.

The research conducted for this book reveals quite indisputably that there is a significant 'gap' between how the EU perceives itself and how it is perceived by citizens, governmental elites, civil society groups and the media in other countries outside Europe.

It also appears as if the 'distinctiveness thesis', that is, the idea according to which the EU is a *different* (read *better*) global actor due to its self-declared goal of promoting peace through integration, human rights and democracy, does not echo with the most common external perceptions. Countries from the so-called 'global south' have grown suspicious of the actual goals of the EU in its trade and economic policies. African countries have publicly contrasted strategies that they consider imposing and tainted by neo-colonial attitudes. Israeli public opinion, political elites and the media believe the EU harbours profound anti-Semitic sentiments. Citizens and opinion makers in Iran and Lebanon point out discrimination against Muslims in most European countries and, along with Palestinians, criticize the decision to disqualify Hamas as a legitimate political movement. Finally, rising regional powers such as Brazil have accused the EU of discrimination and abuse owing to its recent reforms restricting the rights of migrants.

All these perceptions (or misperceptions) are a red light to the EU, for they reveal that its global approval rating might be under strain. As we explained in the introduction to this volume, preconceived notions and perceptions are important factors affecting international politics. Therefore, a lack of credibility in global affairs can be seriously detrimental to the EU as it can weaken its political and economic leverage. In turn, it might even exert a negative impact on its legitimacy at home. In an era of euro-pessimism among European citizens, these external perceptions might further contribute to undermining appreciation of the EU in the hearts and minds of its citizens.

The various chapters of this book point to a potentially inverse relation between 'positive image' and 'policy effectiveness'. The policy areas in which the EU's self-representation is closer to its external perceptions are the more 'political' ones, particularly multilateral governance, international diplomacy and the promotion of democracy. Yet, these areas are those in which the EU's unitary decision making is less developed and its effectiveness deemed quite low by non-European societies. In Muslim countries (from Iran to Lebanon and Palestine), political elites and the media recognize and appreciate the EU's diplomatic approach to international crises and would like the Union to play a more significant role as an independent mediator. Nevertheless, recent experience has fuelled frustrations and disappointment among certain Muslim constituencies. For example, in Palestine, where a number of European governments had long enjoyed a significant approval rating for their political support of the Palestinian cause, the EU is perceived simply 'as an aid donor rather than a credible mediator' (Chapter 6).

By contrast, the policies in which the EU should be in the position to make a real difference due to its 'common voice' and economic leverage – chiefly international trade – are widely criticized by external observers for being tainted with selfishness and short-sightedness. The adoption of conservative policies in the economic field, particularly concerning the Doha Round, has contributed to creating a rather negative image of the EU not only across less developed countries but also among emerging markets. Indians strongly criticize non-tariff trade barriers that prevent access to the EU market for produce exported from Delhi. Brazil and South Africa stigmatize the provision of agricultural subsidies to European commercial farmers. As summarized by a civil society activist in South Africa, 'we know that their trade subsidies are also harming European peasants because they pour money into the pockets of big commercial farmers. Thus, it is also in the interest of common European citizens to change this unjust system' (Chapter 7). In 2007–2008, the dire EPA negotiations were an additional blow to the EU's international approval rating, especially in the ACP countries. Furthermore, European protectionism has also been widely criticized by major global powerhouses such as China and the USA. While the Chinese are mainly concerned about restrictive measures on products with the 'made in China' label, American business and labour have been vocal against EU subsidies to competitive industrial sectors, from aviation (with the Airbus case) to agriculture.

Many factors account for this international image of the EU. First of all, EU foreign policy making is fragmented and inconsistent, which results in a poor understanding of what the EU is and what it stands for in global politics. On the one hand, most citizens around the world have very little knowledge of the EU. On the other hand, although political and business elites have a more defined opinion of the EU, they nevertheless point out the lack of coherence between what the EU 'says' and what it actually 'does'. Other observers also stigmatize the numerous inconsistencies across different EU policies, from development (viewed as progressive) to trade (viewed as regressive).

Since EU foreign policy is subject to consensus among all 27 member states, it often results in comparatively modest initiatives that are interpreted as a sign of weakness by external observers. Thus, the practice of internal multilateralism followed by the EU in most foreign policy areas is widely perceived as a suboptimal approach leading to a lack of visibility and 'voice' in international affairs. While the world would like to see a stronger and more autonomous European stance in global governance (as opposed, for instance, to US unilateralism), their expectations have been frustrated in the past few years, fuelling criticism that the EU has aligned itself with the diktat of the US administration under President George W. Bush.

Furthermore, historical and cultural variables are also at play. EU policies and actions do not happen in a vacuum, but are generally interpreted in the light of pre-existing dynamics. For instance, although trade and economic policies with Africa are publicized by the EU through innovative concepts such as 'partnership', they are inevitably interpreted within an historical context profoundly affected by colonialism and dependency. Such a factor helps explain why the EU's insistence on adopting the EPAs was immediately labelled as a form of 'neo-colonialism'. Cultural variables also contribute to explaining the inclination among Israelis to accuse the EU of anti-Semitism or, by contrast, the accusation of racism and discrimination raised by Muslim constituencies or developing countries whose citizens migrate to Europe in search of a better future. All these factors, which include conservative policies, lack of unity and historical and cultural variables, contribute to shaping the overall image of the EU as a 'fortress': an entity striving to defend itself from global threats by promoting its own interests and refraining from assuming leadership in global affairs.

What can the EU do to reverse such an image? First of all, European institutions and policy makers should improve not only the reciprocal coherence of various EU policies, but also their consistency with the fundamental values the EU claims that it promotes. Our analysis reveals that trade policies are far more important to poor countries and emerging markets than development aid. Therefore, the EU should reform its bilateral trade regimes in order to establish 'fair' arrangements with its counterparts. At the multilateral level, the EU should use its weight to resume international talks and possibly reform global trade according to those very principles of social justice and sustainability that it purports to promote in its documents and declarations.

Second, the EU should take its potential role of 'mediator' between different cultures and civilizations more seriously. While this might have been more challenging during the tenure of the previous American administration, due to Washington's confrontational attitude, it is likely to find much more fertile ground in the coming years under the leadership of President Barack Obama. A stronger focus on international diplomacy and multilateralism might give the EU a rather promising context in which to use its skills and expertise more proficiently. The first targets of a renovated role for the EU would inevitably include: a concerted effort to bring Israelis and Palestinians back to the negotiating table after the atrocities committed in Gaza in January 2009, a new diplomatic strategy with Iran aimed at supporting its civil nuclear plan in exchange for guarantees that Tehran has no intention to pursue military goals.

Our studies reveal that the world would like the EU to become more political and less obsessed with short-term economic gains. Needless to say, such a process will require stronger commitment from all EU member states. While such commitment might have been quite difficult to achieve in the past due to the continuous regurgitation of national prerogatives, the global character of the current threats shaking Europe and the world might make the cooperation of European states easier to achieve in the coming years. The current global economic crunch has shown that individual states do not have the resources to respond effectively to global financial crises. The meltdown of Iceland's economy (which might apply for EU membership as a consequence of financial instability) and the downfall of the British sterling (as opposed to the strength of the euro) are two cases in point. By sharing the burden and pooling efforts, the EU has proven the most effective institution in responding not only to economic instability, but also to other geopolitical and environmental challenges. Energy security in Europe, for instance, cannot be achieved unless common initiatives are taken at the EU level. Furthermore, any credible response to climate change and its disastrous impact on political stability, human rights and sustainable development is unthinkable outside a multilateral arena.

The catastrophic inheritance of the USA's Bush administration has demonstrated that no country can act unilaterally in today's world. Not even the only superpower. The crisis of unilateralism also among conservative politicians and opinion makers has therefore strengthened the multilateral dimension, of which the EU could become the most credible champion. Most of the chapters in this book show that the leading role played by the EU in the fight against climate change (exemplified by the adoption of the Kyoto Protocol) has been internalized by civil societies around the world as evidence of progressive European thinking. In the eyes of civic associations, non-governmental organizations and labour unions, the EU is still perceived as a region of the world in which social well-being is promoted and inequalities addressed. It is from here that European policy makers and citizens should start rebuilding the future of the EU and its role in a changing world.

# Index